Beautiful Town

_____

BEAUTIFUL TOWN

Storioo and Cssays by Satō Haruo

Translated by Francis B. Tenny

University of Hawai'i Press

Honolulu

Library of Congress Cataloging-in-Publication Data
Satō, Haruo, 1892–1964.
Beautiful town : stories and essays / by Satō Haruo ;
translated by Francis B. Tenny.
p.   cm.
ISBN 0–8248–1704–4 (alk. paper)
1. Satō, Haruo, 1892–1964—Translations into English.
I. Tenny, Francis B., 1920–   . II. Title.
PL838.A86A28   1996
895.6'344—dc20   96–25661
CIP

Designed by Paula Newcomb

Contents

Translator's Preface

This book is a sequel to my earlier translations of Satō Haruo published as *The Sick Rose* by the University of Hawai'i Press in 1993. Readers with an interest in Satō are referred to it.

For this volume I am especially indebted to Elaine Gerbert for her perceptive introduction placing these stories and Satō's entire opus in the context of Japanese and world literature. She has provided the literary and scholarly background for understanding Satō in English.

My appreciation also goes to Kazue Edamatsu Campbell and Takeshi Kokubo for reading these translations for accuracy, for their many good suggestions, and for their understanding of the ambiguities of Japanese of which Satō himself writes. Any remaining errors are solely my responsibility.

Satō "gave" his original "Beautiful Town" story to his son Masaya, and it is only appropriate that these English versions carry the same dedication to Professor Masaya Satō of Keiō University, whose cooperation has made his father's stories available for English translation.

Introduction

Elaine Gerbert

Satō Haruo has been called one of the two most representative writers of the Taishō period (1912–1926)[1]—for some a painful and for others an exhilarating transition between the age of Meiji (1868–1912), when Japan began the project of modernizing itself after the model of Western nation states, and the uncertainties of Shōwa (1926–1989), when it was called upon to define its place in a world that had grown ever more complex.

Although he never identified himself as a "modernist," Satō exhibited what some writers on the subject have identified as characteristics of modernism: a complex net of contradictory impulses embracing both the revolutionary and the conservative, revealing both an optimistic looking to the future and a pessimistic nostalgia for the past, and celebrating the passing of old forms of culture while despairing over the loss of the familiar.

The stories and essays in this volume, translated into English for the first time, afford not only insights into the complexity of the work of a particularly sensitive and gifted writer, but also an enlarged perspective of the literary history of Taishō.

EARLY YEARS

Satō was born in 1892 in Wakayama prefecture, a place whose mild climate and natural beauty had been celebrated in verse and prose since the Heian period. His hometown, Shingū, is located on the Bay of

Waka, where white sandy beaches stretch along a sparkling sea, and the air is perfumed by the cypress, pine, and camphor woods of the nearby mountains. It has been suggested that the lyricism of Satō's writings is somehow inextricably linked to the luminous place of his childhood and the comfortable circumstances of his upbringing.[2]

Shingū was still a sleepy country town, cut off from the major cities, when Satō was born, but a local literary culture had long flourished in its inspirational setting, and the Satō family, physicians in the area for nine generations, had been at the center of that literary tradition. Satō's great-grandfather was a waka poet, and Satō's grandfather wrote and published Chinese poetry. Satō's father, Toyotarō, whose haiku name was Kyōsui, composed haiku and kyōka—"crazy poems" that showcased wit and ingenuity—and strove to develop in his eldest son, Haruo, a poetic eye for viewing nature. Young Satō was taken on walks to observe the flora and fauna of the the countryside and on moon-viewing boat rides down the Kumano River.

Satō studied classical Chinese and began composing poetry at an early age. When still a middle-school student in Shingū, he came to the attention of the Tokyo literary establishment as the precocious poet whose tanka had been selected for publication in the literary journals Myōjō and Subaru. He also gained local notoriety by standing up and delivering an impromptu lecture on naturalism when the poet Yosano Tekkan (1873–1935), the critic and translator Ikuta Chōkō (1882–1936), and the painter Ishii Hakutei (1882–1958) came to Shingū from Tokyo to lecture, arrived late, and needed extra time to prepare for the evening event. In a small provincial town in 1910, literary naturalism was perceived as corrupting, and Satō was suspended from school for his impulsive display of knowledge. He took the opportunity to travel to Tokyo and reestablish contact with Chōkō. He also attended meetings of the Shinshisha New Poetry Society in the home of Tekkan and his wife, the poetess Yosano Akiko (1878–1942), who were at the center of an important revolutionary movement in poetry that promoted free verse and the use of colloquial language.

Satō's sense of style, already developed through the study of classical Japanese and Chinese poetry, was further refined through his contacts with Chōkō and Akiko. We may assume that by editing many of Satō's early manuscripts, Chōkō, who had already translated Nietzsche and D'Annunzio and would later translate works by Marx, Flaubert, Joyce, and Dante, helped to sharpen the young man's literary sense.[3] It is also said that Akiko taught Satō to free himself from the emotional restraints that hampered the free expression of his natural lyrical gifts, and that the sharp economy and effectiveness of the imagery in his prose writings are in part the results of an eye that was further disciplined and cultivated under her tutelage.[4]

In 1910, together with Horiguchi Daigaku (1892–1981), a poet and lifelong friend whose translations of French modernist poets and writers later played a critical role in the introduction of modernist literature into Japan, Satō enrolled in the literature department of Keiō Gijuku (now Keiō University). Headed by Nagai Kafū (1879–1959), who had earlier traveled in America and France, the Keiō literature department was associated with a refined urbane literature, in contrast to the more prosaic writings of the faculty of Waseda University, the stronghold of literary naturalism.

In his early years in Tokyo, Satō published tanka, free-verse poetry, poetry criticism, and translations of poems by Oscar Wilde. In 1916 he became acquainted with Akutagawa Ryūnosuke (1892–1927) and Tanizaki Jun'ichiro (1886–1965), writers who shared his cosmopolitan outlook and tastes.

The cosmopolitanism of Satō's early "modernist period" was expressed, among other ways, in the experimental quality of his writings and the wide range of genres in which he worked roughly between the years 1917 and 1929. In 1918 he published the highly innovative mystery novel, The Fingerprint (Shimon) in the prestigious journal, Chūō kōron, a year after the appearance of his fantasy story, "The House of a Spanish Dog" (Supein inu no ie), and his well-known prose poem The Sick Rose (Yameru sōbi), later retitled Gloom in the Country (Den'en no yūutsu). He produced Japan's first utopian novel, Beautiful Town (Utsukushii machi, 1919); the story "F*O*U" (1926), written in a modernist mode; the futuristic novel The Nonchalant Records (Nonsharan kiroku, 1929); and a novel about a woman who undergoes Freudian psychoanalysis (The Rebirth, Kōseiki, 1929). Like Tanizaki, Satō was intensely interested in the artistic potential of film and produced a screenplay, in addition to plays for the theater.

At the same time that he wrote some of the most imaginatively

4 Elaine Gerbert

creative stories of his day, Satō also worked in a more traditional conservative style. His interest in classical Chinese literature, for example, led him to write "The Star" (Hoshi) in 1920, the year he traveled to Formosa, Amoy, and Fukien province. This was followed by the Chinese-style mystery tale, "A Strange Tale of a Woman's Fan" (Jokaisen kidan, 1925); translations of Chinese children's stories ("The Great Journey of the Locust" (Inago no dairyokō, 1926); and "Chinese Childrens' Stories" (Shina dōwashū, 1929); and an anthology of translations of Chinese poetry by women dating back to the fourth century, "The Wagon Dust Collection" (Shajinshō, 1929). Satō also worked in the popular autobiographical "I novel" vein, producing *Unbearably Forlorn* (Wabishisugiru) in 1922 and an uncompleted roman à clef novel inspired by his breakup with Tanizaki over Tanizaki's wife, Chiyo, *These Three People* (Kono mittsu no mono) in 1925.

MODERNIST WORKS: "BEAUTIFUL TOWN" (1919), "THE FINGERPRINT" (1918), "F*O*U" (1926)

Satō's works written in a modernist vein bespeak an age when Japan was subjected to a bewildering array of influences from abroad. Just as the automobile and the airplane changed the way people experienced space–time relationships, the introduction of electric light, motion pictures, and the radio affected how they saw and heard, and new ideas in all fields of learning and the arts challenged the ways in which they conceived the world—especially human relationships. Urbanization had changed the landscape. When Satō wrote "Beautiful Town," Tokyo was a metropolis of 2,170,000 inhabitants (according to the first national census taken in 1920) and was expanding by 100,000 to 200,000 per year.[5]

It was a forward-looking age, whose modernity was summed up in the popular press by the three K's: "*katsudō shashin*" (moving pictures), "*kuruma*" (cars), and "*kafue*" (cafés).[6] It was also a time of alienation and anxiety and unrest. Tokyo was severely overcrowded and polluted. Inflation put pressure on consumers that erupted in nationwide "rice riots" in 1918. A socialist movement was gathering momentum, and "proletarian literature" would gain more ground in the years to come.

Realism and naturalism, which had dominated the world of letters in the first part of the century, gave way to more sophisticated, self-conscious tendencies in literature. There was a new fascination with aberrant states of mind and unusual perceptions, and an interest in dreams and the fantastic. And Satō was outstanding among writers who turned their backs on quotidian reality to explore unconscious drives, strange mental states, and irrational events, and to stress freedom of the imagination and the primacy of art.

Satō's early work also shared with other modernist productions a "high aesthetic self-consciousness" and an experimental quality and sense of what Ortega y Gasset saw as "a view of art as 'play' or 'delightful fraud.' "[7] His early stories are also colored by a strong international flavor that distinguishes them from the work of the Japanese naturalists, who, with few exceptions, situated their novels in readily identifiable Japanese settings, urban and rural, inhabited by middle- and lower-class Japanese.

"Beautiful Town" (Utsukushii machi)

"Beautiful Town" was published as a single volume in January 1920, not long after the writer Mushanokōji Saneatsu (1885–1976) established his utopian village in Hyūga in 1918, and a year before the millionaire Nishimura Isaku from Shingū announced his plan to create a small-scale garden city near Odawara Station, where ten "cosmopolitan homes" (bunka jūtaku) would be built to house artists.[8] This interest in utopian villages appears to have been stimulated both by the appalling living conditions in hastily put-together living spaces in the larger cities and by idealized notions about art's redemptive powers. Satō's fictional utopian town went a step further in the direction of pure art; it was inspired by an artistic drive and undertaken primarily for the sake of the joy of artistic creation.

Aesthetics is privileged in Brentano's "beautiful town," from which practical men of the world—businessmen, politicians, and military men—are excluded. And its magic is enhanced by the fact that it will never materialize beyond the play model in his hotel room. As Satō states in "The Joy of the Artist," for the artist, the joy experienced in the process of creation is everything; whatever work of art results from this process is but a secondary effect that remains to "commemorate that joy."

As a corollary to the notion of the primacy of art over life, connections between the world of art and everyday reality are severed. The site selected for the "beautiful town" is discovered, not by walking through the then present-day Tokyo, but by seeing Nakazu Island in the beautiful distant world of Edo-period artist Shiba Kōkan's copperplate engraving: a timeless world that has little to do with the actual contemporary "rubbish strewn, disorderly Nakazu Island."

Settings of marginal geographic spaces inside Tokyo add to the sense of separation from everyday reality and to the creation of enclosed liminal spheres conducive to the workings of the artistic imagination. Tsukiji, where the exotic Western-style hotel is located,[9] was a foreign enclave during the Meiji period, an in-between zone mediating the domestic and the familiar, on the one hand, and the alien world of the westerners who had settled in Tokyo, on the other.

Another source of inspiration is the foreigner himself. As an Eurasian, Theodore Brentano would have been a rare kind of person in Meiji Japan, and was rarer yet as a leading character in the novel of a major writer. His name links the "beautiful town" to the world of fairy tales created by Clemens Brentano (1778–1842), the German Romantic poet whose name also appears in Satō's essay, "The Art, That Is the Person" (Geijutsu sunawachi ningen).

The electric lighting that came into widespread use in early Taishō and served as a utilitarian convenience is used here, however, mostly for an artistic purpose—to add a touch of magic to ordinary reality. The "beautiful town" is created at night, under the light of electric lamps, and its phantom effect is further enhanced by the use of mirrors that capture its image in reflected form. The brightly illumined hotel room in which the artists work in silence, and the enclosed interior of the automobile in which they speed through the dark city lit up by streetlights at night, provide E and Kawasaki with artificially illumined spaces in which to pursue their private fantasies, separated from the daylight world of the contemporary rationalistic, materialistic society. These glowing lights both stimulate the imagination and serve as objective correlatives for the inspiration that lights up within.

The sense of connection between the "beautiful town" and contemporary material reality is further attenuated by the concentric narrative structure that places O's story within the framework of the story told by the author of "Beautiful Town." Within O's story, the linear flow of time is broken up by the telescoping of different time frames, going back first "eight or nine years ago," then further back to the Japan of the 1880s, the romantic westernizing Rokumeikan era, and further back yet to the Namban era of the 1790s, when "Dutch and Spanish arts and crafts poured into Japan."

"The Fingerprint" (Shimon)

Of all Satō's stories, "The Fingerprint" repudiates realism most radically. It is governed by references not to life but to works of art, most conspicuously, Edgar Allen Poe's tales of mystery and Thomas de Quincey's *Confessions of an English Opium Eater* (1822). As opposed to the conventional kind of detective story (a genre that enjoyed popularity in the Taishō period), in which the detective uses reason to solve the problem of "who done it," in Satō's story, the sleuth is an opium-eating dreamer who leads the reader away from the reassuring features of everyday reality into unfamiliar hallucinatory ways of perceiving. Representation is subordinated to imagination, and the sense of complete disassociation with the real world is created in part through a narrative structure that follows the movement of a drugged mind working its way through different layers of consciousness.

The sense of separation from the real world is perhaps most prominently conveyed through the motion-picture screen. The disorienting effect produced by the hallucinatory suprareality of the illuminated image of the fingerprint blown up on the screen is further enhanced by the doppelgänger effects, interspersed throughout the narrative, of Poe-like signs (gold chain, skull image, secret compartments and spaces in deserted buildings, corpses, walls that sound, dripping blood, black cat, and so forth). The seemingly random, arbitrary manner in which these images are introduced, disconnected from each other, further increases the effect of disorientation. The most prominent of these effects is the ambiguous double ontological status of the actor William Wilson (his existence on the screen vying with his actual movements in the world), which in turn echoes the Poe story "William Wilson," in which

a double named William Wilson follows a man throughout his life, imitating every aspect of his physical and psychological being.

Satō also redefined the figure of the house in the landscape of
modern Japanese literature. In his stories, the house, once associated
with the oppressions, constraints, and security offered by the traditional family system (ie) in the novels of naturalist writers Tayama
Katai (1871–1930) and Shimazaki Tōson (1872–1943), becomes the
means whereby the individual takes leave of society's defining norms.
The house carefully designed by N is the site of opium dreams in "The
Fingerprint." The country cottage is where the artist spins his melancholy fantasies in "Gloom in the Country." The house is a place of mad
deliriums in "White Hot Passion" (Aojiroi netsujō).

These interiors may be viewed as analogues of the mind, in which
normal perception is problematized, distorted, and re-created through
the prism of the hallucinating eye. Cut off from the concourse of daily
life, in these interiors liminal states of consciousness are explored, distinctions between dream and waking, fantasy and reality, night and
day, madness and sanity dissolve, and the categories of a rationalistic
view of the world cease to hold sway.

Frequently, the enchantments of the eye take place within doubly
or even triply enclosed spaces. The entertainment district of Asakusa,
already separated from the rest of the city as an island of fantasy production and consumption within the capital, is the locus of a movie
house; and within the dark enclosed space of the theater there is the
defined space of the illuminated movie screen, upon which a dream-
world is projected.[10] Far from being finite spaces, these enclosures
expand into worlds large enough to lose oneself in. N takes up the
challenge and in pursuing the image of the fingerprint, steps into a
world without limits and never finds his way back.

"F*O*U"

There is in Satō's appropriation of Western themes, motifs, and literary
allusions a definite sense of play. We may choose to interpret this play-
fulness as another sign that in 1926 Satō had ceased to be ambivalent
about the influence of Western culture, and that his coping with that
influence entailed the adoption of certain distancing strategies which

enabled him to resist the literature that remained essentially foreign in spirit.

On the one hand, he seems to have been at ease in dealing with Western culture. His novels, for example, are notable for their characters—foreigners, Eurasians, and Japanese—who have been fundamentally changed as a result of long sojourns in Western lands. And, unlike in Tanizaki's novels, in which Eurasians and westerners figure as minor characters who function to bring out aspects of the dispositions of the main ones, in Satō's fiction such characters are assigned major roles. (Theodore Brentano, for example, was the first major Eurasian character to appear in a modern Japanese novel.)

The interracial love affair between the Japanese painter Ishino Maki and the Frenchwoman Florence in "F*O*U" is completely unencumbered by the sense of difficulty due to racial difference that marked the love affair between the upper-class Japanese man and the German dancing girl in Mori Ōgai's novella "The Dancing Girl" (Maihime, 1898). Nor is there any trace of the feelings of racial inferiority of the kind that Natsume Sōseki wrote about when describing his stay in England at the turn of the century.

On the other hand, we might say that Satō, who never set foot in the West, does not really take on the issue of cultural and racial difference. The West in that sense is not a real problem in these stories but a kind of abstract challenge to be negotiated in literary games.

These games are most obvious in "F*O*U," which is also the most decidedly modernist and Western story in flavor. It was reportedly written under the influence of Horiguchi Daigaku's 1924 translation of Ouvert la Nuit (1921; Open all night, 1981), a work that made its author, Paul Morand (1888–1976), almost as popular in Japan as he was in France. And, indeed, "F*O*U" bears certain surface similarities to the French work, with its theme of romantic adventure with a beautiful foreign woman in a postwar European city, and its exotic touches, such as Florence's room, decorated in the style of a Turkish harem. Morand's exuberant style may also have left a mark on the sudden and striking way in which certain images are joined, for example, the street urchin standing in a "contorted pose, his belly thrust out, the backs of his hands stuck to his hips, and his arms bent like the handles of a flower vase."[11]

However, the names of Apollinaire and André Salmon inserted in the text may be seen as clues to Satō's playful strategy, rather than as suggestions that "F*O*U" was written as a "cubist style" exercise mixing fantasy, realism, and irony in the manner of the experimental works of the two French writers. Reading "F*O*U" as an ironic piece where the motivating force is the swing back and forth between the conventionally real and the fantastic, with elements of satire, fancy, and the outrageous along the way, and with the recurring phrase, "I think so too," marking the beat of this pendulum-like rhythm, may yield a more encompassing interpretation.

Reality is handled playfully in its assortment of picturesque vignettes: a Japanese who thinks he is a Chinese from the T'ang period; statements from Maki such as "I love my brother; I love France even more"; the outrageous proposal to his wife that she come to France and serve as a wet nurse for the baby and as a maid to Florence; the confusion between the House of Tarme brothel and the Château de Tarme, between a pimp and an estate steward; the mocking allusion to the Odalisque of Matisse in the description of Florence's room; Maki, the proverbial impoverished foreign artist, driving a Parisian taxicab; the radio waves he radiates; the hair in the soup—the pendulum marks each vignette.

There are also word games of the sort found in traditional Japanese popular literature written for entertainment, gesaku: texts peppered with cryptic allusions, double entendres, and ingenious verbal allusions intended to tease, challenge, and stump the readers. In "F*O*U" these word games begin with the title and include "Harue" (whose name is the feminine variant of Satō's own first name, Haruo); Ishino's fairy princess, Florence, who has the same name as the city of Dante (who was also guided on an artistic odyssey by a woman) but, unlike Beatrice, is anything but "beatified." Other obvious clues pointing to the "deceitful" nature of this modernist story, and perhaps commenting on modernist art in general, are the fake "1575 vintage wine" and the fake Tintoretto painting. Satō's literary play culminates in the story's completely fraudulent ending, as he forges a "review" of Ishino's paintings by the critic André Salmon.[12]

One should, moreover, take note that "F*O*U" was written in 1926, two years after Satō published his statement on Japanese aesthetics in "Fūryūron" (On elegance) and a year after Ikuta Chōkō published his criticism of modernism in the essay titled "To the New Generation of the Bundan" (Bundan no shinjidai ni ataru), in which he mocked the contrived style of Morand and his Japanese followers and criticized modernism for appealing solely to the desire for sensation without regard for moral or political content.[13]

And Satō's Western-inspired art-for-art's-sake philosophy, expounded seven years earlier in "The Joy of the Artist," undergoes a radical transformation in this story, in which the artist, far from being a uniquely endowed person qualified to create a new society based upon the old, is a childlike madman.

TRADITIONAL WORKS: "THE STAR" (1920), "UNBEARABLY FORLORN" (1921), "A WINDOW OPENS" (1924)

"The Star" (Hoshi)

Satō, who had been introduced to Chinese literature at a time in his childhood when he was living an idyllic kind of life, returned to it, and to the beautiful setting of Shingū, while recuperating from a severe psychological and physical breakdown seemingly brought about by marital difficulties with his second wife, the actress Komezawa Kayoko. She was having an affair with his younger brother Natsuki, who was then living with the couple while commuting to the Shōchiku Studios, where he worked as an assistant film director. After a period of rest in Shingū, Satō went to Formosa to visit a Chinese friend. He spent three months in China. While traveling in Fukien province, he came upon a popular ballad based on an old folktale, "Chen the Third and the Fifth Daughter." This was the origin of "The Star."

The structure of Satō's Chinese story seems straightforward and direct after the concentric narratives and allusive imagery and irony of his Western-style fiction. In "The Star" he turns to the past, to a simple world governed by an inexorable moral law written in the heavens, a world in which wicked deeds are inevitably punished and good ones rewarded. (Satō, in the wake of an episode where human guile and wile had caused him so much pain, may have craved the simplicity of a fairy-tale-like legend in which an absolute sort of moral balance holds sway.)

Chen the seeker looks to the star in the heavens where the ultimate powers reside—the star that is symbol and source of an absolute kind of beauty not to be found in the compromised world of human beings—to find his destiny, and he follows it throughout his life. Fifth Daughter schemes and wins ascendency over Beneficial Spring, temporarily, but is eventually punished for her ambition and immoral acts; indirectly, it is Chen's star that leads to her death by drowning.

Chen, whose deceptions are not as malicious as Fifth Daughter's, is also punished, but less severely, in keeping with his milder offenses. His wish to father a great man is granted, but not in perfect form. Before he can behold and rejoice in his son's success, he falls victim to Fifth Daughter's ruse and drowns.

In the world of "The Star" the wronged are vindicated and goodness is rewarded. The orphaned girl, Beneficial Spring, who is the innocent victim of trickery, survives Chen and Fifth Daughter and becomes the mother of Chen's son, in whom Chen's destiny is ultimately fulfilled. In this respect, her character is similar to that of the poor orphaned girl in Satō's earlier story, "Okinu to sono kyōdai" (Okinu and her brother, 1918), who is rewarded for her virtue after many years of hardship.[14]

Satō's concerns seem to have narrowed to a moral found in a traditional fable or fairy tale, but its simple, even simplistic handling of the absolute notwithstanding, the story projects a subtle concern regarding the relationship between ethics and aesthetics, a theme with which he had struggled the year before in the essay "The Art, That Is the Person." Here the suggestion is that fraudulent ethics prevent the realization of a transcendent beautiful dream.

Looking to the Asian past for ways in which to counter the hegemony of Western culture was a recurring phenomenon throughout Meiji and Taishō, and "The Star" and Satō's subsequent Chinese stories and translations of Chinese literature found a ready audience among a public interested in China and in works that reminded them of the continental roots of their cultural heritage.

It is telling of both the time in which he lived and his individual temperament that Satō chose Chinese themes from long ago to write

about, and that his Chinese stories were written in a way that romanti-
cized the Chinese past. His nostalgic inclinations, expressed in a fascination for exotic ruins and mysterious tales about the unusual fates of
people who lived in the past (as, for instance, in "A Strange Tale of a
Woman's Fan") offer evidence of the romantic spirit that some critics
have found to lie at the heart of modernism.[15]

"Unbearably Forlorn" (Wabishisugiru)

While Satō was experimenting with Western-style fiction and producing stories set in China, the most highly esteemed genre among practi-
tioners of "high" literature of the time was the "I novel" (shishōsetsu), a
novel in which the concerns, feelings, and sensibilities of the protagonist were viewed as reflections of the author's own personal state of
mind. "Unbearably Forlorn," a work composed in Satō's "speak as you
write style" (shaberu yō ni kaku buntai), is taken to be a straightforward
expression of his state of mind, with fewer of the aesthetic distancing
devices that characterized "Beautiful Town," "The Fingerprint," and
"F*O*U." This direct prose style, used to deal with Satō's personal
problems, led some Japanese critics to regard the story as marking a
definite advance in his growth as a writer and his maturity as a man, so
deeply rooted were the values of the "I novel" tradition, in which truthful self-revelation was held to be a hallmark of literary achievement.[16]
Readers playing the literary detective game of finding parallels between
the novel and events in Satō's life were, and are, challenged to look for
literary clues in the "text" of Satō's highly unconventional personal
life—a life so marked by unusually complicated relationships as to
seem almost more fictional than fiction itself.

Of all Satō's "interpersonal experiences," the ones that have
attracted the most attention are those associated with Tanizaki
Jun'ichirō, the writer six years his senior who had not only mentored
the writing of "Gloom in the Country," proofread "The Fingerprint"
and brokered its publication in Chūō kōron, but in a more profoundly
lasting way affected the course of his life.

Somewhat prophetically, perhaps, it was through their mutual
interest in drama and film that the two men came to meet each other
in 1916. Satō, twenty-six and married to the Shingeki actress Kawaji

Utako (his first wife), was introduced by her to Kamiyama Shigehito, a well-known Shingeki actor who had performed both on stage and in American movies. Tanizaki, at thirty-one, was involved in filmmaking, having recently been invited to serve as a script consultant for Taishō Motion Picture Film Studios and having written the sceenplay for "Amateur Club" (Amachua kurabu). His good friend Kamiyama introduced him to Satō's stories and poetry, and Satō became a close acquaintance and frequent visitor at his house following a party held at the Tanizakis' to commemorate the publication of Akutagawa's story, "Rashōmon." The friendship continued even after the Tanizakis moved to the seaside city of Odawara in Kanagawa prefecture, where Satō called often and entertained Tanizaki and his wife, Chiyo, with his ready verbal wit.

By 1920 Tanizaki's marriage to Chiyo had grown cold. Satō's own marriage (his second one, to Kayoko, who was a friend of his first wife, Utako) was floundering, and would soon lead to his departure from Tokyo and eventually from Japan. In the winter of 1921, on his return to Tokyo, he stopped at Odawara to visit the Tanizakis. His visit became an extended one. He moved into an apartment on the second floor of their house and stayed for two months. Sensitized by his own recent suffering to the unhappiness of others, Satō took a deep personal interest in the plight of Chiyo and her daughter, who were left alone in the empty house, unloved and neglected, while Tanizaki was pursuing other women (including Chiyo's own younger sister Seiko, who was starring in "Amateur Club"). Satō offered to marry Chiyo and reached an agreement whereby Tanizaki would divorce her. When Tanizaki suddenly and without explanation backed out of the agreement, relations between the two men were severed.[17] The separation was formally announced in the magazine Kaizō in March 1921. Contact between them ceased entirely when Tanizaki moved his household to the Kansai after the 1923 earthquake.

At this point, Satō entered his so-called wandering period and for four years drifted aimlessly about Tokyo, living here and there, despondent over the ruined love affair with Chiyo, and gripped in the vise of unconsolable, hopeless loneliness. In 1924 he married an Akasaka geisha named Odanaka Tami. The marriage was a failure from the start, and before long Tami was writing to Tanizaki to complain about her treatment at Satō's hands. Her letters were followed by Satō's own, and in due time the two writers were eventually reconciled. Satō divorced Tami and made plans to marry Chiyo.

Thus public interest in "Unbearably Forlorn" was conceivably renewed eight years after its publication, when an announcement appeared, this time in all the major newspapers, informing the public that, following negotiations presided over by Chiyo's older brother and lasting seven hours, a formal statement had been signed in which Tanizaki agreed to divorce Chiyo so that Satō might marry her.

After Satō and Chiyo moved into an attractive new southern European–style house (designed by Satō) in the Sekiguchidai district of Tokyo, all traces of melancholia, pessimism, and groping disappeared from Satō's work. His experimental period drew to a close; henceforth, his writing would take on an assured tone, and his work, committed to a more fixed view of the world, would be more assertive—although perchance less interesting from a literary point of view.

"A Window Opens" (Mado hiraku)

"A Window Opens" represents Satō as literary craftsman at his best. The haiku at the end of the story poses a question—Deep in autumn, the man next door, what does he do?—which the narrative answers through a series of lightly layered levels of perception. Satō leads us up to the window through a series of images and incidents that project the experience of life in a horribly cramped environment on both the physical and the psychological levels. The unbearable confinement of the house in the alley is concretized in the pomegranate tree (a traditional symbol of fertility in Chinese literature), which is dead in the sunless garden but cannot be removed because there is no place to throw it. The sense of confinement and annoying interaction with the neighbor reaches a climax in the innocent puppy's gruesome fate.

At this point in the narrative, "a window opens," which provides a different view on the world outside. It brings the outside in, and as a symbol of the transitional plane between reality and the "inner rooms" of the imagination, it also provides a way into the mind of the first-person narrator. And as scenes viewed through the framework of the window become food for thought and conversation for the protagonist and his friends, the window becomes a socializing force, enabling the protagonist to relinquish his self-absorption and enter the world outside with new insight.

The proscenium of the window frame offers rich potential for dramatic irony and humor, which Satō deftly exploits. As he watches the new tenants next door through the window, curiosity about the couple who have just moved in replaces anger toward their landlord the tofu dealer, and as he becomes involved in speculating about the new couple, imagining how they live, and how they feel, earlier emotions of frustration and anger give way to feelings of tolerance and empathy for the strangers next door.

In a deft, humorous manner reminiscent of *senryū*, the story reveals the human impulse to create narratives in order to make sense of the world, the propensity to create stories about one's fellow beings on the basis of scenes glimpsed from a distance, and the way in which the engagement of the imagination in storytelling may defuse anger and hostility.

As in *haikai* and *senryū*, the story conjoins the earthy with the aesthetic by situating the window in the bathroom. The potential vulgarity of the perspective of the "observation platform" is offset by the sensitivity with which Satō traces the shifts and turns in the protagonist's feelings toward other people and his environment. The delicate evolution of his emotional reactions to the outside world, and the gentle humor that tempers the annoyance produced by the cramped living conditions, makes "A Window Opens" a classic story with the flavor of a haiku in the opinion of one Japanese critic.[18] The story suggests a way of addressing the dichotomy between aesthetics and ethics that was broached in "Beautiful Town." Satō deals with this issue in a different form in his critical essays.

CRITICAL ESSAYS

The tensions and ambivalences that pulled Satō toward Western-style experimentations and back to Chinese literature and classical Japanese aesthetics are as evident in his critical writings as they are in his novelistic works. The translated essays included in this book allow us to glimpse the evolution of Satō's thought on literary matters, from his early Western-inspired romantic ideas about art and the special vocation of the artist, through a reappraisal of the meaning of a classical Japanese aesthetic concept in "Fūryūron" (On elegance, 1924), to a more conservative period in the late thirties and early forties, when a pre-occupation with national and cultural identity took precedence over concerns of an individualistic nature and the earlier optimistic belief in the universality of art gave way to a pessimistic realization of what he assumed to be the nonuniversal nature of Japanese language and culture, and therefore, of Japanese literature.

"The Joy of the Artist" (1919) and "The Art, That Is the Person" (1919)

The ideas, tone, and even format of the early essays, "The Joy of the Artist" (Geijutsuka no yorokobi) and "The Art, That Is the Person" (Geijutsu sunawachi ningen) appear to have been inspired by Western writings. Satō's aphoristic style and his joyful affirmation of the value of playful production may recall the writings of Nietzsche and, before him, Schiller, who asserted that human beings are most fully human when they play at aesthetic creation.[19] The art for art's sake philosophy and statements about the desirability of transforming all human occupations into art, and all human life into art, echo views expressed by John Ruskin and William Morris, who had sought to use art to beautify, humanize, and spiritualize an environment made ugly and mean by the ever-present manifestations of a ruthless urge to "industrialize" that seemed to know no limits.

Romantic notions of the "ultimate self" and the "higher self" that lie at the core of "The Art, That Is the Person" also sound more Western than Japanese. But the circular argument that only a good man can create good art and that good art must be created by a good man (what exactly might constitute good art and a good man are left to the reader's imagination, as Satō fails to define either category) creates a somewhat nebulous, even confused, impression and may suggest that he sensed and yearned for an orientation for which he had not found an adequate form of expression at this stage of his career.

There are signs that the values of Satō's traditional background were already in conflict with an individualism that had been acquired primarily through translated literature and imported art. The romantic references to the "eternal immortal me" and the "absolute me" are modified by a simultaneous realization of the smallness of the self in limitless space. Apprehension of the eternal in the moment, the world within the self, the universal in the particular, the interpenetration of all things—in short, themes grounded in the buddhistic worldview of medieval Japan—were oft-repeated motifs in Satō's work as he groped his way toward new footholds on the slippery slope between Eastern tradition and the intellectual and artistic inducements of the modern West, and would be heard with increasing frequency as the years went by and he came to embrace traditional aesthetics based upon an Eastern orientation that emphasized spirit over matter.

"The Ascetic and the Frog" (Kugyōsha to kawazu, 1919)

Themes that would be developed in a more serious vein in "Fūryūron" were initially explored in a witty allegorical style in "The Ascetic and the Frog." Like "F*O*U," written seven years later, this piece may be read as an ironic commentary on aesthetics—this time, traditional aesthetics—viewed from the perspective of a little Satō-like frog in search of the ultimate.

In playing with the idea of the traditional poetics of *fūryū*, as exemplifed in the haiku of the great medieval poet of *fūryū*, Matsuo Bashō (1644–1694), Satō reworked it from the inside, probed and expanded it, and created a modernist piece that mixed irony, fantasy, and play.

With the wit of an iconoclastic haiku poet, Satō lifts and deftly reverses the images of the revered poem:

> *furuike ya*   an old pond-
> *kawazu tobikomu*   a frog jumps in
> *mizu no oto*   the sound of water.

The frog whose leap triggered the enlightenment experience for the poet-listener in Bashō's poem becomes, in Satō's own words, a frog from Aesop's fable and a seeker after enlightenment. Consciousness, previously seated in the poet-speaker and presumed listener who hears the sound of the water in Bashō's poem, is now in the frog.

Possibly looking at himself with an ironic gaze, Satō has his frog articulate the concern about the relationship between will and the spirit of *fūryū* that he later investigated in "Fūryūron."

Unlike the proverbial Zen patriarch who refused to speak to the suppliant who approached him for spiritual guidance, Satō's avuncular ascetic readily enters into a dialogue with the frog, who, in a modern manner, is talkative and inquisitive. But in spite of the ascetic's easy formulaic explanation of "the point" of the Bashō haiku—an explanation geared to the search for quick, easy answers in the convenience-minded modern world—Satō's frog does not grasp it.

It takes time. The moss that covered Bashō's old pond eventually grows over the frog's body. Comprehension of *fūryū* is not to be achieved readily through the application of will and action after all. It takes patience. One may read the ancients but possibly not "know" them. Not even their poems—not even *"furuike ya"* itself—can teach one how to "really" grasp *fūryū*. It takes the reduction of will to the absolute minimum, to the point where nature can enter and flow through one.

In his version of *"furuike ya,"* Satō's modern frog struggles to find an answer amid distractions produced by the din and politics of the modern world. The frog finds *mu* (nothingness) only after it has ceased to will, when it loses all sense of time, purpose, and, eventually, self—the modern rationalistic self that Satō himself would perhaps attempt to shed.

"Fūryūron" (On elegance, 1924)

"Fūryūron" appeared in the April issue of *Chūō kōron* the year after the Great Kantō Earthquake that struck Yokohama and part of Tokyo on September 1, 1923, killing over a hundred thousand people and destroying several thousand homes. This catastrophe seemed to mark the end of an era, and, for many, doubts and misgivings about the benefits of a half-century's drive to modernize Japan along Western lines seemed to crystallize in the wake of its widespread destruction. For others the challenge of creating a new life in a newly rebuilt capital seemed an opportunity to create a new world order. The proletarian literature movement gained momentum, and many new socialist literary organizations and literary journals came into being. Furthermore, movements such as Japanese versions of formalism, dada, and surrealism were reinvigorated. Many of the older writers who had established their careers earlier in the Taishō period, on the other hand, faced a time of spiritual crisis and loss of confidence. Some changed course abruptly and completely.

The reactions of Satō and Tanizaki, and the courses their writing careers took in the following years, make for an interesting study in contrasts. Burned out of his fashionable Western-style house in Yokohama, Tanizaki moved to the Kansai. Living in the historic region of Osaka and Kyoto, he began to mine its old cultural traditions, melding his vision of the past with private fantasies and dreams in a series of highly successful novels.

During the same period Satō reassessed the issue of cultural identity in a somewhat more rational, objective fashion in essay form. *Fūryūron* conjoined an attempt to define a medieval Japanese aesthetic concept with a sense of what being Japanese meant, spiritually as well as aesthetically. As such, it was part of a larger intellectual movement that had been ongoing ever since the Meiji restoration had turned the country into a modernizing nation-state organized to defend itself against Western powers. The pattern of ambivalence toward Western culture, exemplifed in the late-nineteenth-century movement to "leave Asia" *(Datsu-A)* and enter Europe *(Nyū-Ō)*, followed by a reverse trend in the twentieth century to return to Asia *(Nyū-A)* and leave Europe *(Datsu-Ō)*, colors Satō's works as well as those of numerous other modern Japanese who wrote on Japanese aesthetics. "Fūryūron" is of interest as a historical document rather in the same vein as the art historian Okakura Kakuzō's *The Ideals of the East* (1902) and *The Book of Tea* (1904). Although Okakura wrote his books in English and Satō wrote in Japanese, both writers revealed the tensions and conflicts that the contrast between Asian and Western traditions produced in artists and intellectuals. As Okakura reacted against mistaken Western notions about the tea ceremony as a quaint superficial custom, defending the East Asian spiritual and philosophical traditions underpinning it, so Satō affirmed classical Japanese aesthetics in the face of Western literary and artistic influences. Both essayists sought to define a Japanese style of appreciating beauty and of being in the world as distinct from the ways of other peoples, and each saw a connection between aesthetic orientation and national essence.

Satō's writing on *fūryū*, the uniquely "Japanese" aesthetic, also shares concerns about national identity found in the works of his contemporaries such as the philosophers Kuki Shūzō (1888–1941), Nishida Kitarō (1870–1945), and Watsuji Tetsurō (1889–1960), and the founder of Japanese folklore studies, Yanagida Kunio (1875–1962), who turned away from cosmopolitan civilization to seek a return to the "native place of the spirit" (*Nihon kaiki*).[20]

In searching for a renewed Asian and specifically Japanese identity, Satō came to appreciate the refined elegant aesthetic inheritance of medieval Japan, which was seen to represent human qualities the very opposite of those associated with the rationalistic, materialistic culture of the West. In his literary activities, which became explicitly political as the war drew nigh, Satō's concern about national identity assumed a more radical and actively public form than Tanizaki's (which was expressed in *Inei Raisan* [*In praise of shadows*, 1938] a novelistic exposition on the Japanese sense of beauty).

"Fūryūron" marked a turning point in Satō's career; it was the harbinger of an overriding concern about his country's cultural and spiritual identity and a changing world that would preoccupy him for the next several decades and eventually lead to his appointment as an official correspondent attached to the Imperial Army.

For Satō, the concept of *fūryū* was essentially a spiritual orientation, grounded in the medieval buddhistic view of the universe that was, he believed, inextricably linked to the Japanese character. The characters for "wind" and "flow" used to write *fūryū* suggest an "indefinable" spirit, one entailing a total immersion of the self in nature and freedom from attachment to ego. Ironically, the concept that Satō would use to orient himself in the modern world, and that would offer to others a spiritual foundation, and thereby a source of stability and strength, was founded on the poetically suggestive, indefinable ideas of ephemerality (*mujō*) and nothingness (*mu*).

Satō again reveals his interest in ways in which the play of perspective changes the shapes, sizes, and positions of objects in space. He asks his reader to imagine the long line of which the single point is but the present moment, and the long thread tying the present point to the past, and the plane surface lying behind the manifestation of a single line, and then to imagine the moment of human life today in the cosmos, and the infinite cosmos contained within the single world of today.

These imaginings, generated by unusual visual perspectives—like the hallucinatory visual experiences wherein scenes recede and become tiny, about to disappear, then grow rapidly larger, described earlier in *Gloom in the Country*—are universal, and their phenomenology has been explored, and aestheticized, by writers in the West as well as in Japan. Satō, however, found significance in a presumed difference distinguishing the Japanese response to the "momentary, minute nature of man and the eternity and infinity of nature" from the responses of other people (Europeans in particular). According to Satō, the same feelings that evoked "anguished screams and actions among other people" grew in the Japanese not into religion and philosophy but were soon aestheticized into the "artistic state of the 'pathos of things' *(aware)*." It was in their embracing of the "pathos of things" and "the sense of impermanence" *(mujōkan)* that the Japanese differed from other peoples.

In Japan as Satō saw it, it was the active relinquishing of resistance to the human ontological condition and finding therein a source of spirituality and aesthetic beauty that set the Japanese apart. In this respect, "Fūryūron" may be read as a challenging introduction to the perennial concern of thinkers, East and West: the concept of will in Eastern and Western aesthetics.

"The Genesis of the Prose Spirit" (1924)

As in the case of "Fūryūron," the discursive impressionistic prose of "The Genesis of the Prose Spirit" (Sanbun seishin no hassei) reflects its own genesis: group discussions among writers *(zadankai)*, which sometimes took the form of exchanges of written opinions published in magazines.

In *Fūryūron* and "The Genesis of the Prose Spirit," Satō contrasted two essential aesthetic orientations: the spirit of *fūryū*—medieval, classical in its restraint, and quintessentially Japanese—and the spirit of prose, associated with modernism, rationalism, the spirit of positivism underlying naturalism, and democracy—in short, a spirit originating in the West.

These orientations toward art had political implications that would be realized in the decades to come. Whereas "Fūryūron" stressed uniqueness and an essentially aristocratic sensibility that could not be adequately communicated through language but only intuited and referred to as "that," "The Genesis of the Prose Spirit" described an outlook that crossed national, cultural, and racial lines and was essentially democratic in its communicability and universality.

In this connection it may be interesting briefly to compare Satō with Uno Kōji (1891–1961), who along with Satō was said to project, more than any other writer, the "mood" of the Taishō period; albeit, if classified on a scale of aesthetic preferences Uno's work would be close to the opposite pole of the "poetic spirit."

In place of the "orderly balance, unity, and harmony" embraced by the classical "poetic spirit," Uno's novels display a multiplicity of characters, behaviors, polyphonic articulations, and perspectives on the world. In his hand, the spirit of this modern prose is essentially critical, parodic, and undermining. Instead of aiming for an ideal, it exposes the narrowness inherent in the foreclosing of alternative perceptions that accompanies the effort to attain a unified perspective. Its movement is centrifugal, away from the unifying center. It promotes the eccentric and the irregular, the misshapen, the ill-begotten, the strange and accidental—in short, life in all its imperfections.

Seeking change, chafing against constraint, finding a natural outlet for his views in parody, Uno kept silent during the war years, even defied the authorities by continuing to meet publicly in restaurants with a geisha and the small group of writers who gathered around him. Satō, in search of the ultimate aesthetic form, and seemingly finding it in *fūryū*, lent his support to the Nihon Romanha, an ultranationalistic group of young writers dedicated to the resuscitation of the Japanese classics, and supported the war effort through his writings in the late thirties and early forties.

THE MIDDLE YEARS

Satō's marriage to Chiyo in 1930 marked the important turning point. Thereafter he distanced himself from the more cosmopolitan interests of his early period and focused his attention on traditional Japanese and, occasionally, Chinese, literature. He wrote historical novels based on the lives of the thirteenth-century founder of the "Pure Land" sect, Hōnen (*Kikusui monogatari*, Tale of the chrysanthemum spring, 1936), and the thirteenth-century essayist Kamo no Chōmei (*Kamo no*

Chōmei, 1935); published modern Japanese translations of works by the Edo-period writers Ihara Saikaku (1642–1693) and Ueda Akinari (1734–1809); and, as the Pacific War took a turn for the worse for Japan, he wrote biographical novels about a sixteenth-century samurai who fought against Western colonial powers in Southeast Asia for trading rights (Yamada Nagamasa, 1942) and about a Christian samurai who succeeded in sinking a Portuguese warship outside Nagasaki harbor (Arima Harunobu, 1942).

Satō, who had written at length on the necessity to suppress will in the search for *fūryū*, and whose little frog had turned his back on politics to find transcendence in solitude, was himself caught up in vehement manifestations of will.

In 1934 Satō's activities took a directly political turn with the publication of "Battle Songs" (*Jinchū no kangin*), that is, his commentaries on "Poem Diary" (*Utanikki*, 1907), a collection of war poetry written by Mori Ōgai during the Russo-Japanese War (1904–1905). Soon thereafter he was invited to write newspaper and magazine articles about his impressions of military maneuvers conducted near Mount Fuji, and in 1938 he went to China in the capacity of official correspondent attached to the Imperial Army. Before the war was over, he would also go to Malaysia and Indonesia as a representative of the Japanese writing establishment traveling with the army.

The song Satō wrote praising the national flag ("Under the Rising Sun," "Nisshōki no shita ni," 1938) was broadcast throughout the Japanese empire, and one of Satō's verses ("We Shall Smite Them and Be Done," "Uchiteshi yaman"), in the half-dozen volumes of war poetry that he produced, was made into a major motion picture that set attendance records far exceeding those of any other film made during the war years.[21]

On Japanese Literature and the Japanese Language

In Satō's short essays on Japanese literature and language, written during the war, is heard none of the optimistic belief, voiced by numerous writers during the Taishō period, in the capacity of art to transcend national and cultural divisions and annihilate racial prejudice by revealing the unity of the human spirit amid the variety of its forms. Rather, written after more than a half-century during which thousands of Japanese had devoted years of their lives to attempting to learn Western languages and read the national literatures of Western countries, Satō's essays are a reminder of how one-sided those efforts to transcend cultural divisions through art had been after all.

In "The International Quality of Japanese Literature" (Nihon bungaku no kokusaisei, 1938) he notes that Japanese literature can be comprehended by foreigners if they have the necessary "understanding and love for Japanese civilization." Unfortunately, most do not understand the "humanity of Japanese literature" because they have not exerted the effort to try to understand Japan. Moreover, the most "typically Japanese elements" are those that are the most difficult to translate and the most likely to be "extinguished" in translation. At the end of the century, when yet so few and yet comparatively many more westerners can read some Japanese literature in the original, Satō's remarks are reminders of the yawning chasm that lay between Western nations and Japan in the years preceding the war.

There is a note of pathos in Satō's assessment of the Japanese language and its inadequacy as a tool for effective communication with westerners, whose languages are so much more "aggressive" and "argumentative." The contradictory impulses manifest in Satō's writing are even more in evidence in the curious discrepancy between his emphasis upon the delicacy, lyrical beauty, and "tenderness" of the Japanese language in "The Beauty of the Japanese Language" (Nihongo no utsukushisa, 1941) and the bellicosity of his war poems. The sense of regret over the inability of the Japanese language to be readily understood by non-Japanese, and the sadness and pity for Japan that suffuse this essay, written at a time when Japan would soon be engulfed in a war with America, is a compelling reminder of the unsurmountable difficulties Japan experienced in trying to communicate with the Western world, and of the struggles of individual artists like Satō, who tried in vain to be part of a bridge of understanding that, in the end, failed.

THE LATE YEARS

Satō devoted his last years to the preservation of the Japanese literary tradition by editing, translating, and commenting on the works of earlier writers. During the war he edited the writings of Meiji-period novelists Izumi Kyōka (1873–1939) and Higuchi Ichiyō (1872–1896) and his mentor, Ikuta Chōkō. After the war he wrote biographical novels about the lives of the poet and novelist Shimazaki Tōson (*Shijin Shimazaki Tōson hyōden*, Critical Biography of Shimazaki Tōson the Poet, 1949), Yosano Akiko (*Akiko mandara*, Akiko Mandala, 1954), Takamura Kōtarō (*Shōsetsu Takamura Kōtarō*, Takamura Kōtarō, a Novel, 1956), and Nagai Kafū (*Shōsetsu Nagai Kafū den*, Biography of Nagai Kafū, a Novel, 1960). He edited the Keiō University literary journal, *Mita bungaku*; translated Yoshida Kenkō's fourteenth-century essay *Tsurezuregusa* into modern Japanese; authored many literary memoirs and essays on the history of Japanese literature, and served as a mentor to numerous young writers and as a judge on the Akutagawa Prize Committee. He was inducted into the Japan Academy of Arts in 1948 and awarded the Yomiuri Literary Prizes for poetry in 1953 and for prose, for *Akiko Mandara*, in 1954. Satō received his country's highest distinction when he was awarded the Order of Culture in 1960, four years before his death at the age of seventy-two.

Notes

1. Itō Sei, "Uno Kōji no sekai," in *Uno Kōji kaizō*, ed. Shibukawa Gyō et al. (Tokyo: Chūō Kōron, 1963), p. 246.

2. Fukuda Kiyoto and Okada Junya, *Satō Haruo hito to sakuhin* (Tokyo: Shimizu Shoin, 1966), p. 12.

3. As suggested by Donald Keene, *Dawn to the West: Japanese Literature of the Modern Era*, vol. 1: *Fiction* (New York: Holt, Rinehart, and Winston, 1984), p. 632.

4. Fukuda and Okada, p. 21.

5. Kawamoto Saburō, *Taishō gen'ei* (Tokyo: Shinchōsha, 1990), p. 250.

6. First introduced in 1892, moving pictures had become windows to the mysterious exotic West, and the faces of Charlie Chaplin and Mary Pickford were familiar images of the "high collar," "high-class Western culture" (*seiyō no haikara bunka*) associated with the silver screen (Kawamoto, p. 79). Automobile registration had increased from 210 at the end of the Meiji era to over 10,000 in 1921 (Kawamoto, p. 250). And cafes, where one could indulge in exotic refreshments such as hot chocolate, baked apples, and doughnuts, attracted writers, artists, and journalists, and the avant-garde of the avant-garde: members of the feminist Seitōsha society.

7. Cited in Malcolm Bradbury and James McFarlane, "The Name and Nature of Modernism," in *Modernism, A Guide to European Literature 1890–1930*, ed. Malcolm Bradbury and James McFarlane (New York and London: Penguin Books, 1976), p. 28.

8. Yamaguchi Hiroshi, *Kōgai jūtakuchi no keifu* (Tokyo: Kashima, 1988), p. 28; cited in Stephen Dodd, "Fantasies, Fairies, and Electric Dreams; Satō Haruo's Critique of Taishō," *Monumenta Nipponica* 49, no. 3 (Autumn 1994): 296.

9. According to Kawamoto Saburō, this was the Metropole Hotel, built in 1890 on a site formerly occupied by the American legation (Kawamoto, p. 22).

10. Of the "three K's," Satō liked movies best. In the essay "Motion Pictures Now and in the Future" (Katsudō shashin no genzai to shōrai), which he authored with Tanizaki in 1918, he advocated film as an art form. "I am grateful for living in the age of movies; it is one of the few most eternal of the human material inventions; when I see a good one, I experience a transcendental feeling" (Kawamoto, p. 82).

11. Satō's description of a woman laughing in the street, her teeth sparkling like "little white seeds of a Mediterranean fruit," may have echoed Morand's "teeth small as rice grains" but obviously came even closer to a line from Oscar Wilde's "The Picture of Dorian Gray": "she laughed again, her teeth showed like white seeds in a scarlet fruit." *The Portable Oscar Wilde*, ed. Richard Aldington and Stanley Weintraub (New York: Penguin Books, 1981), p. 372.

12. André Salmon (1881–1969), poet, novelist, and art critic who belonged to the Cubist group that included Guillaume Apollinaire (1880–1918), Max Jacob (1876–1944), and Pablo Picasso (1881–1973). Satō himself was a renowned Western-style painter who exhibited his oil paintings in galleries on the Ginza as well as in exhibits sponsored by the Nika Kai, the most important organization for Western-style painting in Japan.

13. Donald Keene, *Dawn to the West, Japanese Literature of the Modern Era*, vol. 2: *Poetry, Drama, Criticism* (New York: Holt, Rinehart, and Winston, 1984), pp. 553–554.

14. There is an English translation of this story in *The Sick Rose: A Pastoral Elegy*, translated by Francis B. Tenny with introduction by J. Thomas Rimer (Honolulu: University of Hawai'i Press, 1993).

15. Bradbury and McFarlane, *Modernism*, pp. 46–47.

16. Yoshida Sei'ichi, *Kaisetsu*, vol. 1, *Satō Haruo zenshū*, 12 vols. (Tokyo: Kōdansha, 1969), p. 611.

17. The so-called Odawara Affair is described by Takeuchi Yoshio in *Karei naru shōgai* (Tokyo: Sekai Shoin, 1971), pp. 72–87. Tanizaki, it is said, refused

to release Chiyo in 1921 because he needed her for his art; it was after the publication of *Some Prefer Nettles* (Tade kuu mushi, 1929), his novel about a failed
marriage, that he decided to let her go (Takeuchi, p. 83). For English language
accounts of the affair see Van C. Gessel's *Three Modern Novelists: Sōseki, Tanizaki, Kawabata* (Tokyo, New York, London: Kodansha International, 1993);
Ken Ito's *Visions of Desire: Tanizaki's Fictional Worlds* (Stanford: Stanford University Press, 1991); Donald Keene's *Dawn to the West*, vol. 1, and James Thomas
Kenney's "The Life and Works of Satō Haruo." (Ph.D. diss. Harvard University, 1980), p. 96.

    18. Yoshida Sei'ichi praises "A Window Opens" for its haiku-like qualities
of *aware* (pathos) and *okashimi* (humor) (Yoshida, p. 617).

    19. "Over the Aesthetic Education of Man in a Series of Letters," *Friedrich
Schiller: Poet of Freedom*, trans. William F. Wertz, Jr. (New York: New Benjamin
Franklin House, 1985), p. 259.

    20. Tetsuo Najita, "Japanese Revolt against the West: Political and Cul-
tural Criticism in the Twentieth Century," in *The Cambridge History of Japan*,
vol. 6: *The Twentieth Century*, ed. Peter Duus (Cambridge: Cambridge University Press, 1988), p. 735. For a discussion of Kuki Shūzō's appropriation of the
Edo aesthetic term *iki* to define a native sensibility distinct from and "exterior
to Europe's modernity," see Leslie Pincus, "In a Labyrinth of Western Desire:
Kuki Shūzō and the Discovery of Japanese Being," in *Japan in the World*, ed.
Masao Miyoshi and H. D. Harootunian (Durham and London: Duke University Press, 1993).

    21. James Thomas Kenney, Jr., "The Life and Works of Satō Haruo,"
p. 120.

Stories

Beautiful Town

Utsukushii Machi, 1919

I give this story to my
dear child Masaya.[1] It
was written by your father
when he was still young, some
twelve or thirteen years
before you were born.
      Satō Haruo, summer 1947

We are such stuff as dreams are made on . . .
      Shakespeare

My close friend O spoke to me one day about the painter E. . . . Mr. O
had recently had an opportunity to meet this good friend, and E had
inquired about me. (I wonder if O hadn't been speaking about me with
too much interest.) E had borrowed from O's bookshelves a book of
mine that I had given to O. On reading and returning the book he was
reported to have said to O, "I've got a story that I'd really like the
author of *The Fingerprint* to hear. . . ."

Speaking frankly, I have seldom been satisfied with a story that
some kind person has told me I might like to use in my writing. Only in
the case of the artist E did I foresee that I would surely be interested.
Though I did not know him, I had seen E's work at exhibitions now

and then. I would usually linger in front of his work, finding there a certain concurrence of artistic sympathy. The fact that E found my books interesting was not just flattery, I was conceited enough to think. E felt we had something we could mutually agree on, a joint work of art, and he had a story that he wanted me to hear. Thus it happened that one winter's night, escorted by O, I called on E in his studio. As he stoked the fire and I urged him on, this is the story we heard.

As I write this, I express my deep gratitude to both E and O.

THE STORY TOLD ME BY ARTIST E

When you think of it, there was something extraordinary about this story from the beginning. It was eight or nine years ago. I was twenty-one or twenty-two at the time. I received a letter one day. It made me suspicious; the sender had a foreign name. Since I had neglected language study in my school days, I was prone to avoid being spoken to by foreigners and of course I had never been familiar enough with a foreigner to receive a letter from one. The letter was written in good simple Japanese, unduly familiar in tone, and in a clumsy hand on letter paper from the S Hotel in Tsukiji. . . . "Rather than my writing at length, you'll understand everything at once. I want you to come to my hotel at six this evening. The talk will be interesting. I want you to hear a discussion that may please you. . . ." That's all the letter said. Just think of it. I get a letter from someone I don't know. It's uncanny. I get it in the morning when I'm still in bed. All day long it worries me. I wonder if it isn't a stupid petty prank by one of my associates. Students of painting since Buffalmacco in the *Decameron* have diverted themselves by pestering people. Sensing this possibility, I asked some-one to call the S Hotel and inquire whether there was anyone there by the name of Theodore Brentano, and if there really was, whether that person had mistaken my identity in asking me to come. To my surprise, I got the answer that there was no mistake. The call was for me.

By five it was already dark. The streets were lit with the lights of night. All because it was October. In rather dirty attire, affecting a bohemian look, I stood timidly before the entrance to the elegant hotel. To my wonder, far from being rejected I was received politely by a bellhop in a uniform of gold braid and gold buttons who seemed to be expecting me and who led me through brightly lit halls to a room where he left me, asking me to wait briefly. Whoever the unknown person was who had invited me, he did not for some reason appear right away. I sat down at a table where a lot of large books had been tossed. As I glanced restlessly around the room, I was startled by a sight on one wall. An oil painting, a landscape some two-by-three feet in size, was hanging on the greenish-gray wall. I stared in surprise and disbelief. My doubts at last forced me to rise from my chair and go over to examine the picture. It was definitely my painting "Gloom in the City." I had shown it two years earlier in my first exhibition. As I thought about it, there was no reason to be so surprised. Someone must have bought it, even though I put a rather high price on it in my youthful pride and a sense of despair that it would not sell. But now I was astonished to see my own painting on a wall of this hotel. It was so unexpected. I was all the more unable to understand who had invited me here. The man who bought my picture "Gloom in the City"—what kind of connoisseur was he that I hadn't noticed him two years ago? Thinking about this strange day, I returned to my chair and waited impatiently to see the nature of the mysterious person who had invited me, the discriminating buyer of my painting. I slipped my watch out stealthily to look at. It was a little before six. In my anxiety I had come too early. Tiring of the critical examination of my painting, so unexpectedly thrust in front of me, I picked up one of the many big books piled on the table before me. They were all about construction. I looked through them briefly, and my eye was drawn to the abundant illustrations. . . . At that moment footsteps sounded heavily behind me and the door opened. Hurriedly I laid the book facedown, stood up and turned around. Mr. Theodore Brentano? An imposing, stout young gentleman came through the door, wearing a smoking jacket and apparently fresh from the dining room. He was about my age. As I started to bow politely, he smiled and nonchalantly said, "Hello."

Theodore Brentano?

He hadn't lied in his letter. The minute I saw his smiling face I understood it all. Theodore Brentano? I had forgotten my dear friend.

But the blame should not be attributed solely to my insensitivity. Why didn't Theodore Brentano sign his letter to me "Teizō Kawasaki" the way he used to? "Teizō Kawasaki" was my childhood friend whom I could recall without a moment's doubt. When I inquired, it seemed he was not without a secret intent to surprise me, though he did not use a made-up name. Kawasaki was a Eurasian child who went under either name. " 'Theodore Brentano' is right for today," he said laughing. After his mother had died his father took him to his own country to become an American. His father was a wealthy American who traveled a lot and had many business connections in the Far East. His mother was the man's mistress, remaining in Tokyo. The mother died when Kawasaki was sixteen. The boy was taken by his father by ship from Yokohama. The morning that I had gone to see him off at the station, there was Kawasaki wearing a brand-new Western suit and a necktie of mixed purple, red, and green in place of the school uniform he had shed. . . . Kawasaki, his head thrust out at us from the window of the first-class car he was riding in with his enormous father. . . . Kawasaki, who used to carry in his school uniform pocket the gold watch with the gold locket hanging from it that his father had given him. As I listened to the story of his subsequent life, it brought back all kinds of memories. His life, strange as it was, was not as strange as his name. Other than his name, all was but a matter of growing up over the years—his large build, his cheery style of talking, his attractive mouth, the eyes that seemed to bore into one, and then his wealth. He had grown surprisingly fast.

When I thought about him as a child like that, I became a child again myself.

He had been in Tokyo two years before, he said, and pointing behind him at my painting, he added, "That's not bad at all." He said he had studied painting a bit himself. Judging by what he said about my picture, one would not think that he, a complete amateur, was posing as an expert. With self-confidence and unyielding to my dissent, he admired Whistler. We shared lots of talk about the arts. Actually I thought he understood contemporary art better than its self-appointed critics. . . . While we were talking on about the arts, he suddenly changed his tone and began to speak of "a marvelous and most pleasing plan" (as he himself called it) that he hoped to realize in the near

future. As his story progressed, he became excited, and then his excite-
ment spread to me. Before we knew it the two of us were enraptured. I
was ardently drawn to the fantastic idea embraced by my friend, and I
truly had to admire the American spirit it would take to realize it.
There are plenty of millionaires in Japan, but how many among them
would think of a project such as this? It would surely take some kind of
genius to devise such a plan. As I recall it now, in the midst of talking
about his plan he suddenly fetched a book from the next room and
hastily ruffled through the pages to find and read me a passage. I didn't
understand very well, but it was a section from Part II of Faust. (E told
me so and gave me the gist of the poem. It was probably the following
selection. Having arbitrarily so concluded, I quote the following
extracts from Dr. Mori Ōgai's translation):[2]

> Who am I? I am profusion. Poetry am I.
> I am the poet who finds fulfillment
> In squandering mine own greatest goods.
> I have riches too, unlimited.
> Myself I rate no less than Plutus,
> The God of Wealth, whose feasts and revels I adorn
>   with merriment.
> What the God does lack I do dispense.

. . . In a word, he wanted to build a beautiful town somewhere,
investing all his fortune in it. He told me that the legacy his father left
him, his father who had died four years earlier, amounted to some tens
of millions of yen, including a huge gold mine somewhere in South
America and other assets. . . . Converted into cash, such a fortune
could cover a giant undertaking in Japan, but in America you could do
only one-six-thousandth as much. In America his funds might be
enough to build only one mansion, but in Japan he might be able to do
about a hundred at one throw. "But," he said, "what I want does not
require such magnificent mansions. Just a house is okay. In size a single
house should be two stories with perhaps 1,500 to 1,800 square feet. I'd
like to have about a hundred of these. In these houses, everything useless should be eliminated, but they should be beautifully adorned. Truly
good decoration is always indispensable. To think that there is beauty

in needless luxury is a small and yet not insignificant fallacy derived from a larger modern fallacy. Mankind cherishes a love of opulence, but hardly any of our modern-day luxury springs from that love. It is in any case possible to eliminate everything useless and still achieve exquisite beauty. I'd like to have a hundred houses like that. I could build around a hundred. As I say, it's fine if they're just houses. Now how many can there be of which one can think, 'There truly is a house'? Truly only a few. Just as the man is indeed rare of whom you can think, 'There is a man.' . . . Then in these hundred houses I'd like to have a hundred people or rather a hundred families live. I wouldn't rent the houses to them. I'd only want them to live there." He spoke like this. When I asked him what kind of people he would like to have live in the houses, he stammered in distress. "I haven't fully thought about that yet. I can't become an examiner of people. If I can avoid being presumptuous, for the mere reason that I am the one who built the little town of one hundred houses, I'll choose people I like," he said as an opener. I think he went on to enumerate the following points. I don't remember very well, as I didn't pay much attention at the time. He said: "(a) People most satisfied by the houses I built. (b) Couples who have married of their own mutual choice and who both have stayed with their first marriage and have children. (c) People who have chosen as an occupation the work they like best. Therefore they've become most proficient in their work and have made a living from it. (d) No merchants, no public officials, no military. (e) People who keep the promise never to engage in monetary transactions in the town. So they will suffer some inconvenience. Therefore, near to my town but outside of it I should provide some money-transfer facilities for the people of the town. (f) They must have a dog as a pet. If by nature they don't like dogs, they must care for a cat. If they don't like either dogs or cats, they can keep a bird. . . ." And so on.

"I dare not presume to prescribe these or anything like them as requirements for human life," Kawasaki continued. "But provisionally I would like to set these criteria for choosing the people who are to live in the houses I build. In return for daring to undertake this project, I am prepared to accept public criticism that I am a foolish, capricious, eccentric person. Maybe I will have to endure more than that. In order for us to do unusual things, there is need in our world for all kinds of sacrifice. . . . The houses I build must give a nice, comfortable feeling to those who live in them. If unfortunately I don't find anyone to live under such frivolous conditions in houses built by a foolish, capricious man like me, then I'll hire someone to keep my houses nice and clean. And when it becomes night, I think I'll put bright lights in those houses where no one is living, so that the lights will appear beautiful in the windows. Regardless of whether the houses are occupied or not, I will provide funds for a budget to maintain the little town. For about a hundred years—I'd like to say forever if I could—I want the houses to stand solidly for a hundred years. I also forgot to say my beautiful town must be located in the city of Tokyo. It must form a distinct quarter situated in an unexpected part of the city; it must be a place where it will invite scrutiny by many people. I hope that people as they gaze will think how good it would be to live in a place like that and will be surprised to hear that anyone can. On hearing the conditions that enable them to live there, however, they will be puzzled at why some eccentric fellow wasted so much valuable money to build a town for whatever purpose. I'd like to have people raise these questions. People may perceive me as a mysterious man. Above all I want boys and girls, noble beings who though small can think and feel things without preconception, in seeing this town's beauty, to get at one glance an impression they will never forget all their lives, like a fairy-tale masterpiece that had sunk deep into their tender hearts. The way young people will make a detour to see a beautiful girl, children must make a detour to go by my 'Beautiful Town.' "

"I think I can understand something of your happy idea, but I wonder how I can help you with it." I said this looking up at the excited face of my old friend, a man to be loved and admired, a fine young millionaire, a planner to be marveled at. In reply he said that there would be need for a painter like me in carrying out the plans, first in connection with the selection of the overall site, then for the walls and roofs of the individual houses, and finally for the general view of the whole town comprised of roofs and walls blending in harmonious colors. He took out a large notebook with a green leather cover and showed me the plans again in numerical figures. For me, totally unfamiliar with mathematics, it looked like numbers with lots of zeros piled up in layers step by step. He flipped back and forth through twenty or thirty large pages of his notes, explaining his points one by one in a tone I should follow clearly. . . . On this basis I learned that he needed to find four acres of land at a price of some half-million yen. Beyond that everything was a little confused in my sketchy under-standing. I was somewhat troubled by it, but his enthusiasm prevented me from saying that the explanation was useless. I thought blankly that the "Beautiful Town" he had outlined to me was more interesting, not for the figures he had used, but instead as seen shimmering through the purple swirls of heavy, fragrant smoke from the cigar he had pressed on me, the sweet-smelling cigar I was smoking. I was a young fellow at the time, who could brood seriously about the need for a monastery to serve writers and artists.

During our long conversation the night grew late without our knowing it. The sound of the streetcars we had earlier heard had now ceased. That night he put me in a car—automobiles were rare in Tokyo those days. Saying he wanted a little excursion himself, he got in with me and delivered me to my home in Ōkubo. . . . That night was the first time I had ridden in a car. In the car he spoke a little about how he couldn't sleep at night and so slept in the daytime and arose in the evening, and about how, as I was poor, he could give me some support. Then, tiring of talk and changing his attitude completely, he lapsed into almost total silence. Not only he, but the long night streets, the very night itself. . . . Outside were streetlights along a tree-lined road. Suddenly I was passing through places I did not know. I felt I was speed-ing swiftly toward the "Beautiful Town" that as yet existed nowhere.

ⵊ

If human beings were blessed with the ability to do freely whatever they wanted, I think from then on I would have seen in my dreams night after night that Beautiful Town that I knew could be built but knew not how. I did actually have such dreams once or twice. Kawa-saki's marvelous plan had captivated me before I knew it. I had the feeling of dreaming as I walked through Tokyo, aimless but happy in the balmy autumn weather, my paint box clattering and dangling from my shoulder. As a student of painting I had done this before, and now and then I found unexpected places to paint, but I was not now moved to paint them as I used to do. (If it were not for the idea inspired by Kawasaki, however, my series of etchings "Cityscapes" might not have come to be.) At that time, though, I had no mind to set up my easel, whether before a scene with trees, or a scene of just roofs, or along the banks of a ditch, or before a stone wall, or windows lit by the golden light of the setting sun. I was full of thoughts that today I would find the four acres blessed with the qualifications to become the Beautiful Town, the fields where would be sown the seeds of the mythical "blue flower,"[3] wherever those fields may be but we know not where for sure, the fields that will shortly become the living picture of Beautiful Town. If I didn't find the four acres today, all would come to naught, I felt. What I might never see again if I didn't get them today would, indeed, be scenes worth painting.

I did that for nearly two months, wandering the now chilly streets of Tokyo. Every day I returned discouraged. On those occasions when I took my disappointment to him in the S Hotel, he too was disappointed. In the end he had to look at me with displeasure.

Easily enthused yet easily let down as I am, I might soon have tired of this if it had gone on for another ten days. But I chanced onto a "Lucky Idea" (as Kawasaki called it at the time). I think you may know the copperplate engraving by Shiba Kōkan.[4] When I was out walking aimlessly one day, I recalled seeing in the newspaper that an exhibition worth dropping by had opened the day before at the K Club on O Street in Nihonbashi. The exhibition was assembled for the enjoyment of various Dutch and Spanish arts and crafts introduced of old into Japan by the red-headed "Southern Barbarians," as artistic dilettantes called them, and the show was timed to interest the swarms of busy people at the approaching New Year's season. I went out of curiosity. There were all kinds of things—scarlet wools, black velvets with purple and celadon-green arabesque patterns, Dutch plates, flower vases, large broken compasses, heavy handmade pocket watches, and so on. Exhibited side by side for reference were various naive Japanese imitations, mainly ceramics, produced under this Western influence. Deferring these till later and with one tour around, I did not look things over thoroughly. Not that I wasn't interested, but rather than those things, I found myself more attracted to some old prints hanging on the walls.

There were some rare works of Aodo—that was the first I had heard of him.[5] There was Shiba Kōkan too, who gave me that "Lucky Idea," as Kawasaki called it. I had seen his work once before, so I may be confusing it with another of his prints. What I remember now is that green and yellow-brown were the key tones of the copper engraving. It was colored only lightly, and here and there were very light spots of lemon-yellow. These had faded almost to the point of vanishing. The composition placed the horizon below the bottom third of the picture. There was a row of tiny houses, some smallish trees, and several small people and a dog walking on a miniature grassy road. As I recall, there was a clear pink tinge to the peoples' clothing. Very effective it was. The quiet clouds of autumn streamed slanting across the broad sky.

While the picture partook of a certain power of its own, what interested me more and gave me the "idea" was the title, which the author himself had written within the figure of a scroll flying in the wind, in a kind of engagingly childlike, mannered style across the top of the picture's open sky. In print-style Roman letters it said: "TOTO NAKASU NO KEI" (View of Nakazu in Tokyo).[6]

Nakazu! Nakazu!! Nakazu!!! As I shouted the words I fled out of the hall at top speed, but not really like I was crazy. I could not decide whether to go first to Nakazu or to Kawasaki's hotel in Tsukiji, but my hasty steps took me toward Tsukiji. Saying that Kawasaki was still asleep at three o'clock, the bellhop in his uniform of gold braid and gold buttons was reluctant to show me in. I wakened Kawasaki anyway, and the two of us went off to see Nakazu. He kept repeating "Lucky Idea, Lucky Idea." But I was strangely uneasy, thinking, "What if it's no good?" I almost felt I didn't want to go. . . . I've had no reason to visit there since that time, so I don't know how much it may have changed by now. When we went there then, though, I became discouraged at once. That rubbish-strewn, disorderly place gave me a chilly feeling. I didn't remotely have the courage to ask his opinion or express my own.

"Well, it's no good after all," was my only opinion. I thought with pity that my silent companion probably felt the same. As we listened to the jumble of evening sounds, we crossed the upstream bridge; whether it was the one called the male bridge or the female bridge I don't remember.

"Nope. It was a terrible 'Lucky Idea,' " I said, as if to laugh at myself and console my friend.

"Why?" he asked, with a rather triumphant air the moment he heard me. He was completely satisfied with that filthy, good-for-nothing land. The two of us walked in the opposite direction from the Gyōtoku riverbank. . . . Along here was a line of houses on the bank and we could not see Nakazu from the road. . . . Pointing ahead as we walked, he said, "Let's go up and look from the bridge. Shiba Kōkan must have drawn the view from above. I used to go under that bridge on a boat."

Yes. From the bridge! The bridge was the one called Shin-Ōhashi (The New Big Bridge), but that was before the present bridge was built. The former bridge was downstream from the present one, closer to Nakazu. (As Artist E told me the story, he took a sketchbook from a stack on the shelves behind where he stood. Laying it on the tea table surrounded by the three of us, he opened it to a blank page. Then, excusing himself with "Of course, I can't say this is accurate, but if this is the Sumida River . . . ", he drew a sketch with an artist's quick hand and then explained it.)

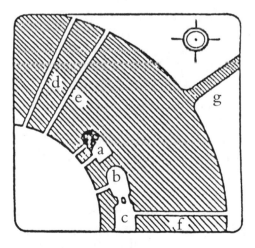

a Nakazu
b Hakozaki
c Tsukiji extended
d Shin-Ōhashi (New Big
  Bridge)
e Former Shin-Ōhashi
f Eitaibashi Bridge
g Onagi River

Kawasaki said, after all, that he liked it very much, very much indeed. . . . Actually, as I visualized from the bridge in the winter's setting sun the Beautiful Town without form but with the potential for any form, and I put that vision in place of the cluster of dirty gray roofs that now existed, it was enough to make me change my mind and like the place. . . . So Kawasaki decided on the area you could see best from the bridge. (As he spoke, E pointed to the part colored black in the drawing.) He would do his best to realize this plan in all respects, Kawasaki declared. He said he would like to buy, if he could, that picture of Shiba Kōkan's, both as a memento of the source of our inspiration and as a way to let people know what kind of place our Beautiful Town had been in olden times. . . . But the art dealer reported that the owner of the picture was a collector of Shiba Kōkan. On this pretext the dealer set an exorbitant price. Kawasaki replied with vigor, "I must respect such an enthusiast for Shiba Kōkan. A man like that should not be overwhelmed by the power of money." So in the end he did not acquire the print.

That evening, the evening we decided on Nakazu as our intended site, our hearts were buoyant. We felt like we were at a temple festival, with its sideshows. I was so elated that I shaved off my ragged three-or-four-month beard before the mirror on his dressing table. I took off my dirty corduroy work clothes and put on an elegant dark suit I borrowed from Kawasaki. That was so I could accompany him to the very strict hotel dining room, which you could not enter without coat and tie. I remember something funny. I was so absorbed in our conversation that night and, heedless of things as I am, forgot I was wearing a borrowed suit and went home wearing it. . . . We drank quite a lot in the dining room. Kawasaki became slightly intoxicated, and on returning to his room he played the piano for me. What he played, whether he played well or played nonsense, I would not know. Music is something I don't understand at all. We continued talking that night of Beautiful Town. He would investigate tomorrow to see if he could buy the land he had seen that day, he said. He also wanted to run an advertisement in the newspaper to hire an architect to design the individual houses for Beautiful Town. He said that he himself was the composer of Beautiful Town, I was the conductor, and the architect he was going to hire would be the string section of the orchestra for all the beautiful houses that would make up Beautiful Town. I drafted the ad for the newspaper as he requested; he said he would pay the architect 3,000 yen per month. . . . I didn't know whether that was adequate or was comparatively high for the service. When it came out in the paper, there were lots of applicants, so I guess it was an adequate allowance. Nearly twenty came for the interviews every evening, but all left after failing to satisfy him.

After we stopped receiving crowds of applicants in the hotel room that became the founding office for this strange town, a short, thin old man with pure-white hair came in one day. His outward appearance had something interesting about it. Forty years before it might have been thought the newest fashion. . . . An elderly architect in a proper morning suit worn with the odd grace befitting it and bearing the stigma of bashful refinement stood before Kawasaki. Kawasaki took to the old man at first sight, as did I some days later. The more he talked to the old man, the more Kawasaki liked him. The architect answered his questions in halting pauses. In the 1880s era of the Rokumeikan,[7] that fanciful, out-of-season flowery time, he had gone to Paris on his own funds to study his beloved "Architecture of Enlightenment." When he returned several years later, the period of unnatural westernization had ended and he encountered a period of even more unnatural retrogression. The knowledge he had taken pains to acquire in his middle years was unexpectedly useless in Japan. The newly returned architect saw himself growing old and poor. . . . In that time all he had been able to do was subcontracted design for some army barracks and movie houses. Once, through a secondhand appeal, he had designed a villa for some nobleman. The plans he drew at great pains and to his own satisfaction were, however, never used. One set was said to be too simple, the other too elaborate. The architect believed that something in-between would not be unsightly, but, already growing old, he declined to try again. He had a dutiful son who became a doctor and supported him. In the meantime he dreamed only of building for once in his life a house that he liked. But no one asked him. There was no land to build on. Still, he imagined all sorts of clients and all sorts of building sites, and he enjoyed working assiduously to design home after home. He had about fifty of these paper plans. Before he knew it he had grown to be an old and white-haired architect. (Like Urashima Tarō!)[8] He said his family had been trying to get him to give up this odd old man's passion, but he wanted, one way or another, for once in his life, to build one of his dream houses on real earth. He confessed that this was his desire for the little remaining time he had left.

"I think this is a man to be respected; we should surely consult him about our project. He has a love for his work that is rare nowadays. Anyway, I told him that I would like to see the plans that he has drawn to no purpose. He should come around 6:30 tomorrow evening. We have as good as got a faithful colleague in him, I think, but it is essential that you like him too. Can you meet him when he comes tomorrow night?" This is what Kawasaki told me the night after the old architect's first visit. When the time came for me to go to the hotel the next day, I saw the old man there a step ahead of me, climbing the stone steps of the hotel entrance. He was struggling with a big bulging portfolio under his arm. . . . Seen from behind, he was wearing the same respectable, old-fashioned, somewhat humorous attire that Kawasaki had described.

That evening I too reached an utterly sympathetic understanding with this elderly architect, just as my friend had the day before.

☖

Thus the architect joined us to make three. Two weeks later the three of us were hurriedly at work to carry out our plans. At Kawasaki's request, the working hours were set from 7:30 to 11:30 in the evenings. For some reason it was not just the set four hours. We were so happy working we were often surprised to find that it was past midnight.

Each of us worked at his own lighted table in his own area of the large hotel room. Now and then, when necessary, we would all assemble around Kawasaki's big round table in the middle of the room. The first evening Kawasaki invited us to join him, and as he served us wine he explained rather concretely his overall plan for the town. From his subsequent investigation he thought he could acquire more than five acres at one end of that tract surrounded by water. To separate it from the other part of Nakazu, a ditch thirty feet wide and rather deep should be dug through the middle. We must build a strong stone wall to demarcate the independent area. The town road should follow the

shoreline to form a ring all the way around. The road should be eighteen feet wide. The side next to the water should be provided with a
stone balustrade—a chest-high parapet. The houses along one side of
the road would run in a smaller ring inside the road and the parapet.
The houses, perhaps fewer than a hundred and each with its own distinct form, would blend harmoniously together, like a castle. The
vacant land in the middle should present a garden, which could be
seen at a glance from the inner windows of every house equally. . . .
This was the gist of his concept. Each house should be two stories high
and should not require much more than a thousand square feet of land.
He said that people who needed a larger residence would not reside in
this town.

For a time I was extremely busy. Kawasaki had recognized that
more than ten of the nearly fifty houses the old architect had designed
in vain would be fully suitable to build on the site we were planning.
The footings and foundations used an abundance of stone. The houses
themselves were to be of wood with the stucco exterior of the traditional Japanese storehouse style. The exteriors were almost pure Western, but the interiors were Japanese mansions designed each in its own
distinctive style. There would be no discord with the exteriors, Kawasaki said in admiration. I took the drawings of the houses one by one,
both the elevations and the three-dimensional projections, and tried to
make simple watercolor paintings. Or I tried coloring over pencil drawings. The most practically designed houses became the most pictorial
when they were converted into paintings. Alongside the houses or
behind them I drew in trees of various shapes that I imagined would
add beauty to the scene. Sometimes I thought of deciduous trees, other
times of evergreens. I fancied various vines climbing the walls. Every
day as I pursued my work, I felt that every existing house my eyes
chanced upon and the treetops I saw showing over mansion garden
walls had become objects of reference for my work just because they
were there. Whenever I looked at the sky, the clouds, flowers in a park,
a woman's kimono, I wondered right away whether that could not be
the color for the walls of my houses, the pillars, the balcony railings,
window curtains, and other household furnishings. That's how absorbed I became in my work. As I painted my pictures, then repainted,
and again reconsidered them, uncertain in my mind and troubled at

the difficulties I saw, Kawasaki would offer some superb idea or thought-ful criticism. He would sit and look up now and then to stare dreamily at a large plat of the area that he had had someone survey and draft for him. Then again he would read from a book. He seemed to like *News from Nowhere* by William Morris.[9] He was always reading it. In those days he would get up around noon, and on the days when he didn't meet with people about the land purchase, he would talk about the houses that he had found to his liking on his walks around town.

In a single night the taciturn old architect would speak no more times than you could count on your fingers. Some days he would say nothing at all. However, the fact that he was in no ill humor was evi-dent from his constant smile. When I needed to go to him for some question to consult about the plans he had already turned over to me, I would have to stand beside him and repeat his name two or three times. There were times when he never did look my way, and I had to give it up as useless. The old man was not deaf. He was just so absorbed, sharpening his pencil, lost in thought, or drawing with his drafting pen.

Our room was lit by necessity with the brightest lights shining like midday. When one of us had to go to someone to talk about business, it was our custom to tiptoe on the thick carpet to avoid disturbing the concentration of the others. Except for when the young hotel bellhop in his uniform of gold braid and gold buttons stealthily opened the door, entered, and stoked the stove with coal, the brilliantly gleaming room was hushed in dead silence. When I visualize us all moving about like silent shadows in that room, it leaves me with a strange feeling. I wonder, is it a scene in a dream reflected in a big mirror, or if not that, is it a single frame from a motion picture. . . ? That's how we worked. We were forever busy. And always happy. The silent bellhop no longer came to light the stove. The time had come instead for the three of us each to throw open the nearest window. Our work progressed rapidly. As we grew accustomed to our work, the old architect and I found our thoughts flowing spontaneously as we sat at our desks. Kawasaki, who had no special work assigned to him, naturally appeared bored. He seemed to be waiting impatiently, unable to bear the waiting, for us to finish our work on Beautiful Town. . . . It was the same with us. Then he thought up some work for himself.

One night when we came into Kawasaki's room as usual, there on the big round table where we drank tea before starting our work lay several gleaming pairs of sharp scissors and knives, big and little ones, and a ruler. Next to them were four of the houses we had designed, built of cardboard and paste on a large wooden board. The paper houses were about two inches tall. Each had the same number of windows and doors, exactly as in the plans, that opened with unbelievable fidelity to the touch of your fingers. The same colors that I had conceived and designated were painted in oil on the tiny outer walls. They were not yet dry. Kawasaki's eyes were fixed on the cardboard with the gravity of a man lost in thought. From that evening on he worked alongside us, diligently building paper houses as his work while the two of us pursued our efforts. He was addicted to this serious pastime with the enthusiasm of a child. As each house was finished we too examined it with the joy of a child. "Look, this little house has exactly the arrangement, room by room. Isn't it fun?" Kawasaki said this as if it comprised the accomplished dream and all the rooms of all the little houses had actually been built for real. Every evening he was absorbed in his work of paper handicraft in a way that others than we would have found absurd. Some evenings he was interrupted in his work. The bellhop in the uniform of gold braid and gold buttons would announce a visitor with a calling card respectfully delivered on a silver tray. It was not really a hindrance to the building of Beautiful Town, but rather a sign of progress. These were agents for the land purchase we needed for Beautiful Town. They withdrew to continue discussions in the room next to where we were working.

As the number of cardboard houses increased, our innocent, enthusiastic dreamer was no longer content with houses alone. Now the assorted trees and vines I had conceived were constructed on that tabletop plank. They were cleverly built of wire and combed-wool yarn. So too the road around the town and the parapet on its outer edge were built piece by piece. For the water surrounding the whole layout, he had laid out mirrors that reflected the row of toy houses upside down. When the mirrors, shining too vividly, failed to create a reflection in the water, he replaced them with translucent frosted glass. His depiction of "Beautiful Town"—this whim made of cardboard— grew more and more elaborate, until even I thought it looked excessive. . . . This happened one night. As I was studying five sheets of plans from the old architect, I was wondering what sequence would be best to match up the houses, and I was trying to draw every combination to find the most beautiful and natural arrangement. As was my custom at such times, I was in the midst of scribbling in my sketchbook, when suddenly the lights went out.

"What's going on?" I yelled out, and the architect muttered something.

In the darkness I heard the hysterical voice of Kawasaki. It was he who had turned off the lights. Startled, he turned them on again. He had become so absorbed in his own thoughts that he had forgotten we were working in the same room. He then asked us if it was all right to stop our work for a while and called us with a smile to come join him at the round table. Again he turned off the lights. I had no idea when he might have worked on it, but in that tabletop Beautiful Town of paper there were lights shining dimly from each and every house. They shone from those tiny windows to reveal to our eyes a miniature world of streets at night. Flickers of light spilled from the windows and were reflected hazily back by the still waters of frosted glass. . . . By his careful preparation hadn't the mirrors been placed at just the right angle to the houses? The many flickers of light were reflected in long, fine streaks, as if they were skimming the surface of the water.

"Then for the next thing," he said, flooding the roofs with the light of a dim green bulb. We stood there side by side looking at the town in the moonlight, when suddenly from above a giant finger reached down and pointed at an open space in the tiny paper town. The timid old architect spoke dryly.

"Um, wouldn't it be better to have a little more light? I was just now working on the design for the steps to this house here. . . ."

. . . Of course this happened only once. We would never play with this toy village every day as if it were nighttime or lit by the moon.

Kawasaki had given a lot of thought to the lighting of his houses in Beautiful Town. He was not satisfied with the idea of buying electricity from an outside electric company. He thought that would impair the independence, the separateness of his town. He could not consider asking his townspeople to use kerosene lamps. "I don't like to see the times do a backflip. That's nothing more than nostalgia. We should look ahead and not fix our eyes on the past. . . ."

My friend, who had reason in his dreams and dreams in his reason, continued.

"When science is perfected, we shall not need to rely on the necessarily large facilities of the electric companies. (That goes not just for electric lights.) There will come a day when people can light their own homes adequately with their own simple electric machines and with about the same time and effort they formerly expended on their oil lamps. The way every household treasures and uses its sewing machine. When that time comes, diverse machines will become objects to be cherished, not feared or hated, because we cannot do without them in our daily life. For our lives as humans to become fully rational and reach their highest potential, science, which is one side of our life, must reach its highest potential in its own way. I think when all of today's useful machines are fully perfected, the mechanical power to drive them will no longer depend on the huge factories that ceaselessly corrode people's health. Just as gentle, well-nurtured, domesticated wild animals, horses, and cows muster their graceful power in the service of humans, and people too through love can become like them, all kinds of necessary machines will become easier to use and will make the most handy tools to help people in the happy pursuit of their handicrafts. When that time comes, machine industry will be the indispensable first step in promoting the arts. Can't we call machine factories militarism in the service of the arts?"

Then again, "the society that we now live in—this is an odd remark about the unlimited power of money—is a dangerous ugly structure of arches in grotesque[10] shapes attached to a grotesque foundation, but the two-legged wingless animal that is man lives calmly in this queer nest. Even the people who call for improvement do no more than add another kind of grotesqueness," he pointed out with relish.

But for me, a person absorbed strictly in my own interests, watching the colors in the clouds and the movements of the stars rather than thinking of earthly matters, and not one with the temperament suitable for his kind of contemplation, I was not up to judging whether what he said was not after all just one kind of grotesqueness. I did not try to make him develop his thinking by interrupting with the question, "Why?" Often I was smothered in the smoke of confusion. Yet I saw the passion of a dreamer in the strong tides that flowed through the depths of those statements, and he and I took pleasure together in the sentiment. "Even that Beautiful Town," he said once, gazing intently at the paper city on the tabletop. "We can only give form to it. Whether Beautiful Town really becomes a beautiful and happy place, only the hearts of each and every person who lives there can make it so."

Before we started our work and after we had finished, we would chat. He often brought up topics like this, but, oddly enough, those ideas interested the old architect more than me. That man retained the thinking of the Peoples' Rights Movement of some thirty-odd years before.

^

The three of us gathering there nightly, absorbed in our work, began in February of 1912 and continued for three years. At the end of the third summer, when the refreshing daylight was changing gradually to autumn, the work began to take shape. From the beginning Kawasaki had divided the project into three stages. It was at least a ten-year plan, but the first phase was accomplished early that fall, four or five months ahead of schedule. That was of course due to the extraordinary enthusiasm and energy of that old architect who lived in a world of nothing but straight lines, horizontal parallel lines, lines that cross or lines that rise vertically side by side, lines that press down on these from above. As the end of the first phase neared, Kawasaki stopped talking of his highly reasoned "two-legged, wingless animals, and grotesqueness," and instead pressed us with the greatest urgency; without limit we were pressed, even as we, exasperated at ourselves, wanted to see the first phase finished.

Then came the night when the first phase of our work was to be finished. We intended to work all night. . . . Those days we often worked all night. As the night grew utterly late, our inspiration soared. I was drawing a stone bridge; it had three arches of polished white granite that divided the flowing water. . . . The arches were reflected upside down in the water at flood tide, but the image of the bridge was ruffled in the roiling waters. . . . As I drew, I saw that view before me.

Kawasaki called us to the round table. There, beside the almost completed tiny paper model of Beautiful Town, stood three bottles of
champagne. Next to them were three champagne glasses. When we
had gathered as usual around three sides of the big round table,
Kawasaki set a glass before each of us and poured the amber wine.

"Well, drink up! Drink up!" he said, flustered. He picked up the
glass in front of him and drained it dry, peering at our faces as he did so.

"The time has come to buy the land. . . ."

He added, . . . but—it's in order now for me to tell you why the
project did not materialize. When I tell you, you won't be too surprised.
That land at Nakazu is even now a dirty, rubbish-strewn place, more so
than in the past. More than being no surprise, that should have been
foreseen from the start of my story. But for the two of us, the old architect and me, and maybe for Kawasaki too, the three of us, though we
can leave him out of it, for the two of us it was completely unexpected.
In a word, that preposterous man simply did not have the money to
build the town!

We drank quickly in succession while he spoke as calmly as he
could, in a moaning voice. . . .

"My dad was a swindler. The son of a swindler is also a swindler."
He said this with scorn for himself, looking back and forth between us
with the eyes of an imploring lion. "My father let it be known around
the Far East that he owned a large trading company in America. In
America he claimed that he held a large trading company in the Far
East. He spent his life deceiving people, even me. When he died, he
left a gold mine in South America. That was no lie. The mining con-
cession was terribly big. My father's estate was full of defects and there
was no hope of my being able to manage it. When I heard this from the
executor, I decided to sell the mine with no regrets. If I sold the min-
eral rights in that enormous mine, it would be enough to redeem my
father's debts and leave a large sum of money in my hands. To have
money these days is everything. To have money these days is one of the
great natural gifts. No, you might say it is the only one. If you have
money, you can make a revolution. It was my choice what to do with
this welcome gift. So what should I do? . . . As a youth of eighteen aiming to be an artist and waiting for my gold mine to be sold, I nursed my
dream and finally hit on the plan for Beautiful Town. I thought of

Beautiful Town as a large living and moving work of art. That was when I began to think that building houses for people was a sacred concept, just like building shrines for the gods was sacred to the ancients. I often dreamed that halfway up a hill somewhere there was a big city of long-lasting stone houses built without sparing money and lined up in beautiful rhythm. My fantasies, those of a man who loves to fantasize, stretched out endlessly. That dream city towered through the vicissitudes of many centuries. Moss grew among the houses, vines coiled, and the whole town was infused with nature. The people of the town did not work to make money as was the custom of their eccentric ancestors. They worked for pleasure alone. As travelers come from other towns to see old temples, so travelers would dismount at the station at the foot of the hill to marvel at the many customs peculiar to this town since its founding and completely contrary to their own. . . . Thoughtful people might see the precious vein of ore that is human life partially revealed in this old town deep in the heart of the mountains. . . . I pictured that in my fancy, but reality gradually reduced my dreams to a meager prospect. . . . That is, the ore deposits in my father's, the swindler's, mine, though the claim was broad, were about to be exhausted. If the veins gave out, I was told, it was most doubtful that another lode would be found on the claim. In the end my big important dream, soaring on giant wings, came crashing down headlong. My visionary town was crushed beneath it, smashed into pieces. Father's mine was abandoned, an empty mountain gaping with crisscross holes like a beehive without honey, and his residence with its double mortgage did not leave enough to pay off dad's debts, they said. Well, they did give me a bare five hundred thousand dollars to get established in the world. The executor of dad's troublesome estate was an uncle of mine, dad's younger brother who came from Germany. As of now I can't be sure that I wasn't cheated by the unscrupulous administrator or by my uncle. It doesn't matter anyhow. I would like to have you imagine my disappointment when it was determined that I would receive only $500,000. . . . You, E the artist and Mr. T the architect, can easily understand that. . . . Your disappointment and surprise at this moment are no different from mine at that time.

"When I came to Tokyo, I had less than a million yen. There was to be no more from anywhere. Twenty million, that would have been enough if only I'd had it, I thought constantly to myself. With twenty million as a base, twenty million I don't have except in my imagination, I began to build 'Phantom Town.' It was a Phantom Town, and once the thought came to me that it could never really be built, I thought I could express it through art, to create the reality in people's hearts at least. At first the fancy was a magic cloud floating in my heart, and I thought of writing it like a prose poem. If that had been the extent of my ambition, I would probably have been safe. . . . That would have matched my capacity. But I began to think I wanted to write it as a novel close to the truth. Then, to make the novel more realistic, I intended to put in a factual record of the designs for planning Beautiful Town up to the point of construction. Thus the hero of my novel unfortunately dies when the plans are completed, and Beautiful Town exists on no earthly map. The readers of my novel would be confused as to whether it falls into the realm of poetry or that of history. Even if they understood as they laid it aside that my book was poetry, they might have believed that, because of the passion I put into it and the totally intelligent and rational design, and if only I did have the money, that city truly would have been built there right before their eyes. Then among my ardent readers there might be a wealthy man so moved by my book that he would build that town himself. . . . I thought there might be. What a dreamer I am. I have read lots of books about building houses. In doing so, I had my father the swindler's heart in me. That heart deceived me first. . . . There were moments when I was convinced I actually had that much money in my own bank account. Those moments expanded into minutes, then grew long enough for me to visualize Beautiful Town. I'm like the hero in a story —in the daytime a hermit in a humble monastery, devoted to a life of submission, who every night gives himself over to debauchery as the gaudily dressed lover of a dissolute noble lady. When I was planning Beautiful Town—that was at night after all—I was a man of unlimited wealth. No, not only at night. Somehow I could think like that all the time. What convinced me was half in myself, the other half in everyone else I met. My thoughts that gave no heed to money, that scarcely respected money at all, and my disposition to leave things to chance, may have led to my being seen by the world as a billionaire with two or three thousand times the amount of money I actually possessed. They were lionizing me. That's not unreasonable. After all, I valued two thousand yen the way common people value two hundred. Anyway, I was no common crook robbing large sums from other people. I was just a queer imposter squandering his own money on expenses that common people would see as entirely meaningless. That is, in order to make my fantasies real, I invested in the purchase of my own sense of reality. Even though that way of doing business has existed in the world, no one has done it more vigorously than I. Common people, therefore, may have had no need to be wary of me. . . . Except for that foolish real-estate agent. But it wasn't only the common people who were easily convinced that I was wealthy. I'm sorry about you two. Sad to say, when I asked for your help, noting that my own knowledge and ability were inadequate to weave the planning story into my work of art, the two of you believed without misgiving that I was wealthy enough to bring it off. Didn't you? . . . Of course, that was when I had no doubt of my own capacity. You two foolishly believed me the way other two-legged, wingless animals put their blind faith in the grotesque. So you were deceived. You worked as hard as you could, like people in a dream laboring to make money. You're bewildered now just like those people when they wake from their dreams of the grotesque! If sometime, any time, you had only asked, either of you, 'Can you really do this thing?' I could have confessed easily and honestly by saying, 'No, it's nothing but an idle dream.' Oh, truly, how much I sometimes wanted you, either of you, to give me that opportunity. If you wonder why, it's because I thought the time would come sooner or later, as it did tonight, when I would have to confess everything to you, how I had tricked you so easily and misled you with false hopes. Yet I could not say it to you on my own. . . . Mysteriously, I began to feel there was a kind of mental tension to the pleasure in this uneasy world where I am forever pursued by something. Just like men and women who are unlucky in love. Should I confess, I worried about crushing your enthusiasm. I didn't want you to think me like a coldhearted man dallying with a young woman whom he plans to abandon in due course. I do resemble the young man who indulges in his love with the one he knows he cannot marry, who steals that love in order to prolong it, and yet who lacks the courage to confess his intention to leave until he is cornered. . . . Don't you see me that way?

"We can imagine that the Beautiful Town that looms so clearly when we close our eyes is now lying in ruins many long years after it was built. Or maybe we destroyed it ourselves after we finished because we didn't like it. Then later we think it was not something that had to be destroyed, but rather a thing that should be honorably regretted. No, I'd say it's better not to deceive ourselves any longer. To say that the vision is more beautiful than the reality was my kind of stupid remark until yesterday. The vision is beautiful. So the actual is more beautiful, but our Beautiful Town is an impossibility! Because I don't have the money! That great natural gift needed for it—money—is not there. I'm like the artist who decieves himself that he has talent, who puts on airs because others see him as having talent, and who then, forgetting his limitations, rashly undertakes some large work of art, only to become frustrated in the end when he realizes he lacks the talent. Now the time has come when I must clearly acknowledge as much. . . . The day after tomorrow at 7 P.M. the real-estate agent will come with his crafty kind of compulsion to get my answer. To meet the payment of many million yen I don't have thirty thousand. That's just one-third of the agent's commission. The guy swallowed it whole. I would not be at all unhappy to see the boorish look on his vulgar face. Three weeks ago I bought a steamship ticket on the liner K——Maru. Tomorrow I leave Japan—at least I'll be gone from Tokyo. At first I thought I would go without saying anything to you two either. . . .

"But E, and Mr. T, the work you've done for me is surely not all in vain. All the effort you have put into my phantom town has enabled me to see it much more clearly. You have given me such good ideas and revealed such wisdom that even now I can fully picture the town. I haven't given up the idea of writing a book about it—under the title *Nisi Dominus Frustra* (All in Vain, Without God). When I do, I plan to dedicate it in honor of you two, my devoted collaborators who have bravely endured the same big disappointment as I. My trunks are full of your work. I own scarcely anything else. . . . I am penniless with infinite wealth."

As he talked on, Kawasaki gradually calmed down. He was a proud man, and rather than apologize for his own wrongdoing he spoke in a tone of bravado, threatening and consoling us. But the look on his pale face and his glistening tears belied his voice. There was nothing to say, nothing we could think appropriate to say. The old architect and I fervently held our silence. I don't know what I did, but oddly enough old Mr. T kept lifting his already empty glass in vain as he tried again and again to drink, his hand trembling and his mind unconscious of the lack of any drink. At long last Kawasaki appeared to notice. He refilled the empty glass with champagne, then filled mine. "So, drink to the swindler!" he said. We three were sunk in a deep silence that may have lasted an hour or more. Meantime the cuckoo clock in his room next door sounded once in a voice like an owl—was it four o'clock? At the window facing the city where I continued to gaze to no purport, I saw the dim light of morning through the slats in the blind. Supposing I suddenly dared to laugh out loud, I wondered how my voice would echo through the silent daylight of that big room.

"That's the way it is," Kawasaki said at last. "From tonight I don't expect to be here and you won't be coming either. And so, E, I sent a letter to your home this evening. And to Mr. T's home too. . . . I think I will leave without saying any more to you. It is already morning and the streetcars should be running. I think I'd like to have you go now. . . . At ten this morning the used furniture dealer is coming. I'm selling all my household things here. Until then I'd like to sleep soundly."

As he spoke he rose and opened the door himself as if to spur us on. Then he led us down the staircase, awakened the hotel man, and had him open the front door. We parted from him silently and left the hotel. The strange night had fully dawned but morning fog hung low over the city below a still sunless sky. Streetcars were running with few passengers. My head in its odd condition was suddenly invigorated. I had no intention of feeling any different than usual. Then I was struck by a sense of confusion at some unexpected words from Kawasaki. The old architect and I would always say good-bye casually in front of the hotel and then go our separate ways. Only this time we did not part but walked on together. I accompanied the old man as he trudged along; it was in the opposite direction from my destination. We walked side by side for quite a long time, crossing one of the many bridges in that neighborhood, whatever it was called. By the time we had crossed the bridge without saying a word, I had almost forgotten the old architect was with me, when suddenly he spoke in that timid voice of his. . . .

"That man, after last night we shan't meet him again. But you'll meet with me again, won't you? You've become my friend. I'd like to talk with you from time to time. About that 'Beautiful Town.' "

So saying, he grasped my wrist with his chilly hands. As I was about to reply, something suddenly occurred to me, a terrible thought that had not previously crossed my mind.

"Mr. T. I'll talk with you later. Now I must go back to the hotel. I've got to see that man right away!"

Mr. Architect T appeared to think I was angry at Kawasaki. I shoved the old man aside as he tried to detain me, and without looking back I raced toward the hotel. I pictured my friend groaning on blood-soaked white sheets. . . . He had said he was going to Germany. . . . That was a lie. . . . He intended to die. . . . "The hero in my novel dies unfortunately when the planning is completed." Hadn't I heard him say that earlier? . . . Wouldn't a fool like him put himself into the story he was writing? A man like him thought nothing of death. . . . I recalled the man in the Russian novel who said, "If anyone asks, tell them I have gone to America," and then pointed a pistol at his head and pulled the trigger. . . . What he said could be considered a riddle about death. He said he sent a letter to my home. Was it to be a post-humous statement? My heart was beating hard; its echo pursued me as I ran. I was dizzy with the worry. I kept cool, though. Wasn't this the same street I had raced along so fast from the K Arts Club to Kawasaki's place that day when I had the "Lucky Idea" about Nakazu? . . . Oh, the sun was rising, I thought as I stared at my long shadow on the ground. I stepped on my shadow; I chased it as I walked. Hurriedly. When I turned a corner and saw the hotel, all was quiet. The lights in the win-dows had gone out. I leapt up the front steps and pushed on the door. It had been locked after our departure. Had nothing happened? Had no one discovered him? As I wondered I rang the bell by the door. . . . There was a long interval.

One of the bellhops that I had become familiar with over three long years, rubbing his eyes and hooking up the gold braid of his uni-form, greeted me with a sour look and led me to Kawasaki's suite. The room was the opposite of what I had expected. The door as usual was not locked. When we opened it, a large leather briefcase lay on the round table. The paper city was crushed beneath it. The room next door where Kawasaki slept was quiet; Kawasaki was not dead. He seemed rather to be sleeping like someone dead tired. I was ashamed of my pathologically nervous fantasies, and to cover up for having told the bellboy I had urgent business with Kawasaki, I said it could wait until after he woke up. Adding that it would be a nuisance to come again later, I lay down to sleep for a while on the sofa, as I always did after a long night's work, in the room where we worked—no, the room where until last night we worked. . . .

"Oh? What? Dead?" I called out crossly and jumped up, shaken out of my sleep roughly by the shoulders. . . . I was half asleep. The nervous delusions I had had before I went to sleep had continued in my sleep. My fitful sleep was haunted by all manner of Kawasakis hovering on the border between reality and dream. Though troubled by the bright morning light in the room, I had finally gotten to sleep.

"Hey? What kind of a dream are you having? . . . Get up quick!"

That dead Kawasaki was shaking me awake from my delusions.

"Get up quick! If you don't, I'll sell you to the furniture man along with the sofa."

Kawasaki's bad joke was accompanied by a burst of laughter from a merchant fawning before his classy client. I looked and saw two men standing behind Kawasaki. One was the hotel manager whom I had seen before; the other I assumed to be the secondhand-furniture dealer. Smiling wryly, I washed my face at Kawasaki's suggestion and went with him to eat in a corner of the dining room. Because it was a little after eleven we had lunch. Then it was time for Kawasaki and me to part. It seemed he really was going abroad. He was just like always. Although his facial color was poor, his smile had its usual cheerful charm. It was inconceivable that he was the protagonist of last night's scene. I was angry at myself for panicking, not so much last night as this morning. "The bellboy said you came back on urgent business?" he asked. "No, it was a nuisance to go home to sleep for nothing," I had to answer casually. Then I chanced to think: this man, the man now before me, if he had died, think how I would have been questioned in that flustered state. Kawasaki seemed not to notice what I was thinking but was instead rather jollier than usual.

We finished eating leisurely as we chatted pointlessly about these and other topics. How the furniture dealer came on schedule. How if the stuff was going to the dealer and if he would drop the word, the hotel would probably buy it up. How the hotel manager rattled on tediously and so it was better to leave the whole discussion to the two of them. How it was only the piano he hated to give up, and so he had played a piece this morning as soon as he had gotten up. When Kawasaki said that, how it was no dream when I thought I had seen him from the back, sitting and playing the piano in my dreams. How pleasant the ship's cabin would be on such a clear early-autumn morning. And how beautiful the sky really was. Even as I worried over it, I said nothing about the letter he said he had sent to my home last night. For one thing, I was posing and did not want him to think I was worried about it. For another thing, I didn't want by raising it to bring on last night's reaction in the presently rather calm Kawasaki. To tell the truth, I felt a little sad gazing at Kawasaki, whom I shall probably never see again. I am overly sentimental and more solicitous than others. For lack of sleep, or for whatever reason, this feeling of separation was curiously stimulated by the color, the very sight, of the fresh green apples on the table. . . . Even today green apples bring back the feeling of that day.

I parted from him there in that noisy room where the hotel manager and the furniture dealer were giving orders to move things about. I would never see him again—up to now. He said he was leaving on the 7 P.M. train. I spent the day sleeping. When I went to his place just before six to see him off, he had long since left at about four o'clock. The familiar bellhop answered the door and told me that. I barely missed the old architect, who came later for the same purpose and then went home. The architect had phoned around noon to ask the time of departure and Kawasaki sent the reply of seven o'clock. However, Kawasaki suddenly changed his plans and told the bellhop over and over to give us his regards. As I could not see him off in person, I could not help feeling he was somehow still there in the hotel. Not only that, I had been going to that hotel every night. The way we had been working there for three years I still could not believe it had all collapsed in a night. . . . I felt I should hurry on as always to the hotel to continue the work. But among all the brightly lit hotel windows only two on the front corner, second floor, that where we had worked until last night and Kawasaki's room, were dark. I looked back as I walked in a daze.

All I could think of was Beautiful Town. I don't know where or how I walked. I walked around the night streets. Like a young man hopeless in his love. . . . It struck me that Beautiful Town had actually become my love. That was a simile, I thought as I walked. It was something more than a simile. No matter how far I pushed it, I felt the resemblance was perfect. Had my feet taken me to Shin-Ōhashi (New Big Bridge) before I knew it? . . . Just as the hasty feet of a lover pining for his love take him unconsciously to the vicinity of her home. When I noticed I had come thus to the bridge, my steps slowed naturally to a stroll. Suddenly I saw, some twelve or fifteen feet ahead of me, a man leaning on the railing and gazing out unconcerned and oblivious to passersby. It was the old architect for sure. He was wearing the old morning coat as usual. When I knew without a doubt who he was, I turned hastily back in the direction from which I had come. I did not want to wake him from his dream. If he were to see me inadvertently and say a word, any words, I would burst instantly into tears. I should not like that at all. I realized that my nerves were totally prostrated from that strange night just past.

⌂

Beautiful Town! Beautiful Town! I thought I would forget that crazy idea in no time. The very next day I went out, wandering around with my paint box dangling from my shoulder. I tried setting up my easel here and there, hit or miss. It was no use. If I painted a tree, it reminded me at once of the garden in Beautiful Town. If it was a view of roofs, I thought of roofs in Beautiful Town. If I went to the art institute at night, my charcoal left off sketching the nude woman and drew a line of small houses on a corner of her figure. I was often uneasy with myself. I thought maybe I was possessed by something.

It happened on one of those days. I had an unexpected visit one evening from the old architect. He asked me to do something really strange. I already knew of his extraordinary personality, but when I heard this request, even I had to find the moment strange. Since the planning of Beautiful Town turned out to be fake and his work was now useless, he simply could not tell the facts to the family he had been reporting to day by day. . . . So for the last ten days, like this night, he had been going out before seven, killing time till nearly eleven by walking around town and seeing movies he did not want to see before returning home to pretend he had been working on Beautiful Town. He could not be expected to continue this unreasonable, boring behavior forever and sometime would have to confess the truth to his household. He could not possibly do that himself. I asked whether his family had come to count on the pay from his work for their livelihood. That was definitely not the case, he said. . . . He was proud of his son, who was a medical doctor and professor of pathology at a medical school. The unselfish son dutifully provided them with almost all of his salary from the school. They—the old architect and his elderly wife— enjoyed what the world calls a comfortable retirement. As the old architect spoke awkwardly but quietly in his usual timid tone, I visualized a household where a nagging old woman taunted her unfortunate husband about everything. I tried to ask as indirectly as I could whether she was like that or what was the reason he could not tell her that Beautiful Town could not be built. His answer was the exact opposite of my unhappy surmise. She thought it would be great if her husband's houses could be built, and she was waiting as expectantly as he to see the realization of the plan, the construction at last of a long row of those wonderful homes. . . . That's why he felt he simply could not face his wife. From what he said, I inferred that the old couple's household was both an oddity matching the childlike shyness of the old man himself and a blessing of the highest order. When I undertook his request, therefore, I came to like him all the more. Thus we met again from time to time. Sometimes he came to visit me, at other times I went to him. We who were farther apart in age than father and son became longtime congenial friends. As I viewed their life, so filled with gentle love and serenity, I thought how dear it was to find such lives in the middle of the noisy city—on a back alley in downtown Nihonbashi.

I thought old Mr. T was the happiest man ever. Even if his worldly life was a failure, he was a person of such peace, with a good wife, a good son, good daughters, good grandchildren, a warbler singing in his sunny window, and even more good things in his everyday fancies. You could hang the title Beautiful Town onto that happiness.

But, with the verbosity of an old man, old Mr. T kept talking of Beautiful Town until I was completely worn down. As he spoke I became strangely sad—until finally I was as oppressed as if I were hearing news of a lover I had barely forgotten.

E's story went on and on. It grew long in becoming the story of old Mr. T. . . . I will stop my writing here, though. It has somehow become very trivial. A story heard from someone else that may seem a bit interesting when you start to write will usually end up worthless. As author I ended up writing that kind of worthless story. . . . Still, if I find later by some chance that I want to try to continue, it is not impossible that I might write a sequel to "Beautiful Town," even if there is no point to it. Before I hurriedly end this tale of two twenty-year-old youths ignorant of the world and a sixty-five-year old man who can still dream—a fairy tale told for the same kind of people as the heroes in my story—I must add a few words. Old Mr. T did finally build one of his dream houses, fulfilling his earlier wishes. That one house was Mr. E's celebrated studio, the serene workroom with its nooks where we had listened to this story into the long night. That faintly tinged "Portrait of an Old Man," reminiscent of the French painter Carrière, that made E famous in the exhibition of 1916—that was painted from the old architect T. Old Mr. T died last year, leaving as his last request the hope that his granddaughter and Mr. E would have a happy life together. This spring E's wife happily carried out her grandfather's wish. Next year (because it would not be auspicious this year of her wedding) she will get a dog, according to the rules for Beautiful Town. My dog, Leo, will likely have pups next spring. Leo always has good ones, so I promised her the best of the litter. Old Mr. T's prized warbler in the cage the old man built so diligently is even now cared for tenderly in the window of the alcove by E's vivacious, beautiful young wife. What about Theodore Brentano who was Teizō Kawasaki? Wasn't he a spy? The paper model of Beautiful Town, didn't it resemble a fort somewhere? Who would have raised such an absurd and yet at first blush not unreasonable question, and why? How well built was E's studio, and on what land? Where did the money come from to build such a fine studio? Why were the three names of T, E, and Kawasaki carved on the cornerstone along with the date of construction? What kind of a household did E have, the man who rightly held a home from Beautiful Town? I can't relate all that in a word or two, and it is not impossible that I may feel like writing a sequel to "Beautiful Town." I may give it a try.

I think I will dedicate this rough and incomplete story to E and his wife as a token of my friendship. E, my magnanimous friend, can you bear with me that the interesting story you told at such great pains has ended in these muddled notes of mine? To atone for my faults I think it fitting to end with this famous poem by Akiko.[11]

> *How sweet to walk*
> *that little path,*
> *not one of life's grand avenues.*

Notes

1. A son, born in 1932, now a professor of psychology at Keiō University.

2. From the Boy-Charioteer's speech in the Masquerade Ball Scene, Part II, act I, scene 2 of Goethe's *Faust*. Translation from the Japanese with reference to the German original.

3. Also used by Satō in *The Sick Rose* as a symbol for an idyllic age, taken from a novel by Novalis, eighteenth-century German poet.

4. 1738?–1818. Artist, painter, and engraver who studied Western-style perspective and technique from the Dutch in Nagasaki.

5. 1747?–1822. Western-style painter and printmaker.

6. Although the spelling on the picture is given as NAKASU in Roman letters, the correct name of this district in Tokyo is Nakazu. This kind of discrepancy in the use of Roman letters and in pronunciation is not uncommon.

7. An elegant palace of culture in the Tokyo of the 1880s for Japanese to display their interest in Western high society.

8. A Japanese Rip Van Winkle from a popular legend about a man who spent many years in an undersea palace and returned home to become instantly old.

9. English writer and artist, 1834–1896, who wrote of a utopian socialism where art is the salvation of mankind.

10. Satō repeatedly uses the German word *Grotesken*.

11. Yosano Akiko, 1878–1942, well-known Japanese woman poet. Translation by Carol Tenny.

The Fingerprint

Shimon, 1918

THE MYSTERIOUS TALE OF THE LIFE OF MY UNFORTUNATE FRIEND

N[1] was my only close friend from childhood. At twenty he went abroad to observe more widely the arts that he loved. I well remember his interesting letters sent to me now and then over several years from Paris, Florence, and London. (They are among the most masterly writings I have seen in the Japanese language.) The last to come was a postcard dated August 11, 1907, two years after he went to London and six years after he left Japan. His letters gradually became shorter; then suddenly they stopped. I kept on writing in the hope of not losing contact. Probably he saw my letters. Not one ever came back to me as sender. But there was never an answer. For a while I lost track of my only close friend. In case you wonder, his mother had died before he went abroad and he had no relatives. As he was not writing me, it was inconceivable that he was writing anyone in Japan. I imagined that he might have fallen in love there in that strange land. If so, I thought maybe he would write me about it, but that was a vain hope. I could think only of the old saying "Out of sight, out of mind." Then four years later a postcard arrived with a London cancellation of July 11, 1911 (he put no date on it himself). It was addressed to me out of the blue and it reported merely that he was returning home. After that, picture postcards with no message arrived from Cairo, from Singapore, from Hong Kong, from Shanghai. Finally, late in 1912, a year and a half after his card from London reporting his intent to return, he appeared, a sudden and unexpected visitor at my door. The moment I saw him I thought, "My, how his health has failed!" He looked like someone who had exhausted his vitality. It could not be attributed solely to the fatigue of travel. He in no way looked like a man of thirty. It was a strange kind of ageing, like an old man but also like a man in his prime. His expression was dull; only the light in his eyes shone brightly like a jewel. From this description you may not clearly picture his appearance at the time. You can guess that it was not a very happy look. I'll be satisfied to leave it at that for now.

Meeting again after more than ten years, he would not talk very cheerfully with me. I thought back on what a brilliant conversationalist he had been when we were boys, and I wondered that a man could change so much. To my questioning he replied only in a weary tone. When I asked him if his health had suffered (to tell the truth, I imagined he had syphilis), he answered in a word, "I'm okay." I did not think it was good, though, to doubt his friendship for me. At least he had come to see me straightaway on arriving in Japan. That was not all that I failed to understand. Although he said he "intended to live in Tokyo," within two or three days he suddenly told me unexpectedly that he was leaving for Nagasaki. At first I interpreted this to mean "I'm going on a trip to Nagasaki." Nagasaki was his old hometown, after all. Then, when he corrected himself to say that he would live in Nagasaki, I felt that for no clear reason I failed to understand him. He was born in Nagasaki but he had been raised in Tokyo since he was an infant. He had some unpleasant relatives in Nagasaki, but he had broken all contact with them, he said. He used to hate the very soil of that town.

He left hastily for Nagasaki. I received notice of his arrival. I had no cause to write, however. He broke his departure promise and failed to send me his address.

My friend who had been very open with me ten years ago was a puzzle to me now. If I had not seen him later and had only the impression he left at that time, I would have thought that for several days I had been living unawares with the ghost of my best friend, perhaps through the medium of some spiritualist. Somehow I had to feel that way. After half a year, though, my "Enigma Friend" was back again at my door.

This time he looked somewhat better. On reconsideration he had decided to live in Tokyo and he wondered how I would feel about his living with me—that is, he'd like to be a lodger in my house even though I was now married.

"If you don't object, I'd like to build a house for you, but——"

Saying that, he stared at me, unable as I was to give an immediate answer, and then he added slowly in a low pleading tone, "Hide me, please, won't you?"

"Hide me." When I first heard those words I had to anticipate something terribly serious. The thought struck me suddenly that he might be crazy. Fortunately, my worry and doubt eased a bit as I listened to his explanation.

He spoke generally as follows, in English. Maybe he didn't want anyone else to hear. He may have thought that English was more appropriate to a subject like this. If that was not the case now, he had at least applied this kind of artistic sensibility to real life before. So if I could transcribe his story exactly the way he told it in English, it would be most interesting, but I cannot manage that. Not even a great master of language could do so. The English that he spoke at that time was simple and lucid but full of bizarre words and extremely intricate rhythms that one would think he had chosen deliberately. He said:

"I forget exactly when it was, but while I still had the energy to write you, I think I may have recommended Thomas De Quincey's 'Confessions of an English Opium Eater.' Or maybe I didn't do that. It was around that time. One day I met a man in London's East End. He said he was a sailor. He acted like a sailor. I met him in a pub. We took to each other warmly as we drank together. The drunker we became, the fonder we got, though we were complete strangers. As I think of it now, I was too curious. . . . My whole life illustrates the moral that 'a man should not have too much curiosity and too little will.' I told him, 'I would enjoy your company any time.' Finally I added, 'Take me tonight to your most interesting place.' The place he took me to, what do you think it was? It was an opium den. . . . I began frequenting the place. Of course, you probably don't know the drunken feeling of opium. In a word, it is the ecstasy which is art itself. It's a beautiful extravaganza that echoes through the whole body. Yes! At least that's what I thought then!"

He sighed as he spoke. Then, absorbed for a bit in his own thoughts and with an oppressive, gloomy look, he fell into a deep silence. Truly profound. The unforgettable silence of that moment has become an inseparable part of my recollections.

After a bit he continued.

"Within three or four years I needed the equivalent of some 4,000 drops of opium a day. I lost the energy to write you one line of a letter or a single postcard. For better or for worse, I retained my ambition for the arts. I had not become quite so decadent as to be content with my addiction to opium. I put all my efforts toward reducing the amount of opium. It was almost useless. That's when I determined to return to Japan. There are no opium dens here. If I returned quickly, I could regain a healthy life. I made up my mind. Sato, old friend, I used to see you often in my drunken drugged dreams. . . .

"At last I decided to carry out the decision that I had postponed day after day. On the night before I was to leave for Japan on my way home to a proper life, and thinking that this night would be my last time, I followed that road I had walked so many hundreds of times before, that narrow course no ordinary man would travel in a lifetime, to creep through a door narrower than the gates of heaven. That night in the underground room the sailor James (that was surely his name) was waiting without money, counting on my arrival. I told him 'Starting tomorrow don't come looking for me.' When James asked why, I answered honestly that I was returning to Japan. James said that was too bad because there were no edens (opium dens) in Japan. I said nothing. James kept wheezing in my ear like a devil. . . . 'It's no good, sir, when you've reached that point. You can't quit this drug. If you are bound to go home no matter what, at least go to the ports. I'll tell you all about them, the opium dens in the ports. No, for a moneyed man like you that's no good. Instead, when you land in a port, slip some money to a policeman—the more the better. Then pretend to be absentminded and try asking him, "Where is that place, anyhow?" That's to show that you are absentminded. That's a signal. Don't forget it. No, it's okay, because even if you forget other things, if you forget the appearance of a lover's face, if it's anything about opium there's no fear you will ever in your life forget. Even if you now intend to forget opium completely. When you find the place, find it for sure, say this to the fellow in the house, "A skull with three eye sockets told me." As you say it, he will pull up his shirt to bare his chest, revealing on the curve of his shoulder a tattooed skull with three eye sockets.' James talked on in a voice like a devilish guitar. He pestered me so much I tossed him coins. . . . Later, as a vision in my ship's cabin, I saw James' three-eyed skeleton swaying from the tall mast of that devilish ship plying the serene and moonlit sea. . . .

"When I boarded the ship, I deliberately took only 3,000 grains of opium in tablets. That would do me for only fifteen days. I vowed that on the boat I would secretly use only a little, gradually reducing the amount so that when we met again I would no longer be an opium eater. Don't censure me for not succeeding. On the pretext that I would verify whether what James had said was true or was delirious raving or a made-up story to extort money, and out of my own curiosity, as well as, I must confess, because my opium was running out, I ventured to try out James' suggestion when I went ashore at Cairo.[2] Everything that James had told me was true. Forgetting the date and everything else, I fell asleep in the opium den. I missed the sailing of my ship. I spent some bad days in Constantinople. In Singapore, Hong Kong, and Shanghai too. I tried hard over the period to reduce the amount. I had definitely not changed my determination to arrive in Japan no longer an opium eater. This thought stemmed from my moral conscience and even more from the inconvenience that there were no opium dens in Japan.

"It was when I was in Shanghai, though. A Chinaman in the opium den there told me, 'If you return to Japan, go to the house of a Chinese named Liu at Number 19, M. B. Machi in Nagasaki.' Needless to say, there is an opium den there."

When he had gone this far, he shut his mouth in surprise as if his words had suddenly run into something. I listened spellbound. He was speaking of such dark truths that, as I listened to his words, their realistic impact instilled a fancy that I was reading some child's nursery rhyme. Then too, it opened up his riddles to me one by one.

When I think of it now, this was no more than the merest beginning of the mysterious tale told by his life.

Far from losing his energy, he seemed to maintain an almost insane enthusiasm and inspiration. Forgetting all else, he began to plan the design for a house. Day after day he would say not a word to me. An expert who saw the designs was astonished at such detailed and precise, indeed mysterious, floor plans. Within six months the house was completed on the brow of a south-facing hill. (That's the house I live in now. It's not large, but it is charming and really comfortable. Along with the many letters he sent me from abroad, it is an artistic creation that he bequeathed to the world.)

"I will absolutely stop taking opium. It is not something I can do instantly. I will reduce the amount little by little over fifteen months until I have ceased completely."

As I trusted his firm commitment, my house became his private opium den. I had to keep the secret that I was harboring an "opium eater." To prevent that from leaking out, I had to give up having a maid. He was even more cautious than I on that score. He had two rooms to himself in the seven-room house. One room was in the attic. That was where he indulged his secret. How he did it I had no wish to see. It would have been horrible to observe. If inadvertently I went near, a single look might make me an opium eater too. My nature is susceptible to temptation. I had no knowledge of opium other than what I heard from him. But I can tell you the attacks of his opium dreams were most unpleasant. His moans reached me by night or by day as I slept or read. They came from the third-floor attic through the ceiling into the second floor and spread throughout the house, through my whole world. Frightful sounds they were, like a sick man or a sick animal facing death. They startled me, tormented me, grieved me, worried me, and to tell the truth, angered me too. When they continued too long, I felt like moaning in concert. Sometimes I did.

One day, forced to listen to that awful moaning and howling and not knowing what else to do, I was driven to rush into bluebeard's room. Excited equally by my worry about him and by my own anger, I flew impulsively up the steep and narrow stairs to the attic room. I stood there briefly with a ghastly feeling, then with difficulty regained my determination to enter the room. There was a strong lock on the little door. I took out my passkey. . . . I wondered by chance if he was dead. I pushed the door open a crack and peeked around the room. It was broad daylight and a band of winter sunlight from the small window streamed into the dimly lit room. The tip of the beam shone directly on the side of his face where he had fallen motionless on the couch. The small south-facing window was like a window in a jail. For some reason he had inserted a strong iron grating like a jail window. The sunlight that lit the floor projected the shadowy stripes of the grillwork. Peacefully asleep in that small spot of sun was his beloved kitten. Its unperturbed air was sickening to me. I strode resolutely into the room and called out to him. Moaning, he asked, "What." Trembling and shaking, his face contorted in an expression of pain, even so he spoke like a normal person. It was weird. I shook him awake. He opened his eyes at my action and glanced up briefly as if I were some strange person he did not know.

"Oh. Satō. It's you!"

He spoke abruptly and rose to his knees, reeling on the couch. Attempting to embrace me, he burst into tears. How sad. My friend, depraved in the head, stark mad without a doubt, I thought to myself. In sentimental sympathy I too was about to cry.

This was one of his really bad times. He had two or three of them a week—groaning and moaning. Fortunately, he did seem to be reducing the amount of opium little by little. Tranquil days came at least once in every ten days. (I never knew how it happened.) On these days he would fascinate me by describing with clarity such strange notions that won my sympathy—arguments built oddly out of strange matters, or observations from his limitless experience in splendor and fairy-tale fancy. His opinions on everything were really strange. He seemed to think his views were quite ordinary, however. To cite one example: his attitude toward the movies. Movies were the newest and a splendid form of art—the only art to which science had contributed so directly, he asserted. That made for a vulgar, grotesque, fantastic kind of beauty. He explained the reasons to me at great length. It pleased me that his arguments were faultless and were presented in a form of prose poetry. (I would like to record them all here. I regret, though, that the number of pages and the deadline for this manuscript do not allow me to dawdle. I promise sometime to find the opportunity to write about what impressed me among the things he told me.) It was more than a topic of discussion for him; he did have an extraordinary love for the movies. He liked movies more than children do. Movies were like the everyday fare of an opium dream. "I often used to see those things right

from the beginning of my opium dreams. For me they were dear and sad
things, too," he said. So at least once a month, on a day when he could
go out, he would invite my wife and me to go to Asakusa. My wife did
not like to walk around town with a half-crazy man, or even more to
live with a half-crazy man. She was reluctant to say so, even to me. I
understood very well. She was not unreasonable. When he invited us
to go out with him, no matter how busy I was I would go along. That
was my duty to my friend. It was also my duty to my wife.

Then one day it happened. Again I had to go with him to the
movies in Asakusa. By his choice we went to see the movie *Gun Moll
Rosario* at the D Theater. I remember it was Sunday, a day when we
were crushed by the crowds in the streetcar and in the theater. *Gun
Moll Rosario* (You may have seen it) was one of the great productions of
the American film company Green Flag. It's a detective film about a
gang of thieves led, as the title would suggest, by a woman. There is
nothing very unusual about the plot, but the photography has a pictorial freshness to it. The actress who plays the gun moll of the title, as
the movie talker in the theater explained, is "the leading vamp actress
in America today." Indeed she was a charmer. The parts where she
appeared in a man's riding togs were especially good. From the beginning of the film when you see the Green Flag Company's green-flag
trademark flapping in the breeze, he was like a man enjoying a vision
in broad daylight. He had forgotten the place, the time, even the fact
that he was sitting next to me squashed in a big crowd. He was lost in
rapture. That expression of joy on the face of such a helpless man made
me sad—not only this time but every time it happened. The picture
rolled on. Then the vamp Rosario, sitting in the corner of a bar, whispered some scheme into the ear of her follower, the driver Johnson. . . .
The picture expanded into a close-up of her face. At first you could see
only Rosario's face. Her appearance was that of a young lady, noble,
lovely, revealed in large against the strong backlighting. Then she
smiled sweetly, showing her white teeth. Truly a bewitching look.
Johnson nodded, acknowledging Rosario's instructions, and turned
around to reveal his striking face.

"Oh!"

Suddenly hearing a low sharp cry, I was surprised to have my arm
grabbed roughly.

"Hey. What's up?"

With a sudden throbbing in my heart I stared in the dark at the man who was clutching my arm. I wondered if he wasn't seized by spring madness there immersed in the steamy crowd, but he said: "No. Nothing. It's nothing."

As he spoke, he let go of me and quickly wiped the sweat from his brow, though he should not have been particularly hot. I felt relieved that his voice now was unexpectedly calm. I said, "Let's go," but he made no effort to answer. Again enthusiastic but not entranced as before, he stared with brightly shining eyes. . . . The Rosario gang always wore gloves, but Driver Johnson's gloves were worn through at spots. Johnson had not noticed. He had lost the sensation in his fingers through his work. Carelessly, then, he would leave fingerprints at the scene of a crime. One of these prints was projected on the screen in eerie large scale, looking like bacteria under a microscope.

"Okay. Let's go."

He cried out again, grabbed my arm, held it firmly, and with a great show of jostling quickly shouldered me out of the theater.

"Yes. He really is crazy," I murmured to myself as he dragged me out. I wondered at first if he intended to do something to me. No, that did not appear to be the case. When we came out into broad daylight and I could see him, he wore a thin smile on his exhausted face. Silently, saying not a word, he walked beside me. He boarded the streetcar with me. The next time he spoke was when I told him to change cars at Suda-chō. I stood up, but he kept his seat and said, "I'm going to Maruzen Bookstore." I could do nothing about this madman. I had to accompany him to Maruzen. He stood up impatiently as we reached Maruzen. He led the way off the streetcar. I rushed impetuously after him up the U-shaped staircase at Maruzen.

"Do you have any authoritative works on fingerprints written in either French or English?" he asked the store clerk. There were some in English but the ones in German were better, the clerk answered. In that case, he said, he would take all those in English and in German. He seemed dissatisfied even after receiving two or three bulky volumes, and he had the clerk search through the reference catalogues for more titles. He asked to have them all ordered and sent to him as quickly as possible. He added books necessary for the study of German, grammars and dictionaries, and seven or eight of the stock Japanese volumes on fingerprints in the store, so that altogether he ended up with a stack two or three feet high. He put one English volume in his pocket and asked to have the others delivered as quickly as possible. He wrote down my name and address. (He usually gave my name, not only this time but whenever he had to identify himself. A weekly movie magazine published in Los Angeles, U.S.A., that he subscribed to, was addressed to me. If this article of mine accidentally comes to the attention of anyone at Maruzen, the commendable researcher who bought so many odd books that few people read is really not I. Ever since then I have been receiving, under my name, the "Lamp of Learning" from Maruzen. I want to record that here.) Needless to say, that strange, assiduous researcher on fingerprints was N. No sooner had he left the store than he took the book from his pocket and began reading avidly in the streetcar.

For two or three months my mad and miserable friend was absorbed in the study of fingerprints with as much mad enthusiasm—no, many times more   than when he was designing his house. What surprised me most was the fact that he deliberately began the study of German in order to read German books. I was astonished to see the superhuman results. However well he may have mastered English and French, this madman had been able in less than twenty days to comprehend fully the books written in German. To someone like me with no talent for languages, it seemed like the miracle wrought by the Apostles after the Ascent of the Master, when the Apostles scattered to the four quarters to preach the Gospel and immediately were able to speak and understand foreign languages. I often saw how, as he read, his beloved cat would sit transfixed, staring at the books along with its master.

I spoke to my wife to advise her to be careful not to cross my unhappy friend.

Suddenly one day the fingerprint researcher said something disturbing: "Let's go to Nagasaki, but this time not to get opium. I need to have you come with me." It was getting to be autumn. I had done some paintings with the intention of entering them in a certain exhibition, but I set them aside, knowing I could not rest unless I accompanied my mad friend. He was in good spirits those days, perhaps because of the weather, but even more because, miraculously, he had stopped the use of opium and the moaning after becoming a fanatic for the study of fingerprints. Anyway, I could not let him go there alone. I went with him. He kept his usual oppressive silence on the train, but drew letters constantly with his fingers in the air before his eyes. At first I thought they were arabesque designs. Then, as I looked, I noticed they were the same letters:

If   If   If   If
     If   If   If   If

They were repeated over and over again. After he had continued for some hours, words gradually emerged to form a phrase. In the tedious hours on the train with a traveling companion but no conversation partner I had nothing to do but watch. At first I could not understand the words. He wrote the letters in the air extremely fast, and also my knowledge of language was inadequate. Gradually I became able to read them to some extent. I am certainly not proud of my powers of observation. It just shows how the letters were repeated and repeated. The letters in the air ran on like this over many hundreds of miles: —PROVIDED THAT THERE ARE TWO FINGER PATTERNS QUITE SIMILAR (in English)—. Beyond that, I could not understand at all. "If there are two identical prints," I translated. Well, well. Still a matter of fingerprints. What do you suppose he is thinking about, I wondered. His mood engulfed me.—PROVIDED THAT THERE ARE TWO FINGER PATTERNS QUITE SIMILAR—I said it under my breath. I had trouble keeping the words from coming out. Finally, as we passed through Hiroshima, I spoke the words involuntarily—PROVIDED THAT THERE ARE TWO FINGER PATTERNS QUITE SIMILAR—As I spoke, he overheard with his sharp ears, but he did not appear particularly surprised. Instantly he said, anxiously, in Japanese: "Yes, but actually there is only one. That's the core of the problem."

As he wished, I had to accompany him straight to Nagasaki without leaving the train en route except for a two- or three-hour wait for the connecting ferry at Shimonoseki. We arrived at the Nagasaki station in the morning of the third (?) day after leaving Tokyo. Without giving me time to look around, he strode off, walking as fast as when he raced up the stairs at Maruzen. Straight ahead to the south as you went out of the station a large avenue opened out along the waterfront with shops on one side. After walking straight ahead for five or six blocks (or maybe more) he turned back a bit in his tracks and said, as if to himself and then as if consulting me, "Here is where we should turn." With that he turned sharply up the hill toward the east. The road followed a ditch about eighteen feet wide. A hill loomed clearly ahead, and halfway up could be seen the gate of a temple. The sun had risen above the summit. Horns hooted from the ships below. We walked a couple of blocks up the road, observing children here and there apparently on their way to school. Here was an old round-arch stone bridge with square stone railings. As we crossed the bridge and looked back, I saw the dazzling reflection of a pane of window glass in a towering black church steeple. Looking under the bridge, I saw floating on the incoming tide a still-green inedible tangerine, fresh as if it had just been thrown in. We turned again to the south and walked along a narrow, irregularly winding road, paved unevenly with natural rocks like whetstones. On the right was a house with a birdcage hanging from the eaves. The road gradually steepened, finally becoming quite steep. This appeared to be the old part of Nagasaki. It was dirty, the houses were small, but the area had its own character. When we had climbed the slope, I straightened up, stopped, took a cigarette out of my pocket and lit it. In the space of some three feet between the houses we could see the harbor, the sea, and part of the cape enclosing the port.

Perhaps a bit tired too, he stopped there with me. Then he started walking again before I did. The stone-paved road curved in a semicircle around the middle slope of the mountain, then emerged onto the flank of the hill. The sun struck our faces from directly overhead. The houses on both sides were the shabbiest yet. They seemed to be sliding down a wild slope that you could not believe was in the middle of a city, even with houses on both sides of the street. The sound of banging on sheet iron in the factories, characteristic of a port, shivered the whole town and clanged in my sleepless head. The road flattened out. N called out something to me, but this time I did not want to answer. We came to a row of small Chinese restaurants, at least every fifth or sixth house looked like one. Appearing to lose confidence, he turned left, went ahead five or six blocks, then turned left again. Then soon he turned right. This road was paved with stones like the earlier ones, but it was a much narrower alley, at most about six feet wide. The alley continued straight for three or four blocks, more like a deep ditch than a road.

I don't remember too well after that, perhaps because I was inattentive, but more likely because the route was so complicated. . . . Soon we stopped in front of a house. "Oh, it's vacant," he said, and then went into the house next door. It was a bar. A freckle-faced woman of thirty who looked as if she had just gotten up was standing in a room she had just finished sweeping. She was a foreigner, but I didn't know what nationality. N asked in English for tea. She prepared black tea. He said something simple that I did not understand to the woman when she brought the tea. The woman said something too, which I failed to understand—though they were both speaking English. I judged they might be exchanging some rather crude joke. As the woman spoke she sat down on a chair next to us. Resting her elbows, she settled her double chin on her fists. N watched her. He took his cigarette case out of his pocket and tossed it on the wooden table in front of her with the gesture of a man dealing cards. He started to say something. The woman replied, then chatted on at length. For the most part I did not understand. She spoke too fast, and it was all slang.

Not that I didn't understand some parts, though. . . . For example, "Is that vacant house next door for rent?" "Yes, but if you rent it, what are you going to do with it?" "I thought I would open your kind of shop and go into competition with you. . . . Anyway, is it for rent?" "A house for rent is a house for rent. But if there is no one to rent it, it doesn't get rented and occupied." "Why? Is it so dilapidated?" "No, but besides being in bad shape, it is haunted!" "Haunted! I don't believe such a crazy thing." "People have seen blood dripping from the ceiling of that house in the night. Everybody who has lived there, five families, at least twenty people in all, have heard the same drip-dripping sound. I heard the words right from their own mouths. None of them stayed more than a week. There's nobody in the neighborhood now who doesn't know about that house. . . ." "Who's the present owner? Where does he live?" "I don't know the owner, but there's a Japanese barber. If you cross the bridge behind us and go straight ahead, you'll find a Japanese barbershop and they'll know."

N stood up, saying something. He took a silver fifty-sen coin out of his pocket and tossed it onto the table. It bounced with a clink and fell to the floor. He took out another coin to replace it. The woman picked them both up with a winsome smile. N seemed again to have forgotten that I was with him. He walked briskly out of the shop. "Hm. Blood drips? Blood drips?" He muttered the words to himself as he entered an alley about four feet wide, just enough for one person to pass at a time between this house and the vacant one. (Was that the former opium den, I wondered?) We came out of the alley. There was a ditch there and an open space of about six to nine feet behind the back walls of the bar and the vacant house. Almost straight ahead as we came out of the alley was a rough wooden bridge about four feet wide spanning the twelve-foot ditch. When we emerged into the open space between the exit from the alley and the bridge, he suddenly stopped. He stood there and took his bearings.

"Why are you standing there?"

"Hm. Maybe here. Yes," he said. But not to me. He was talking to himself. Then he seemed to notice me for the first time since we had left the dirty little bar. He turned to me as he spoke.

"You. Remember this place, please!"

As he spoke he pointed to the spot under his feet where he was standing. Stepping back two or three paces, he made an X mark by stroking the ground gently with the tip of his umbrella. Then he walked on toward the bridge. . . . "May the earth be light upon thee," he murmured. (That's what a foreigner in mourning says.) There was a lot about this man's actions I could not understand. But of all the things he had done in the last year or so, nothing was more incomprehensible than his actions and expressions at this time. I thought there must be a deep meaning to them. But I discarded that idea at once. Somehow he was deranged. As for me, my nerves were exhausted from traveling with no sleep and no rest. Another ten days of this and I would be like him for sure.

He found the "Japanese barbershop" right away. Asking me to interpret for him, he made his request to the barber through me. "Are you the agent for the haunted house across the stream? If so, I don't care about those rumors. I might rent it. Sorry to trouble you, but could you show it to me?" The sullen wife of the sullen barber led us back along the road we had come by. She walked ahead, jangling five or six keys. We crossed the narrow wooden bridge for the second time and passed the X mark. Opening the back door of the vacant house, she showed us in and stood at the door with a look of annoyance at our curiosity. The dimly lit interior smelled musty. A cricket was chirping somewhere. By the light from the doorway we had just entered, N opened a window. Rays of sunlight glittering like gold danced cheerily into the room. It reminded me of looking into his attic room at my house. I was filled with the desire to return home at once or, failing that, to have a good sleep once again. N was looking around eagerly, entirely indifferent to our feelings. The exterior of the house was old brick, but the interior was made largely of wood. The floor was almost entirely of old brick.

"You. Remember this house please. I brought you here on purpose because I wanted to show you the house."

N whispered in my ear. "Look. The ceiling" (pointing at it) "is old. In contrast, the floor" (looking down) "is very new. The house must have been remodeled three or four years ago. Just the time when I came to you asking to be hidden," he continued. Taking me into a corner that had now become the kitchen, he added, "Look. The entrance used to be here, a cellar entrance. See." (He tapped the point of his umbrella on the floor, then repeated the tapping in another place two feet away. He compared the tapping sounds.) "How about it? It's like this. You can tell the difference in the sound if you pay attention." To be honest, I didn't hear the difference. He seemed to sense my doubt right away, and he said, "I see you don't get the difference yet."

He walked over to the sink. Two sides of the sink utilized the walls of the house. The other two right-angled sides were built of old brick. Several wooden drainboards were fastened on top. The sink seemed to be newly installed. (Four years before, he said.) The workmanship on the wood was very rough. With no one living there, the water that didn't run out had opened cracks between the new boards. He examined them meticulously. I wondered what he was doing when he took off one of his silk-knit gloves and bit it loose. The glove unraveled quickly into a thread more than six feet long. I wondered again as he took off a small gold medal attached to his watch. He hung the medal from one end of the thread and dropped it through the crack between the drainboards. Pulled by the weight of the medal, the unraveled thread on the drainboard slithered down, gulped into the crack. Appearing to be immensely satisfied with his impromptu idea, he looked at me with a complacent smile. Without thinking, I called out.

"It's deep, all right."

At that moment a call came from the barber's wife, who we thought had left the doorway and gone somewhere.

"Are you still looking around?"

She peeked in the door and shouted, partly suspicious and partly annoyed. Her voice sounded odd as it echoed drearily through the house. N whispered to me with the smile still on his face. "Give the woman one yen. Tell her it'll be a minute or two, anything as an excuse. I'll be right out."

I did as he asked. Refusing the money at first, the woman then accepted it. N came right out. Treating us rather curtly, the woman spoke slowly in a local Nagasaki dialect I was unfamiliar with:—Better not to rent that house. Mysterious things happen there. When curious people try staying overnight, nothing bad may happen, but as soon as someone moves in to live, strange things like the rumors say—every night from around 9 to 2 the sound of blood dripping from the ceiling.—N listened closely and carefully with a conspicuously gloomy expression. We left the barbershop lady at once. He spoke anxiously.

"I pulled up the string too quickly and the medal dropped off the end. It fell into the cellar. I wonder what I should do about it."

"Is it something you valued that much?"

"No. The medal is nothing. But it's dangerous to leave it there. I could be traced."

"What?"

He made no move to answer my question. Raising his hand, he hailed a waiting rickshaw. The jinriksha man looked at N and asked "Where" in funny English. (That wasn't unreasonable. N had lived abroad surrounded by foreign faces for so long that his appearance was more Western than Japanese.) "To the station," he replied in English. Our rickshaw passed through neighborhoods like the back streets around Nihonbashi and parts of Shitaya in Tokyo. . . . I was so tired I dozed off in the rickshaw. I didn't open my eyes until the rickshaw stopped and the shafts were set down. We were back at the station. When I had heard him reply "The station" to the rickshaw man who asked "Where," I thought it was to find an inn in the area. That did not seem to be the case. "There's a train at 3:15," he said. I was astonished.

"Hey. Can't we stay the night somewhere? I've come all this way on purpose. I'd like to look around a little bit. First, though, I'm terribly tired. I fell asleep in the rickshaw."

"That may be. But you can sleep in Hakata, or in Moji, or Hiroshima, or Osaka, or Kyoto. Even better, if we go back to Tokyo you can sleep all you want. . . . The farther from Nagasaki the better. Nagasaki is an awfully bad memory for me. Please forgive me." That's what he said. Then, searching through his pockets, "Yeah. I forgot. . . . I'm tired too. . . . I've got to mail these." He held out two letters prepared in advance and addressed overseas.

"These letters will determine my fate."

Needless to say, I did not understand what it was all about. Thanks to this demanding, mad, busy detective of a friend I saw nothing of Nagasaki. I was without sleep. Breakfast and lunch were in the station restaurant, and I had to take the 3:15 train. My head was in confusion as we boarded. The strange saying that I remembered from the train down recurred to my lips, troubling me as it merged into the reverberating sound of the wheels: PROVIDED THAT THERE ARE TWO FINGER PATTERNS QUITE SIMILAR . . . PROVIDED THAT THERE ARE TWO FINGER PATTERNS QUITE SIMILAR . . . PROVIDED THAT. . . . PROVIDED THAT. . . . THERE ARE. . . . (How many hundreds of times). . . . Damn the man! Did he want to make me mad too?

He came suddenly into my room on a rare visit, holding an open magazine in his hand. It was at dusk one day. Whatever he was holding he thrust in front of my eyes as he spoke with unusual vigor. "Look at this! Here!" To tell the truth, I had gotten over my anxiety and concern about him. Instead I had become curious about everything he did, so I took the item from his hand and looked at it. What? Wasn't that the movie magazine? Fifteen or sixteen lines had been underlined in red ink. The ink was a vivid new red. The meaning of the English text could be translated something like this:

William Wilson, exclusive actor with the Green Flag Company who premiered in XYZ and appeared in other films such as *Gun Moll Rosa-*

rio and *The Train Robbers*, known for his supporting roles, recognized by movie fans and the public for his poignant style of acting and considered to have a great future, disappeared suddenly on October 27. The reason is not known. Although he has been using an English name, he is considered to have a Germanic appearance. In view of the current war, it is rumored that he might be a German spy and his mysterious behavior may have resulted from fear of being exposed. In any case, as movie fans we can only regret the sudden disappearance of this promising young actor.

He stared at me as I read, and as soon as he saw I was finished, he spoke.

"Hey. That William Wilson was the driver Johnson in the film *Gun Moll Rosario*. . . . Come up to my room. You seem to think I'm crazy. Maybe I really am. Today I am going to confess the real reason why I wanted you to hide me in your house."

At this invitation I went to his room and sat down facing him in front of his desk. He was lost in silent thought for two or three minutes while he considered what sequence to follow in telling me the circumstances. Suddenly he stood and picked up his gloves from a trunk in the corner of his disorderly room. He snapped them to shake off the dust and for some reason pulled them on both hands. (Even earlier he had detected with a kind of insane sensitivity that I thought him insane. He expressed his displeasure at this, but his actions one by one were those of a madman.) Gloves on, he returned to his desk. Fumbling with his gloved hands he opened a locked drawer in the desk and carefully took out a gold watch. He pushed the stem with his gloved hand and opened the case on the dial side. Then, as if he had just thought of it, he asked me to light the candle on his desk. I did as he asked. All the objects in his room cast double shadows from the electric bulb and the candle. He held the watch up directly in front of the candlelight.

"How about it? Can you see the fingerprint on the underside of the cover?"

Yes, as he said, one fingerprint was clearly, distinctly, delicately impressed where you would notice it on a surface that was as shiny as glass, porcelain, or metal. The print was of course made by the skin oil of a person's finger. I recognized that as soon as I saw it. I held out my hand to take the watch and look at it. "You should wear gloves when you look at the watch, so as not to make any other fingerprints on it," he said. I withdrew the hand that was making trouble, but he added grumpily, "Take it and look at it." I borrowed a glove from him for each hand and then took the watch and scrutinized the fingerprint. After I had looked for a bit, he spoke.

"Take a good look. That's William Wilson's fingerprint. At least it is the fingerprint of Gun Moll Rosario's driver Johnson, who left it on a corner of the mahogany desk. If you ask why, it is exactly like the fingerprint shown in the film."

"That may be, but," I said, in pity for my mad friend's delusions, or more in compassion, "I could never recognize the huge blown-up fingerprint from that film. No matter how much you blow up finger-prints, they are not something you can fix in your mind. It's like seeing in a dream the most complex map of the world. You can't fix that in your memory."

He nodded. "What you say is completely true." He agreed fully with my slightly sarcastic comment, then continued as if to himself. "I guess that isn't the way to start my explanation." He stood up and walked around the room. Then at last he began speaking again as he walked.

He said: "You. You know there is, or was, an opium den in Naga-saki. No, of course you knew, and you'll remember that you went there with me to see what's left of the place. I'm a bit muddled in the head. I'm not crazy, though." (An insane person who declares he is not insane is the most difficult to handle, I thought.) "I went to that opium den right after returning from abroad. There was no way I could live without opium. I hid it from you and went there to live for half a year. I acted like a foreigner. I paid lots of money to that Chinaman to live there and eat his opium. At the time I felt it was all right to waste my life there. I resigned myself to my opium addiction. Still, I came back after half a year. There was a deep reason for that. You'll forgive me, won't you? I've kept a secret even from you. I fled to Tokyo when I thought I might have accidentally killed a man in Nagasaki. That's why I asked you to hide me. But rest easy. I am surely no murderer. The murderer is that guy! Definitely that guy! . . . It's William Wilson. Not the movie actor Johnson. . . . It's William Wilson." He walked around and around nervously without a pause. He spoke as if to himself. Occa-

sionally seeming to remember me, he would call out: "You, Satō old
fellow," but his talk would continue like a monologue. He continued
along these lines.

"One evening. I was besotted with opium as usual. I could see
things drowsily in my narcotic dream. What I saw in my dream that
night was the panorama of a lake. . . . I often saw that lake view in my
dreams. It was perfectly still, pure blue, vaster than the sea. But I knew
well it was a lake. On the far side of the calm, still water, vast as the
sea, there was a building equally huge. It was twelve times larger than
the background. The view I saw that evening across the water was, as I
say, an old castle twelve times bigger than natural size. Behind the
castle were Islamic-like domes of a palatial building at least twelve
times natural size. The domes rose in tiers half-hidden by the crenel-
lated battlements. The contrast of the Moslem buildings behind the
castle walls made a most extraordinary combination, if you thought of
it intellectually, but in my dreams it had a very rational harmony. Yes.
Bright moonlight shone on it. . . . If I looked at the water, I saw the
moon. If I looked at the moon, I saw the water." (See the piece entitled
"Moonbeams" appended to this story.)

"It was a dream of a vast expanse of water like the sea. It was rain-
ing silvery rays of light. Now and then lilacs sprouted from the water
and quickly grew into large trees with flowers blossoming. They were
white flowers. Because they were white, maybe they were not lilacs.
Maybe they were pear blossoms. Countless other trees grew up to
flower like the first, and in the course of one night's dream they became
a deep forest. A forest in full bloom. The forest appeared to be in the
water. Just as the sea may roll gently in big swells, so the flowery forest
floating on the waves was pitching and swaying ominously, giving me
an unpleasant feeling of seasickness. It was an elegant yet idiotic and
majestic view. At other times I saw in my opium dreams a giant
machine soaring into the sky (an intricately constructed metallic shape
that you might call 'an ordered disorder,' looking like something
sketched by Albrecht Dürer). It was built of odd shapes and scraps of
metal with one gear silently meshing into the next as it stretched gradually outward, a strange structure that moved sluggishly like a giant
mechanical contrivance. These things appeared intermittently in my
opium dreams, pleasing me as they threatened, intoxicating me as they

tormented. I shouldn't be explaining to you the various kinds of opium dreams. If you want to know about them, the quick way is to read De Quincey. . . . On that particular evening I saw the romantic view enlarged twelve times natural size. The old castle, the domes, the vast expanse of water washed with silver, all were there. Moonlight streamed on the domes. Looking carefully I could see in the foreground a long bridge over the water and on the bridge a numberless horde of cavalrymen advancing from afar. As I recall it now, they were in the full regalia of English dragoons, like the ones I had seen at the coronation in England.

"With the appearance of the mounted troops the atmosphere of the spectacle changed suddenly. It became animated and boisterous. It seemed as if the earth was filled with all kinds of noise, but I could hear nothing because I was totally deaf. Through something beyond the five senses, or if not through the sense of hearing then perhaps through the sense of touch, I could perceive beyond the disorders of the atmosphere. Then suddenly an armed rider appeared in my dreams. (My dreams were often of ancient and medieval times.) Somehow, but I know not how, the warrior passed quickly through the castle walls and came out facing the water. Then I noticed, there on the blue water, blue as the robe worn by the Holy Mother, the Virgin Mary depicted in old paintings, the figure of a person lying motionless, asleep or dead, floating on the surface like a boat beached on the shore. The warrior came through the wall carrying a long spear. The tip of the spear glittered in the moonlight. The rider and the body of the man stranded like a boat out of water were as big as the background scene. I saw them both in six-foot profile, bathed in moonlight: the man floating in water and the rider with a helmet. Suddenly the rider thrust out his lance. At the sound of an explosion blood spurted from the side of the floating man. Blood spread across the blue water of the Virgin's robe and colored the lake red. . . .

"A man's groaning voice resounded in my ears like an echo from afar. There was the clattering sound of feet rushing upstairs, or down. As I moaned aloud I noticed the sound of another's moaning. I moaned alongside and suddenly opened my eyes. I stared. In front of me, almost exactly as I had seen in my dream but smaller, was a fallen man, moaning. Like what I had seen in my dream except he was reduced to normal life size and was lying on the wooden floor and not the water. He had fallen over, moaning, in the dark, round shadow of a plate that held a dim candle over his head. At his pillow was a midget lamp—used to light the opium—but the light projected from the candle shone directly onto the man's forehead and nose, coloring a one-foot area dimly red.

"Hoisting my heavy body up on one elbow, I stared without emotion at a human form about six feet from my unbelieving eyes. I was confused; I could hardly discriminate between fact and fantasy. My power of decision was so weak. I lay on a straw pad placed on a wooden bunk; the groaning, bleeding man lay directly on the floor. I was half in doubt. I reached up to bring the dim candle down from its position in midair so I could see by its light, out from the shadow. Then suddenly I saw that the candle was no longer there in midair. Someone was holding it. I saw the hand and looked to see the face of someone there. It was the old man who ran the opium den; he must have come running when he heard the noise. I realized that my other elbow, the one I was not leaning on, was being hauled up by the Chinaman's strong arm. I saw too that he was pressing against my face. The room was not so dark. In my dazed perception of things I seem to have mistaken the natural sequence. As I looked up at his face, he looked down coldly and moved the candle in the hand that I had thought was floating in space. He was showing me the limp figure of the man whose blood was oozing onto the floor. The Chinaman poked his toe at the man, whose moaning had now stopped, and glared into my face as he did so. No, he may have kicked the man after he looked at me. No, he poked the fallen man's shoulder once with his toe and then he kicked him. The fallen man was a shabbily dressed foreigner, I thought. Or was he wearing a spanking morning coat. I forget. I remember my dreams very well. In my dream his coat was a nondescript blue. In later dreams that was the case.

"Generally there were ten people, or maybe six or seven, in the opium den. The night before, or two nights before, the cellar was full of narcotic sleepers. This night in question there were only that other man and myself. Maybe it was a matter of ship schedules; there were almost no seamen in port. The Chinaman who ran the place—he was a man of forty-eight or forty-nine with a big pockmarked face—said I was a murderer. His words brought back my dream. Perhaps while dreaming I had walked in my sleep and really had stabbed and killed the man. I had to think so. At least I had nothing to establish proof that it was not I. I said to the Chinaman: 'I have absolutely no connection with the dead man. Therefore I had no reason to kill him. However, it is not impossible that I killed in my dream. You are in a shady business. You are in no position to make public a murder done mysteriously by me or by anyone else. Therefore, because of my involvement with this place I am now going to give you'—(that Chinaman, that is)—'one thousand yen.' I discussed that with him. He seemed rather pleased. I turned over to him the cash that I, as a homeless foreigner frequenting this place, kept hidden under the arch of my feet, between my socks and the soles of my feet. I got his agreement that he would remove and dispose of the body. Then, leaving that unpleasant topic, I turned my face away and rolled over in bed. I faced the wall. My bunk was right next to the wall. The wall was a dim white and the light from my midget lamp glowed dark-red on the whiteness. I thought I would go back to sleep, and asleep the impressions of this unpleasant reality would become something more supernatural. . . . When anything unpleasant becomes supernatural, it becomes beautiful. I tried, but even if I saw a nature that was truly extraordinary, the opium had no power. No matter how much I smoked, I could not reenter my dreams. If I really am a madman, that must be when I became insane. My nerves bristled, crystalline as smoky quartz. Suddenly I heard in my ear the sound of TICK-TOCK, TICK-TOCK, TICK-TOCK. Well, I thought, as I listened closely, that sound is being transmitted through the wall and into my ears. Instinctively I looked to confirm my guess. There where I looked was a watch. In the wall. Clearly visible through the wall. I saw it clearly in the daylight about two feet in front of me. I stared at it for thirty minutes, then it disappeared. I could still hear the endless TICK-TOCK, TICK-TOCK, TICK-TOCK.

"Suddenly the sound of a far-off whistle pierced the air. It must have been morning, the dawn whistle from the shipyard. I got up. Got up cheerfully. I decided to wake the Chinaman and break open that wall and get the watch. I rose and started to walk out. I nearly stumbled over the corpse. That Chinese fellow had given his word, had agreed to take care of it right away, but there it was. I had spent the night only six feet from that blood-smeared corpse. As I think of it now, it was frightful. At the time, though, I was angry at the Chinaman for break-ing his promise. I beat on the door of the room where he slept. I kicked it. 'Hey. I'll give you another five hundred yen,' I yelled. The China-man came right out of his wife's room. I told him, 'If you'll let me break down that wall, if you let me do it right away, I'll give you five hundred yen.' He followed me, rubbing his eyes. I went down into the cellar and pointed to the wall behind my bed, saying 'This one. If a watch comes out of there—I'm sure one will—it'll be mine.' The Chinaman agreed with a nod; that would be all right. We pulled out the bunk where I slept. On looking, we saw that at the base of the wall hidden by my bed were twenty or thirty holes about this big" (he made a circle with his thumb and forefinger) "pierced through like a honeycomb. I was aston-ished. The Chinaman was not at all surprised. I broke through the wall at that place. It was made of very thin wood. I was even more surprised, so surprised I called out. Still, the Chinaman was not a bit surprised. He explained to me that the holes, big ones in the earth and smaller ones in the wall, were provided to let air into the room. Well, I did feel a breeze on my face and on the midget lamp I was holding, coming from an astonishing pit about three feet in diameter.

"I took a step in and there it was at my feet. The watch, just as I had clearly seen it a little while ago! That was this watch. The watch with the fingerprint. As the Chinaman directed, I grabbed the corpse by the feet. Definitely the feet. The Chinaman held the head. You know, a dead body weighs twice as much as a living person. We carried the corpse into that hole the watch came out of and the wind blew through. The Chinaman had dragged him by his ankles about six feet. At the entrance to the hole where I was waiting he handed the legs over to me. Pressing our backs against the earth at the top of the hole, we carried the body in like a couple of ants. Holding both feet in my two hands, I crawled in backwards. The Chinaman let go first. The corpse's head fell to the ground with a thud. The Chinaman whispered 'Good' in a somber, reverberating voice. I let my hands go. The three-foot cavern was almost completely blocked by the large corpse dropped there on the ground. When I crawled over the corpse, lying on top of it, the corpse's face and my own were almost rubbing. I felt myself on the point of kissing the dead man, but at last I got out.

"The Chinaman clambered out carrying red leather shoes in one hand. They were shoes from the corpse, I thought. I can't forget holding those dead, bare, cold feet, like marble in winter. I saw a line of blood drawn by the fingers of the giant (as he appeared in my dreams), a blurry line looking as if it had been swept by a feather duster and leading from where the corpse had been to the hole. I stood and looked into the hole again. Why I did this I do not know. I saw grayish morning light coming through from the other end of the cavern. It leaked into that underground pit, flowing over the dead man's chest to his face.

"The various scenes of that night reappeared identically in my later opium dreams. My recollection of that one night has surely never left my head, dulled as it was by the use of opium. What on that night was merely a strange agitation later turned to extraordinary terror. The more time passed, the more frightful it became. In my later opium dreams I saw myself as the murderer. I was there in the hole; my body had crawled over the corpse I had killed. I was lying on the dead body, my nose rubbing the corpse's nose, my lips touching the icy lips of the dead man. I was embracing the corpse as if it were my bride. I cried. I yelled, endlessly, endlessly, as I trembled in animal fear, in human penitence. Hearing me call out, the Chinaman came running in. I cried out even more in grief at being captured.

"When I opened my eyes, it was not the Chinaman. It was my kindest friend. Oh Satō. It was you. How my tears burst out involuntarily when I realized this turning point, when my most extraordinary dream changed in an instant into something so wildly different as the warm friendship of the real world. Oh Satō, how many times I have clung to you in my tears. Not only in my opium dreams, not only in that opium den in Nagasaki, but even unconsciously I've come to wonder if it wasn't I who killed the dead man. I killed him while I dreamt. I would repent too in my dreams, wouldn't I? I began to cling to you in tears of repentance. The criminal that I believed I had discovered through my subconscious or through my sixth sense—wasn't that I? The watch that was evidence of the crime, wasn't that my watch? Actually I did have a gold watch. It got lost on some occasion. (I forget how. I have always forgotten such tedious, trivial things right away. After I started using opium it got much worse. Whether I gave the watch to someone, or I dropped it, or sold it, or whether it was stolen.) I spent all day on one of my good days comparing my fingerprints one by one with the fingerprint on the back of the watch lid. The one on the lid was clearly different from mine. I knew that from staring through the magnifying glass at the whorls of the fingerprint impressed on the watch. That fingerprint was imprinted deeply onto my eyes' own optic nerves. In addition to the fingerprint on the watch and my own ten fingerprints, Satō old friend, I can remember yours and your wife's—especially the thumb prints and index fingers—because you left your prints on both sides of the glossy paper frontispiece in my cinema magazine.

"I forget lots of things, but when it comes to things I have wanted to fix in my memory or things I have once been obsessed with, I never forget. Even if I seem to have forgotten them, when it is necessary I can make them reappear suddenly in vivid recollection. Mostly, it is related to my vision. I discovered that vision was my singular ability when I saw the movie *Gun Moll Rosario*. Yes! That time in the big crowd, you were in the seat next to me, to my right. Satō, you've got a good memory. Think about that time, how frightened I was. The man shown large on the screen—the face of the driver Johnson in profile next to Rosario's large smiling face at the moment when he suddenly turned toward us. The face on the screen was washed by backlight. I knew by intuition that the face was identical to the moonlit face of the mounted rider of my dream. I realized, too, that it was a face I had seen again and again in the opium den in Shanghai. Right away, though, I thought my intuition was crazy. The moment I saw his face, so big in my dream, I decided the dream had been caught up in the film, and I rejected the idea. Otherwise, anything I saw could appear mysteriously like an opium dream. In a flash I feared that the dream of myself as murderer could recur anytime, even when I was not taking opium. The movie reverted from close-up to normal scale. With this thought, my feeling that he was the lance-carrying rider of my dreams diminished a bit. I could not help but feel, though, that he was surely the man in the Shanghai opium den two-and-a-half or three years ago, or was it three-and-a-half years earlier? The sight of the man walking through the door of the Shanghai opium den was clear. When the film switched to a close-up and I glimpsed the fingerprint on the screen, I saw it as identical to the print from the gold watch that had been impressed on my eyes. They were so identical that the only difference was in the size, one small and life-size on the back of the gold watch lid, and the other, taken from the mahogany desk in a tycoon's library, enlarged ten or fifteen times life-size into a picture for the world to see! In the pattern of the fingerprints, in their most intricate and miniature contours, there was not the tiniest difference. I am sure of that. I'll show you some reliable proof, but for now, believe me, please. Then: CAN THERE POSSIBLY BE TWO OR MORE FINGERS IN THE WORLD WITH PRINTS THAT ARE IDENTICAL OR THAT HAVE PATTERNS EXACTLY ALIKE?

"This was now the important problem for me. There are sixteen books about fingerprints; I read them all to find a reliable answer to the problem. Was there a single line on any page stating, 'There may be fingerprints of identical pattern?' There was not a single report or bit of research to this effect in any of the books. However, if you say that 'the mysteries of nature are not exhausted by human research and reports,' then there is no reason to say that mysterious nature will not reveal the facts about a murderer through the subconscious of a narcotic man, leading to the intuitive identification of the criminal. If you insist that there may be two or even three fingerprints that are identical, I still have the right to insist that the man in the movie is surely the murderer. The crux of the problem is not so ambiguous. I set out to determine objectively and coldly for myself that that man, the driver Johnson in the film *Gun Moll Rosario*—that is, the actor William Wilson— was without doubt the criminal. Perhaps I could clear myself of the frightful suspicion that I was the murderer. I wanted to escape those awful nightmares. That was my purpose. In reaching that conclusion I wanted to assure myself of more cheerful feelings. That's why I began to read those books about fingerprints with such scholarly enthusiasm.

"The strange thing was that I came to think it was all a dream— what I had seen in the Nagasaki opium den—or indeed everything related to the murder. You often see very realistic things in a dream. That makes reality feel like a dream. Can you see that too? Because even if you don't see the situation that way, it is the reality of my own experience. I came finally to think that the fact of an opium den in M. B. Machi in Nagasaki, the city where I was born, was itself a dream. Yet at the same time I believed that the facts in the case were beyond doubt.

The feeling that it was all a dream resulted from my low, mean-spirited intent to escape from the unpleasant affair I had been through. One part of me reproached myself on that score. The part of me that wanted to recognize these facts as facts took you to Nagasaki. I wanted to see for myself, but even more I wanted to have you as a third person see there was an opium den in Nagasaki, or at least the traces of one. Even though the times had changed, there should be something left in that place, I thought. It's become a ghost house now—blood drips from the ceiling. Blood drips from the ceiling. That may be true. The blood dripped; the sea that was bluer than the Holy Virgin's robe grew red. I know that for sure. . . . The blood was smeared on the wooden floor. We dragged the body into the earthen pit that provided cellar ventila- tion. When I took you to Nagasaki to the place where I made the X mark, where I stood after coming out of the narrow space leading onto the little bridge—that man, the man killed by William Wilson, is buried there.

"First you must admit the following. If you don't, there is no reason for me to continue talking.

1.   There are never in the world two or more identical finger- prints.
2.   A man who frequented the opium den in Shanghai must have known of and could have frequented the Nagasaki opium den. Just as I did.
3.   There is no general principle that a murderer cannot appear in a movie film. Therefore, it should be possible for a man who commits murder in Nagasaki to be a movie actor in America. But the murderer is unknown to the world.

"You may hesitate to accept No. 3 for being a bit too romantic. Can anyone assert, however, that such a thing is totally impossible? Moreover it is a fact. After I had done some research and thought about it a bit, I accepted these three findings for myself. Believing ten- tatively in my own intuition and my subconscious, I sent out two letters from Nagasaki. For one of them, Satō old friend, I borrowed your name and address. That was addressed to the Green Flag Com- pany in Los Angeles." (I thought to myself at the time that it would have been better if my mad friend had not been so ready to misappro- priate my name.) "The other letter was addressed to William Wilson, exclusive actor with that company. Even if he was not exclusive with the company, he appeared in their films and had some connection with them. This is what I wrote:

> Through the rigorous efforts of the police an opium den has been dis-
> covered in Nagasaki. The (chance?) coincidence of identical finger-
> prints on the gold watch you lost in a cave there and the print shown
> to the world in the film Gun Moll Rosario appears to have aroused the
> interest of the alert Japanese police in connection with the murder
> that you were involved in there. If you recall this and if you don't
> protect yourself immediately, you will be in grave danger.
>
> From a good friend of yours in the Shanghai opium den.

"I showed you earlier the news column in the cinema magazine that I received today. In my happiness I showed it to you prematurely. I mailed those two letters from the station in Nagasaki. You saw me do it. We were in Nagasaki on the fourth of October. That's important. Ordinarily it should take twenty days for mail to be delivered in Los Angeles. Postal conditions are very irregular now because of the war. My movie magazine often comes late, making me impatient. I do know about when William Wilson saw my letter."

While he was speaking and before I knew it he came over and sat down at the desk beside me. From the largest drawer in the desk he took out a letter that contained a photograph or something. He handed it to me.

"This mail was sent by the Green Flag Company. I received it from your wife ten days ago. I had written to the company asking them in your name to send me a catalogue of their movies, if they had one. Not that I wanted the catalogue; I wanted to see the date the company mailed it. They sent it out November 16. My letter to them must have arrived a little before that. I had no difficulty in concluding that the letter I mailed to William Wilson the same day reached him about November 16. I don't know whether he got it immediately, but it is fair to assume that my letter was in his hands by November 24—the day he disappeared. He disappeared after reading my letter. Let me see that thing for a minute. I sent for the film catalogue as an expedient to find out the date my letter was received, but it is unexpectedly useful. The first film listed for William Wilson should be XYZ. The news item in the magazine said that was his first. XYZ was made in 1914, according to the catalogue. Before 1914 William Wilson was not a movie actor. That has to be the case. He killed the man in Nagasaki in the summer of 1912—that must be so because it was in the summer of 1912 that I returned from Nagasaki. That was no movie actor hanging around Nagasaki and Shanghai. You'll probably say this does not determine that William Wilson was the murderer." (He grinned triumphantly.) "If I didn't have confidence in my own subconscious and my own powers of intuition, I would have to face these two questions about the case. That's what I think.

1. Suppose William Wilson's disappearance was not because of reading my letter.
2. Suppose the fingerprint on a corner of the mahogany desk in the film *Gun Moll Rosario* was not that of the driver Johnson—that is the actor William Wilson—but was someone else's.

"These were the two questions. Someone who did not believe me would conjecture that much. They might think that my reasoning was the arbitrary outcome of madness, the product of a narcotic dream about finding the gold watch with the fingerprint in that wall and about everything else I had seen. Actually, I thought that way myself on occasion. This is an important point, though. 'Can there be two or more identical fingerprints in the world?' Where, on what line of what page is that suggested in any of the sixteen books about fingerprints, all written on the basis that fingerprints are important grounds for evidence because every fingerprint must be different from every other. If there can't be two identical fingerprints in the world, and if a skeptic doubting his own eyes would not think of gouging them out, we are left with one thing only that we must accept:

(1) The fingerprint on the underside of the lid of this watch is identical to the fingerprint shown in the film *Gun Moll Rosario*.

OR, for people who are a bit more inclined to believe me:

(2) The fingerprint on the underside of the lid of the watch I picked up near the murdered man is identical to the fingerprint shown in the film *Gun Moll Rosario*.

THAT IS:

If it is impossible for there to be two fingers in the world with identical prints, then in either of the cases above the two fingerprints must have been made by one and the same finger.

Well, the more people come to believe me, as I believe myself most of the time, the more their confidence in No. 2 above will match my own. They will agree that 'William Wilson was without doubt the murderer in the Nagasaki opium den.' "

My friend pursued me with his preposterous talk and with a logic that rambled on and on through a labyrinth. Presently he opened his desk drawer for the third time and took out something like a thick measuring tape. It was movie film. "I bought this," he said as he unrolled it. Excited, his eyes gleaming weirdly, he called me over under the light and held it up for me to see. Sure enough, it was ten feet of the film *Gun Moll Rosario*. Three detectives were shown entering a plush room decorated in rococo style. They discovered something on a desk. One of the detectives pointed it out, and the picture enlarged to a close-up. On a corner of the mahogany-grained desk a single fingerprint was evident. Very carefully, so as not to scratch it, he wrapped a piece of satin from an old necktie around the film segment that showed the fingerprint. Then he rolled the film up again with the cloth inserted at that position. He handed the whole thing to me and spoke in a confident tone.

"Here's the proof. This and the lid of the watch you held with the gloves I loaned you. If you don't recognize right away that these two fingerprints are absolutely identical, that's all right. I would rather have you confirm the fact for certain by leisurely and scrupulous examination. I've got a magnifying glass. In my attic I have set up a magic lantern for viewing films. There are machines sold for this purpose, but the one I have devised is the easiest and clearest to use. I turn all this over to you. I do implore you, though, to be careful not to lose the film and not to wipe out the fingerprint on the watch."

By the end of that evening his zeal and the dignity of his speech had impressed me after all, even if he did entreat too much. I took a look to compare the fingerprint on the watch with that on the film *Gun Moll Rosario*. He was right! There was not the slightest difference!

Later I looked through the magnifying glass. I projected the film and compared fingerprints. There could not be the slightest doubt. I had to believe my eyes; the prints were identical.

That was more than three years ago.

It was the second week of September 1917. I boarded a night boat at Wakanoura to return to my parental home. Out of boredom on shipboard I picked up a newspaper in the cabin. It was three or four days old, not that day's paper. Turning to the crime and scandal page, I noticed a diagram that surprised me. It was a place I had seen before. It was a map of the neighborhood of the onetime Nagasaki opium den in M. B. Machi. At the spot where N had made his X mark this map had an X mark. I shuddered in horror at the coincidence. I ran my eyes over the story. Under the headline of Nagasaki's "Ghost House" the subhead read "More Comes Out, Stranger It Gets." If I had known nothing about it, I most likely would have paid no heed, scorning such everyday trash. This one I read. I had to read it. As I scanned it: . . . M. B. Machi in Nagasaki is a mixed residential area of lower-class foreigners, mostly Chinese. House No. 19 is vacant. A brick foreign-style structure, it was until some years ago the residence of a Chinese couple. Vacant since then, it has occasionally been rented, but the occupants have stayed not more than five or ten days or a couple of weeks at most. The occupants have reported that the dismal sound of blood dripping from the ceiling somewhere echoes for several hours in the evening between eight or nine and midnight. People have seen the drops of blood from the ceiling spreading over the floor. Some daring young people have tried lodging there in the face of those awful rumors. The mystery is that when these bold investigators are in the house nothing strange ever happens. On their assurance that nothing has happened the house is rented again. Once the house is occupied the rumored sounds of dripping recur. No one has lived there for the last three or four years, and two or three days ago the owner hired a man to demolish the house. To everyone's surprise a large underground room about ten mats in size was found under the floor. Who installed it and for what purpose are not known. When they looked to see what made people nervous, it appeared that the sound of water running out of the kitchen sink and dripping in the underground room may have suggested the dripping of blood. They guessed it might be a leak behind the sink drainboard. Even if this was the actual state of things in the "Ghost House," the workmen still discussed what the underground room was for. One man noticed a cool breeze from a corner of the basement, and when he approached, he found a cave. Where did it lead, he wondered. He crawled in two or three steps, yelled, and crawled back out. People asked him why, but he was speechless. He just pointed at the hole. When he did open his mouth after a bit, he blurted out that there was a skeleton in there. Uproar ensued. They sent for the police to come and investigate. There it was, sure enough, arm and leg bones, skull and all. The build seemed larger than a normal Japanese, so they surmised it must have been a Chinese or other foreigner. In searching every nook and cranny they found a bright, newly minted gold medal the size of a one-sen copper coin. It was solid gold, weighing about one ounce and inscribed on the face with the Latin phrase meaning "Art is long; life is short." It was identified as a rare commemorative medal from the literature department of some foreign university. The investigation of a basement unknown to people of the city, along with the discovery of the gold medal and the skeleton and the fact that the skeleton was located some ten feet directly beneath a street, all suggest that the more that comes out of the Ghost House the stranger it gets. The nature of the place suggests, too, the developments in an eighteenth-century tale. Because city police are steadily pursuing their secret investigation as to what significance this may have, the details will soon be exposed. Strange things happen even in these days of the twentieth century. Truth is stranger than fiction. . . . Like a country newspaper the report rambled on and on. (It was a Fukuoka paper.)

I was astonished. No one could have been more surprised than I to read this item. What I had heard as part of a madman's fancy was true after all. He had said, "I carried it in there myself." He had said it was a foreigner. They had actually found the skeleton of a foreigner. Spread across the ceiling of my rolling ship's cabin I saw side by side the identical fingerprints from the film *Gun Moll Rosario* and from the lid of the gold watch. How much should I believe of what N had told me? Outside my porthole the moon glimmered on the night sea to the rolling motion of the ship, suggesting various visions that he had related to me. . . . My belief strengthened gradually until I reached his level of conviction. Didn't I agree with him at last that "William Wilson was surely the murderer in the Nagasaki opium den?"

I took the Fukuoka newspaper home with me. N had died the year before. I put the newspaper in the box that held his mysterious collection of objects: the cinema magazine underlined in red, the catalogue from the Green Flag Company, the gold watch that he had heard and retrieved, the strip from the film *Gun Moll Rosario*.

Even today as I write this I can discover no difference in the two fingerprints, the one on the film and the one on the watch lid. . . . I cannot doubt my own eyes. That would be more of a sacrilege than not believing in God.

When I stare at these fingerprints, I find in them another world. That strange world has become familiar to me. . . . My wife worries that I talk too much about fingerprints, and she seems to think I may be mad. She is said to have asked my friend K, a researcher in mental illness, whether "madness is contagious." I am surely not mad. I say so to my wife. I say so to my readers. To tell the truth, I've recently come to think that N was not mad either.

᚛

Moonbeams

Tsukikage

(A fragment from the unpublished writings of N,
the principal character in "The Fingerprint")

PREFACE

Those of you who have read "The Fingerprint" will, I daresay, have found my confused record to be hard reading. You may have been annoyed at my writing. However, I may have stimulated some curiosity about that character, my friend N. I should like to have such people read this fragment, "Moonbeams." I should like also to demonstrate the literary influence which that man had on me.

After N's death from illness, I dumped out and examined the contents of his desk drawers with the intention of putting his things in order. There by chance I discovered some of his unpublished writings. They are almost all written in English, mere fragments without head or tail to them. As I read them through here and there, I came across this opening line. When N had spoken of his dreams in the Nagasaki opium den, he had said, "If I looked at the moon, I saw the water. If I looked at the water, I saw the moon." I guessed from this fragment that he might have painted such a picture while abroad. For me it was a new discovery about him. As I read more fragments, they all seemed to be records of opium dreams. I wondered if he hadn't collected them in an effort to emulate De Quincey's "Confessions of an English Opium Eater." That's what I thought when I recently received and read a translation of "Opium Eater" from my friend Tsuji.

As I am so completely absorbed in my recollections of N, I will start by quoting his opening segment in English. I will then translate the whole text into Japanese. Not because I think this is the finest example of his writing, but because I think his writings (which portray other things as well) will serve to make up for my own inadequacies in depicting the dreams in "The Fingerprint." The original is in my good friend's handwriting, and thus, as you can see, my translation is not necessarily word for word. I hope it may convey the meaning of the original text without error. Because I am not an expert in languages, I had my friend Sawada Takuji look it over when I had finished. It had no title, but for convenience's sake I added my own title of "Moonbeams."

My introduction has been rather long, but the import of N's written fragment was as follows.[3]

$$\text{\Large ⧆}$$

"Night after night I passed sleeplessly. If sleep at last came over me, I would find myself wide awake after a little while. When night advanced, I became more wakeful, like an old man though very young. I resorted in vain to several kinds of narcotic, and what I thought to be effective in some degree I tried, taking double the maximum dose and half again as much; yet no desired effect was produced. The fear of getting poisoned prevented me from using greater amounts of the drug. I never wanted to invite slumber at all cost, because sleeplessness ceased to cause me so much suffering as before. The consequence of being kept awake many nights running was, however, very unpleasant; I got unnaturally drowsy toward morning and slept it away, so that I never faced the forenoon sun in those days. All afternoon I used to sit in my room, dull, weary, and utterly dejected; sometimes I vacantly gazed at the serene magnitude of heaven from the window; and I went on being melancholy. Tears would flow even at the sight of the clouds, if I happened to discover any picturesque hues in them; so easily was I affected. The day was short in that part of the year, and moreover in my case the daytime was thus shortened into half of the whole span; nevertheless, I found it awfully long and tedious. True, nothing is worse than ennui. I was no more able to paint pictures, nor in any mood to do so. But with the arrival of night, my mental functions turned terribly active; no, 'active' is not the word; it was really an inspiration, or rather the untrammeled activity of soul itself. Exquisite thoughts continually rose up in my mind, one thought following another in the most wonderful series of imagination. . . ."

Although I cannot sleep, I suffer not at all. Tedious it is not. Lovely moonlit nights follow one upon another. I used to think a moonlit night was awfully commonplace. Now I feel exactly the opposite. I cannot get enough of the moon. The more I look at the moon, the better it is. Once one savors the moon deeply, one can be called a lover of the moon. The moon grows to maturity, ages, and is reborn. That elates and saddens the hearts of her lovers and demands ever greater love from them. It leads me to a fuller understanding that I cannot sleep without first a glimpse of the moon. People should drink their fill of those feelings for the slim brilliance of the three-day moon, shining in a narrow curved golden ring, or for the bright mirror of the full moon, flooding the night through with silver. That does not end it. The daytime moon, when her lovers look on that beautiful dead face even from the midst of a big, noisy city—looking up for a moment one thinks of eternity and one's heart becomes cool and serene. I must pity the common man who has forgotten his love for the moon. . . . I have, therefore, chosen to sleep in a room where the moon shines in. The moon now is so bright I can see the hands on my watch. I could write poetry by this light. If I leave the curtains open, the light floods in like water through the full width of the window. The gentle light falls on my bed and freezes there.

It was a night like that. I was still awake in the night. From time to time I sensed the sound of water cascading over rocks. It kept me from my sleep. I pricked up my ears. The off-and-on sound of water gurgling —was it water? Or the very faint sound of insect wings? The reeling of thread? The lamp wick burning? Reverberations of some sound echoed with a BEE-BEE-BEE-BEE as if sewing up the silence of the night. I wondered if it wasn't the sound of a fountain. There should be no fountain here. I strained my ears. The noise subsided before I knew it, but the faint echo persisted. How suspicious. When I climbed into bed, I left the curtains open to watch the moonlight as I lay awake in the night. As always, the moonlight streamed onto my bedside. Not as bright as usual this night.

I rose up a little from my bed. In order to see the moon. The moon wore a large halo. Wasn't the world shrouded in mist? I don't like moonlight nights to be clouded in mist.

I got out of bed and pulled an extra jacket on over my nightgown. I thought to look out of the window at the misty moonlit night. It is foggy all right, I thought. Dense fog. It is beginning to clear slowly. . . . As I watch, something very big can be seen faintly moving in the fog. Then another. They seem to be pushing through from right to left. Silently. Silently. I cannot make out what they are. They are like low-hanging clouds. Very big, though. As I stare, they grow larger until I feel they have spread across the entire scene. They are gray. I watch and the fog slowly lifts. There seems to be a cluster of these large undefinable things. . . . With the clearing I can gradually recognize the strange shapes. They belong to a sailing ship. A big sailing ship that slips gently through the sea like a giant dream. Indeed! Very big. What shape are those sails? Not a spread of sail you would see around here. One rather large sail each fore and aft with many small triangular sails above and to the sides of the larger ones. Every sail is puffed out to its own fancy by the wind. (As a result the ship's speed is rather slack.)

The light of the moon slides down, caressing each curving line of every wind-filled sail, large or small. Each of the tautened sails has a radiance of its own, shining dimly in silvery gray. More beautiful than you can say. The rhythm of the billowing sails piled one upon another is so agreeable to the eyes. Seldom have I seen such beauty as lies in those graceful lines and the calm and gentle hues. . . . As I watched in wonder, I felt a kind of sexual desire. Absurd, but it was true. I must line up my fingers and curve my palm into a gesture imitating the sails beyond the glass of my window. My hands tingled with bodily passion as if from afar I was fondly caressing a beautiful sculpture or, to put it more directly, the body of a beautiful woman. In truth those clustered sails do resemble two embracing, dancing female nudes painted by a cubist. The fog lightens and the sails can be seen rather clearly. The fog does not altogether disperse, and the ship continues its course through the mist. Where it is headed I cannot tell. The air has cleared above and the moon shines brightly, but near the surface the fog hangs heavy and dense. The ship must be sailing on water, but you could think it on sand. I wonder if it isn't floating in space. It is in front of my nose, and I would have said I could touch it if suddenly I reached out my hand. . . . Then it becomes clear. Below the moonlit, wind-filled sails I can see a house. A row of houses with roofs piled upward and outward, gleaming white on one side as if covered with lingering snow, untouched by the sun. Behind the sails, and before them as well, I see tiers of similar roofs, shining on one side. I watch, and the sailboat looks to be slipping through streets between roofs of houses. . . .

Yet how the scene changes. Everything grows beautiful in the light of the moon. Long have I known that moonlight makes a man's heart transcendent. That makes me love a moonlit night the more. Moonlight conceals the arts of magic, doesn't it? But I am not surprised. I am as happy as a man whose prayers are heard. I break into a smile, despite myself. The mystery opens only for one who truly loves. Thus has the moon rewarded me.

I walked across to a window on the opposite side from the one I had been gazing out of. Almost unconscious of my actions, I put out a hand reluctantly to draw aside the greenish curtains. My heart throbbed like a child. My feelings tensed as I wondered if this poor viewless window might show me something other than walls and roofs of houses.

Wanting to leave my feelings unchanged for a bit longer, I refrained from drawing the curtains to their stack in the corner. I had the eager feeling of the scientist at the moment he is about to see the results of his unprecedented experiment. Resolutely I opened the curtains. . . . I looked. There was a river before my eyes. The round moon floated on water still as a sheet of glass. Far off on the opposite bank were houses, casting shadows perfect in every detail. The mystery was not that the water looked like a mirror but that the water was not in fact a mirror. It was a sight anyone could have seen his fill of from antiquity. The sight annnoyed me. It was a new kind of dullness. Imagine that a beautiful princess appeared suddenly on the surface of the calm water, followed by a spate of countless maids-in-waiting in funeral procession, one after another marching gracefully over the water. If it were not a fairy tale, you could never endure it calmly. I wondered as I looked at the scene. The moonlit night was green like movie film. Was it Amsterdam or Venice, cities I have never seen? Maybe I'm looking at one of those cities now. . . . Is it a photogravure, a painting, an etching, an opium dream? It is at least a view I have seen before.

Suddenly there was a flash as if from ice on the still water. It came not from the procession of the beautiful princess, but was no more than a stealthy flutter from the wind. The passing breeze roused a waterlike feeling from water that seemed not to be water. By natural connection I thought of the sound of water I had heard earlier as I lay awake. I had forgotten that sound when I was drawn to the sailing ship. Now I recalled it, and my ears again pick up the delicate reverberations. The sound makes me nervous. I look across the stream, but I cannot tell what made the noise. I think the sound of water comes from those city streets.

I returned to the first window. I was seeking the source of the watery sound. The cluster of sails slipped behind the antique houses lit by the moon and past a towering black gothic steeple. Silently. Silently. . . . The sound of the water is below this window. I pushed the window open and leaned head and shoulders out—when suddenly before my eyes I understood the suspicious noise. A fountain. Diago-nally across from my window in the square at a four-way street intersec-tion in the old town there is a big fountain. Slender streams of water from the fountain gleam in the moonlight; they are bright silver threads entwined in dirty white velvet. Like an earthbound thing yearning for the sky, the water is thrown continuously aloft, thrown upward only to fall back. This must be the mysterious sound that echoed like a hallucination at my bedside.

A pale white something appeared from the small black doorway of a large stone house facing the fountain.

A person emerged from the shadow of the house and into the bright moonlight. With a better look I see it is a woman. She carries a water jar in one hand. When I think she has reached the fountain, the dying sound of the water becomes suddenly intense. Water gushes in a spray of thick white silken threads flashing brightly as it shoots from the fountain's basin. Water filling the big basin is sloshing out. This is the noise I had strained to hear from my bed, the sound of water tumbling over rocks. I watch. How long have they been doing this? How often have people come in turn to draw this water?

Across the street a human figure can be seen approaching. The figure grows larger as it nears. It goes straight for the fountain. The woman turns in that direction. She watches the approaching figure intently without realizing that water is spilling from her jug. The figure comes closer. The woman raises her arm in signal. The figure steps up its pace as it nears. The larger figure bends down and embraces the smaller. The second figure is a man. He must be young. The woman seems finally to notice that the water is slopping over from her jug. She manages to stem the flow of water that spouts from the side of the basin. The water in the basin gleams from now bigger ripples. The sides of the jug are damp with water, damp with moonlight. They shine brightly as if the jug were set with jewels, and the ground the jug is set upon looks black and soaked in water. The woman picks up the jug with both hands, and while she is stooped over the man seems to shove her aside. He picks up the jug lightly in one hand. Water spills from the mouth of the tipping jug and drops with a tinkling noise to the ground. The man pays no heed as he carries the jug to the dark doorway that the woman had earlier come from. There the woman takes it back. Staggering under the weight, she disappears into the dark interior. The man goes to rest by the wall. Traces of water spilled from the jug run across the road, leaving a black line upon the ground.

Soon the woman reappears in the dark doorway. Now she is

wearing a black hood covering her head. The man embraces the woman in black and leads her away. The pair of shadow players appear not to notice that I am watching from the window, and they walk toward my window. I hide myself in the window. Not that I don't want them to see me, but because I think they may not want to be seen by me. I steal a glance as they pass the window. He is a big man and young. The woman is small and slim-waisted. She looks like a girl who would snap in two if you embraced her firmly. She is wrapped in a big black robe. At least that's what I think. The woman points, and at this invitation I look that way and see the sailing ship. The man nods. He's a man of the sea, I think to myself.

Soon the phantom pair disappears, and a feeling wells up in me: I want to see that street; I want to walk in that pure and beautiful moonlight. Until I saw those figures pass my window, I had not thought so.

I notice that if I go out the door next to my window and down seven or eight stone steps by the wall of my house, I will be in the town. I am grateful to the moon. Even the structure of my house has been utterly changed by the magical favor of the moon.

When I went down the silvered steps, my feet took me naturally in the direction of the fountain.

The fountain is bigger than it looked from my window. The black figure spouting water from its mouth is apparently made of bronze. The antique round pedestal for the statue and the big basin as high as my chest are made of snow-white marble. The whole is a translucent blue, cold. Looking up at it, I pace slowly five or six steps around the basin.

The figure spouting water is a naked youth. In a slightly twisted pose and standing on tiptoe, both legs are perfectly aligned. The figure is drawn up, head held high, back stretched, the right hand extended as high as possible. The other arm is twisted and thrust out behind in natural pose. The head leans back as far as possible; the line of the throat makes a right angle with the chin. From the face pointing at the sky, from the mouth no doubt, the water spouts in a fine stream three or four feet into the air. In its cramped position the figure yet looks to be not uncomfortable. The symmetrical beauty must have derived from an ample study of nature, for the beauty penetrates the bronze body. The figure of the youth was black in contrast to the white stone of the statue's pedestal and basin, and one feels the youth might be a black man. The youth's head is too large and the body is emaciated. It would be hard to call this beauty "classical." The weird appearance is a more modern style of beauty. The upstretched hand looks as if it were trying impatiently to grasp a bunch of grapes hanging down like breasts from an unseen high branch. The figure looks to be chasing a dream that flew away like a butterfly. On a moonlit night like this, was it reaching impatiently to touch the round moon hanging in mid-sky? A thin stream of water spews continuously in a faintly shining white thread from the mouth of that face staring at the sky. A breeze comes and goes, blowing the thread of water into a spray that dissipates in faint white mist. Blown sometimes high, sometimes low, it looks like the breath of the fountain, the breathing of the youthful black figure. At moments when the moonlight, bright as day, passes through the spray, a tiny rainbow will float there, only to fade away, then reappear at exactly the same place, exactly as beautiful as before, and again fade away, appearing and disappearing, appearing and disappearing, like an artist trying with his brush to capture beauty in delicate lines on his canvas. Either for lack of ardor in his creation or for lack of skill, the artist must paint it in and paint it out, paint it in and paint it out, over and over again. He must redouble his efforts though they are in vain.

The cluster of big sails slid slowly ahead, soon reaching a point directly behind the fountain. It was so big I had to look up at it. Gigantic, it was. . . . (The writing continued but is here omitted.)

Notes

1. Satō calls his protagonist "RN," but because of the coincidental correspondence with the name of an American political leader, I have shortened the name to "N."

2. Satō is exercising poetic license, as Cairo is not a port and ships transiting the Suez Canal normally call at Port Said or Alexandria.

3. The following paragraph, marked by quotation marks, is Satō's English as printed in his Japanese text; I have made only minor corrections of grammar and spelling. Satō's next paragraph of "translation" of the same passage into Japanese is here omitted. Retranslation would be redundant even in slightly different English. The remainder of "Moonbeams" by Satō (purportedly by N) is written in Japanese and rendered into English by me.

F * O * U [1]

Alternate Title: I Think So Too, 1926

He stood up, glanced again at the beautiful play of sun and shadow on the row of great round columns and the broad steps of La Madeleine and the flower market next to it, then stepped out of the Restaurant LaRue. There in front he saw it, the splendid all-chrome automobile parked next to his pitiful little Citroen.

> *The car had not been there earlier.*
> *It was a Rolls Royce to knock your eyes out.*
> *He had never seen a shape like it.*
> *It sparkled and glittered all over.*

He thought he'd like to get in. He got in. Taking the wheel, he drove off in the direction the car was pointing.

On its own the car merged into the crowded Rue Royale. Swinging right around the obelisk in the Place de la Concorde, it came out onto the Champs-Elysées. The Rolls Royce vibrated not one whit. Emitted not a sound. He gunned the engine; the car remained silent. Surprised to note that the speedometer read 120 kilometers, he slowed down. Slowing, he passed the Arc de Triomphe and reached the Bois de Boulogne. On entering the park, he thought the Rolls Royce was starting to act funny. He stopped the car and got out.

As he opened the hood to look at the engine, a youth of about twelve wearing knickers appeared beside him, watching curiously. The boy stood there importantly in a contorted pose, his belly thrust out, the backs of his hands stuck to his hips, and his arms bent like the handles of a flower vase. To look at him, he was a specimen of "gamin de Paris."

A "gamin de Paris" is one species of mankind. To explain that a "gamin" is a "bad boy who makes his home playing in the streets" is to miss the mark entirely. You might say they are modern elves. Although they are children, they have the sagacity of an adult. They have a way with words. They act like adults. They do mostly bad things. For example, they spot someone out walking, looking rather shabby. They block his path. They look his outfit up and down. They'll look him up and down again, glare in his eyes, and say: "Hey, you. It's spring. It's Sunday. You're young. You're out for a walk, aren't you?"

With another glance, from muddy shoes to weatherbeaten hat, they will leisurely saunter away. If that's all they do, that's all right, but sometimes they do outrageous things. Recently a thirteen-year-old child, with the help of two followers and his mistress (a thirteen-year-old has a mistress), murdered a wealthy old woman. Although the criminals were known, they could not be found anywhere. The case created a great sensation, and after some time had elapsed they were finally arrested in Marseille. The criminals were terrifying, precocious, mentally twisted kids. They differed from adult villains in the fascinating vitality of their wits. Their types would not exist except in a wondrous city like Paris. Once having come into existence, they cannot be overlooked as a topic for sociology. There is a big volume of research on what has been dubbed the "gamin de Paris."

The child who was watching him fix the engine of the Rolls Royce seemed to be one of these types.

Suddenly the child said: "You. Is that your car?"

Surprised, he looked up at the child. With his special smile he replied. . . .

"What? No, it's not mine. It was parked next to mine at LaRue's. I wanted to ride in it, so I did."

"Indeed," the gamin said. "But wouldn't it be a good idea to return it to its owner?"

"Oh dear! I think so too."

At this reply it struck him suddenly. At least, he hastily hopped into the idling Rolls Royce and returned to LaRue's.

There at the front entrance was a gentleman looking all around. When he saw the shining Rolls Royce flying back, he threw up his hands in happy wonderment and shouted.

"It's here! It's here! It's come back!"

From the stopped car he called out.

"Well, I'm back."

Smiling in his own peculiar way, he got out.

"You. Where did you go?"

"To the park. The Bois de Boulogne."

"I was worried," the owner said. On looking at the other's beautiful smile, his anger subsided. He corrected himself.

"That's all right."

"I had some trouble with it, sorry to say."

"Well, now," he said, as they crouched down to examine the car.

"What? It can't be helped. It's nothing."

The owner spoke in a rather consoling tone and got into the car.

As he watched the Rolls Royce glide away, "What a great car," he said to himself with evident admiration. He was about to get into his own car when the manager of the restaurant came out and called to him. He felt someone grab his arm brusquely. It was a policeman.

"Wait a minute. Let's talk."

On arrival at the police station he was, as always, smiling. He handed over a calling card. On the front it said "M. Marqui Icino."

On the reverse, in Japanese characters, it read "Ishino Makio."

He told them all the facts and his feelings after his lunch.

Presently the police chief asked, "Do you know anybody in this city?"

"Everybody among the Japanese," he replied.

"What about the French? Aren't there any that you know?"

The chief asked again.

"There is," he said, "Florence de Tarme."

"Where is the lady?"

"Rue d'Alésia in Montparnasse. Number. . . ."

As he spoke, it slipped his memory. He took out a pocket notebook and showed them where it was written in.

It seems they called Florence de Tarme. She came soon. Seeing him, "Oh! Maki!" she called out.

"Do you," the police chief said as he stared at the woman called Florence de Tarme, "know this young oriental gentleman?"

"Yes! Sure I know him. Why?"

"How did you come to know him?"

"That is," Florence said with a beautiful side glance at the police chief. Then, turning the same glance toward Maki she continued, "He's my sweet Maki."

After speaking she dropped her eyes to look at the table where her hands rested. In the tabletop dust she drew three big letters:

F O U

She took out a handkerchief and wiped her slender fingertips as she spoke.

"What on earth has happened to gentle Maki?"

She squinted one eye and smiled, showing a dimple in one cheek. The police chief eyed the stylish woman and nodded as he read the letters she had stealthily written in the dust, concealed behind her body—F O U (madman).

"When did you come to this country?"

"Just a year ago."

"Well then, you speak quite fluently. . . . By the way, excuse me for asking a rude question, but has anyone ever before, somewhere, in your country or here, said that you were mentally different from others, that is, abnormal?"

After Florence de Tarme had been sent home, Ishino's Japanese friend Senkichi Inagaki had been called. In the interim the chief and he had begun the interrogation and response. Ishino laughed gently, as always. . . .

"People sometimes say that about me. Why, I have doubts whether I am Japanese or not. In my thinking, we—my family, surely came to Japan as visitors. We stayed too long and are disliked. We cause trouble, too, by our different customs. Probably we are Chinese—Chinese from some flourishing period there, like the Tang dynasty. As proof I would say," (as he spoke he held one hand in front of his nose as if dividing his face vertically), "I see a star this way. With one eye the star looks like a dog; with the other eye the same star looks like a hunter. . . . That surely proves that I am Chinese, they say. With that, my family says I am crazy. It appears that the Japanese government misunderstood things in thinking I dislike being Japanese. They sent a squad of soldiers to arrest me. I shaved my head completely. I disguised myself, too, and escaped. I hid for two days between the walls of a house in a village that was traditionally loathed and scorned for no good reason. I knew that these people who were despised and scorned were really kind. In the end I was caught. It wasn't by the troops, though. It was by my older brother. My brother proposed that I go into a hospital for a while. The hospital provided extraterritorial rights, he explained. But in no time I didn't like the hospital. At the hospital, too, they said it wasn't necessary for me to stay there. When I came out of the hospital, I continued to be anxious all the time. I thought I might likely be killed. My uncle had been killed. . . . When he made some antiwar statements, he was hit in the head by stones thrown at him. I suggested to my brother that we stop being guests in Japan and go instead to France. My brother did not agree, but he did consent to let me come here alone. I love my brother. I love France even more. Florence is here, and there is a very nice gentleman who excused me today for riding in his very nice Rolls Royce without his permission, and then there was a child who gave me the best advice. . . . He instructed me wisely that it would be good to return the car to its owner. . . ."

When Inagaki arrived, the police chief, glancing back at Ishino, said to him, "Please put your friend for a while into a hospital that we will designate."

The chief gave Inagaki a piece of paper he had written on. It was addressed to an insane asylum.

⌂

When Florence visited him at the asylum, he was drawing pictures with a pen on scraps of paper. From each window of a big tall building there was a person looking out. The design showed a school of fish looking like birds and swimming in line toward the windows, holding people. He stretched out his arm, holding the paper farther from his eyes. He looked at it, showed it to Florence, and said: "How about it Florence? Isn't it interesting?"

"Really interesting, yes."

Suddenly he drew several messy lines across it.

"What did you do that for?"

"The picture is a little too offhand. . . . That's all."

"Maki," Florence said. "It's sad that you've come here. But it's better than jail, I guess. I have to see you every day. If you're here, I can visit you. I'm the one who got you sent here. Don't be angry, will you? You'll get out of here soon. . . . But what did you do to make the police detain you?"

"It was a beautiful car I rode in for thirty minutes, forgetting it belonged to someone else."

"My goodness. Such a thing. It's really a pity. You're not so uncomfortable here, though, are you?"

"Uncomfortable?" Maki asked. "It's a comfortable enough place, and you come to see me. . . . The only bad thing about it is, they don't have a bed for you here."

"It's only for ten days. Then, if you get out of here, I'll live with you. That will be more pleasant than the way it has been. Definitely."

"Yes. I think so too," Maki replied.

They embraced tenderly, and Florence started out of the room. He called to stop her and give her money. Florence refused, but in the end she accepted. That is, rather, she would use the money to prepare a place for their joint home. Japanese currency was strong in the foreign-exchange markets, and these days Maki had much more money than usual. He had exchanged money at the bank yesterday before going to LaRue's.

When Florence had gone, he continued to think about how happy he would be to live with her. Then he remembered meeting the child in the park yesterday and the boy's advice.

"Wouldn't it be a good idea to return it to its owner?"

"I think so too."

It was good that he had replied that way, he thought.

". . . This time I will live with you. That will be more pleasant than the way it has been. Definitely."

"Yes. I think so too."

To recall these two conversations made him very happy. A smile sprung to his lips like water gushing from a spring and sparkling in the sun. He murmured over and over with his lips: "I think so too. I think so too. I think so too."

Florence came to see him the next day bearing supplies for water-color painting and some early blooming hyacinths.

"These stupid hyacinths aren't for you to paint. I brought them, that's all. They're what girl students paint."

"I think so too. . . . It is a beautiful flower."

Ishino smiled sweetly and laughed. Truly, there was no more inno-cent smile than this. . . . Just to see this smile, Florence may have believed, was the value in living with him.

Ishino always ate his meals at a place called Au Bon Coin in Montpar-nasse.

One evening he overheard a woman complaining behind him. . . .

"My, how disgusting. It's gross. . . ."

Ishino turned around. He thought it might refer to him.

There at the table behind him was a woman holding up a soup spoon and frowning. The sharp-eyed woman saw that Ishino had turned around.

"Isn't this a disgusting place? There's a hair in my soup."

The woman spoke in a tone half appealing to him and half apolo-gizing.

"Is that so? That's strange. It's outrageous."

Ishino replied. He thought the woman was beautiful. He winked eagerly. He was happy to agree with her.

He thought he had encountered the woman two or three times before at this restaurant. After the hair in the soup incident they would speak to each other. As they noticed each other now and again, they gradually became more friendly.

One evening, as she sat facing him, she invited him to come by her house. He followed her to her rooms in a house up the slope of Rue d'Alésia.

Florence opened her door with a key. He followed her in.

"Sit down, please," she said, pointing to a chair.

Florence went directly into the next room, leaving the door between the rooms half open. The chair she had indicated faced that door.

He looked around the room. Florence had hung deep-red curtains from the ceiling on all sides of this parlor. It gave the idea of being in a tent, he thought. There was a light that was modeled on a hanging lamp from a Turkish harem.

After leaving him there, the woman did not come back from the next room. From the sound of rustling silk, it seemed she was changing her clothes. He looked involuntarily through the half-open door and caught a momentary glimpse of her in a chemise only. When her figure disappeared, her feet could still be seen, thrusting out under the light from the purple gauze shade. That room had a bed in it.

Resting his chin on the knob of his cane, Ishino, like a gargoyle on Notre Dame, peered steadily into the next room. No matter how long he waited, Florence made no sign of reappearing. He grew tired of waiting and got up from his chair. He wrapped around his neck the new muffler that he had earlier taken off. (It had become quite cold recently.) He put on his hat and called out.

"Good-bye."

He went out of the room.

The woman could not be made to understand the man. The man could not be made to understand the woman.

As Ishino headed home, he wondered if it wouldn't have been all right to go into the next room. He regretted not having done so. If it happened again, he mused, but then he felt the woman was a bit dignified.

His studio at 209 Boulevard Raspail was not far from Florence's place.

At the next opportunity he had to meet her at Au Bon Coin the woman laughed uproariously. She stared at him with a more beautiful sidelong glance than he had ever seen before.

He asked if it would be all right to come to her place again. She replied: "Yes. Yes. Anytime!"

She looked at Ishino intently with a smile that showed her teeth, white like the seeds in fruit.

Maki Ishino had that Italian kind of beauty. Charmingly short in stature.

The third time he visited her marked the beginning of a truly strange romance between Maki Ishino and Florence de Tarme.

"What a timid, uncertain boy you are! Maki. My Maki. Maki, aren't you really a marquis? A young nobleman?"

"No. Why? I'm just a commoner."

"Still, I've never seen such a refined gentleman."

It was no lie that Florence had never encountered a man who treated her as elegantly as he did.

"I love you," Ishino said.

Florence replied with a kiss.

In response to her questions he talked of various things. The fact that the same star seen with different eyes appeared to him as a dog and as a hunter. The question of why his uncle had died. The woman listened in silent surprise. She said he must be about the same age as she was. Although she told people she was twenty-three, actually she was twenty-five, she said.

"Twenty-five? I'm twenty-five, you say? Really I'm thirty-six."

She did not readily believe what he said. When she finally accepted it, she said:

"You're really like Dorian Gray, that English nobleman."[2]

The woman seemed to think Dorian Gray was a real-life English lord.

"Well, do you have a wife at home in your country?"

"I do. . . . She's probably reached the port back home by now. Last year she came to this country with me, but then she went home because she got pregnant. The child should be born around next February."

"My. What a fortunate woman your wife is. What's her name?"

"Harue."

"Haruè?"

"Yes."

". . . Well, it can't be helped."

Now it was the woman's turn to discuss her situation.

She began by saying she had never before revealed this to anyone.

The lineage of the woman who bore the name of the historic de Tarme family gradually became clear to Ishino. . . . She came from the Château de Tarme in the hilly country of Touraine overlooking the Loire valley. That was Florence's home and birthplace. Florence wanted to live a free life and she had left there at twenty-one. (There was no better place in the world than Montparnasse.) Back at the château where she was born there were lilacs. There was her father, completely white-haired. Her father was still living, without loss of vigor but in the spirit of feudal times. Florence thought of him as no more than a ghost.

Inagaki visited the insane asylum to see Ishino and met with the attending physician. He thought he should report back to Japan how long it would be necessary for Ishino to remain in the asylum.

The attending physician spoke. "I simply cannot predict. And not only the prospect for the length of his stay in the hospital. Also the condition of the patient. I don't think that you can find such a refined, amiable gentleman outside the asylum." (He laughed.) "Actually, the nurses say so too. But to be too placid doesn't signify the absence of illness. To send him back into society, even if something quite abnormal were to happen, I believe there is virtually no reason to fear that he may harm anyone. As he is now, that is. . . . But, as you know, with mental patients there is a worry about the occurrence of gloomy or violent behavior in reaction after a period of cheerful mildness. . . . Has Monsieur Ishino manifested such tendencies before?"

"Absolutely not," Inagaki answered. "Formerly, I won't say he never did anything malicious, but for the last half-year he has been

living in a cheerful, kind, grateful manner. The improper things bor-
dered on the ordinary, and even then I think his madness was under
control. In that sense his madness can well be left uncured." (Both
speaker and listener laughed.) "To be a little abnormal is natural. . . .
He's got a lover named Florence. When she saw that Ishino had been
summoned to the police station, she thought the simplest way to clear
things up was to say he was mad. That's what she said, it seems. As we
look at him, though, I don't think he's very crazy these days."

"I see. So that's the situation? It looks all right. Let's keep him here
for another week and observe him carefully, then we'll issue a certifi-
cate of diagnosis to the police that will sanction his release."

. . . Ishino was in the asylum for thirteen days.

A Turkish-style rug—though it may not have been made in Turkey. A
clothes rack of oak that she had picked up somewhere. Then the big
deep-red curtains that made the room like a tent. The brass harem
lamp. An oval mirror in a rococo frame. Then, fifteen or sixteen popular novels. A terra-cotta figure of the Greek god Pan. A cloissoné
flower vase made in Nagoya—it had more than thirty swallowtail
butterfly wings on it. A bed that might originally have had spiral
posts.

These were the things that Florence had newly brought to Ishino's
studio. Ishino had begun living with Florence right after he came out of
the asylum.

Florence was not home between 9 A.M. and 5 P.M. She had to work
at an office every day. Her office was a secret to everyone. She didn't
even want to tell Ishino if she could help it. When she said as much, he
asked no more. She did explain that it was the office of a secret society
where a lot of Russians gathered. If that became known, it would lead
to suspicion of the people there. That was all she would tell Ishino.

Although he was bored being alone, he was happy even in his
boredom. The woman came home at precisely 5:30.

One day Inagaki came to visit. After inquiring about Ishino's illness, looking around the room so changed in appearance, and ascertaining that Florence was not at home, he spoke.

"You love Florence, don't you?"

"Yes. Why?"

"Does Florence love you?"

"Yes. Why?"

"Please listen. This is what people who don't know the two of you are saying. They're all saying that Florence probably doesn't love you. No, maybe she really does, but they all disapprove of your living with her. They all say that woman seems to have a secret life."

"That's true. . . . That's why she's out now. In the daytime except for Sundays she's always out. You people don't know that woman well. I'm the only one who knows her. If you knew her as well as I do, any of you would have to love her," Ishino continued. "Why don't all of you approve? Why am I so happy, always smiling so? None of you can see the reason. Think about that, please. My personality has changed completely since I met Florence. I've lost my inferiority complex. I've stopped distrusting people. I've been liberated from a hard heart. I've stopped being prejudiced against people. That's how it is. In a word, I look at the world like a contented child at the side of its mother. Isn't that delightful? I think of who has brought me such harmony. It's not the gods who brought it. One woman did. Florence, it was. . . . Despite that, why do you all disapprove? The joy that gives harmony to one's heart, what's so bad about that?"

Inagaki remained silent. Ishino's words showed such genial, heartwarming pleasure. What's more, they were true, and he should not oppose them. . . . Or maybe Ishino's sincere and innocent smile made it impossible for anyone to say anything to the contrary.

"Do you paint during the day?" Inagaki asked.

Ishino replied: "No. I don't think of it. My life is too happy for that."

Then he added: "Anyway, my pictures are too poor. I'm disgusted with them."

"Pictures, you say they're bad, but if they give pleasure, there's nothing better than that."

"I think so too," Ishino said, smiling.

At the end of July they made a swing around the Swiss lakes at Florence's behest.

⌂

When they returned from their travels in September, two letters had arrived from Haruè. A photograph was enclosed. It showed the young mother holding the newly born child. The letters reported the child was a girl. For a name, elder brother had said what about Mariko, as the child was conceived far away.[3] After the birth the mother wasn't as well as might be hoped, but little by little she seemed to be recovering, and anyway she was sending a picture taken at the time. The second letter was about being lonesome because there wasn't much recent news, and about the photograph not coming out too well, and other matters, but he did not read it with much enthusiasm.

Florence said she wanted to see the picture and he did not refuse.

After looking at it for a bit, Florence said: "What a lovable child. She's just like you—annoyingly so. But to me, she's a darling. That child, Maki, I'd like to have her for mine. What's her name?"

"Mari."

"Marie. Darling Marie."

Florence pressed the photograph against her cheek. She talked a lot about Marie. She said nothing about Haruè, however.

Touching Haruè's face in the picture with his finger, he asked Florence, "What about her?"

Florence tilted her head. She said nothing.

"What do you think?"

"People from one country are not good at seeing the beauty in people of another country," Florence replied. She shook her head and added, "I don't see her as beautiful."

"Is that so? I think so too," Maki replied.

"Marie. Darling child. Maki, I'd really like to have that child for my own. Yours and mine."

"I think so too," Maki replied.

Letter sent from Makio to Haruè:

I've seen the picture. The child is darling. She's a good child. She resembles me a lot. Mari is a very good name for her. I'll return on a trip and bring the child back with me. Can you talk to my brother and have him send me money for that?

Reply from Haruè:

. . . I was so happy to get news from you after such a long time. I read the letter over many times. Mari is growing more lovable by the day. Everyone who sees her says she looks exactly like you and doesn't resemble me at all. (Parts omitted.) If you want to come back on a trip, that's one thing, but you don't need to come here to fetch me. I'll come to Paris alone, bringing Mari with me. Your brother says that's the less wasteful way to do it. I can come by myself. When I left you in Paris, I came home alone. This time I'll be coming with Mari to the place where you are. Everyone on the ship will take care of us. Since I had the previous experience, I won't be worried at all. . . .

Cablegram from Makio to his brother:

(Unnecessary Haruè come. Details by letter. Need money.)

Letter, as above:

(First part omitted.) Haruè told me that she would come by herself, but there is no need for her to come. If she does come, it won't be helpful. I want to bring Mari back alone. If I had money for that, I'd leave right away, but I don't have quite enough, so I ask for help. Please send me a little of the balance in your custody. There is someone else from here that I would like to bring with me. When we meet I'll explain everything.

Reply from Older Brother to Makio:

(First part omitted.) As usual, your letter is too simple and one-sided. We don't know how to interpret it here. While it is all right for you to come back to Japan, if you are thinking of returning there, it should be more convenient for Haruè just to go and take Mari. If she doesn't and if you come back to Japan, how could you do such an impossible thing as to return there taking Mari but not the mother? You are always asking for funds, and you should understand that the money I am still holding for you is rather depleted. Although I can't send you the extra funds you ask for, I presume you may have some shortage for living costs away from home, and I enclose a money order. Anyway, after due consideration I hope you will send a more specific and detailed letter. Until then Haruè will not travel. I think it would be a good idea, therefore, for you to use these funds to return to Japan for the present at your convenience. (Latter part omitted.)

Letter from Makio to Haruè:

I've read brother's letter. As you have known ever since we were married, brother is a little unreasonable, and so I am writing this letter to you. I am now living with a woman named Florence de Tarme. She's the daughter of the owner of a château in Touraine. I trust her and I think you would trust her too. Florence saw the picture and said she wants to have Mari. We will take Mari to be our child, Florence's and mine. If you come here, you'll be just one person extra. That's why I thought it was unnecessary for you to come. If you do want to come, I understand and you may do so. Because Florence will be Mari's mother, you would be her wet nurse, and you could also double as servant to Florence and me. Tell brother, get the money, and you can come here right away.

⛩

To enjoy a happy Christmas and New Year's, Florence proposed to Maki that they go to Italy.

On the express to Rome, Ishino whispered with an expression of fear: "You're being followed. Look." (He pointed surreptitiously.) "That man. Maybe you didn't notice. If he's a spy, he's been trailing us since our summer travels in Switzerland. That man. In the elegant outfit, he's dressed up like a stout American."

Florence was surprised. She stared at his face.

"Me? Why is he following me?"

"Well, it's your secret society."

"Oh. Yes. But that fellow—it's nothing. You must be mistaken, aren't you?"

"No. I'm sure. I saw him at the hotel where we were in Switzerland. When we went back to Paris, I saw him on the train too. That man, without a doubt. I'm sure I recognize him."

"So, we must be careful," she said as she stared at the elegant, stout gentleman. After a bit she said to Ishino: "As you say so, I recognize something about him. But he's probably not a spy. . . . Yes, I know. He's a steward in my father's château. I remember. There's no doubt about it. I've got to go ask him."

Florence stood up abruptly. She went directly to stand in front of the stout gentleman dressed in American style. No sooner had she spoken to him than the gentleman got up from his seat, bowed repeatedly as if apologizing in a very polite manner, and said something to Florence.

She came back smiling and laughing and slipped into the seat beside Ishino. She spoke.

"Yes. My eyes were right. He's a steward of my father's. . . . Father does such unpleasant things to me. He worries about my living an independent life and so he secretly puts that man on my trail. . . . It's happened before. He seems to think something bad may happen to me. It's silly. He thinks I'm still a child. He thinks we're living in the ancient past. I told that fellow to get off at the next station and go home. But let him do his duty while we were traveling, he pleaded with me. . . . He will protect me while staying mostly out of sight. He would have no excuse for his lord if it were found out, he begged. It can't be helped. Let him do as he wishes. Anyway, Italy is not a place to be careless. That retainer of my father, if I am not mistaken, is a powerful boxer. And if by any chance we are short on traveling expenses when we get there, we can look him up and get him to pay."

Florence laughed cheerily. On seeing the steward she appeared to recall the château where she was born. She talked of things from her childhood. Her clever chatter and the views of country scenery slipping by outside the window were to him as beautiful as a fairy tale. He gazed enchanted at her expression as she talked, an expression that changed more beautifully than the scenery out the window.

"I never get tired of traveling with you," he said.

"Yes. I think so too."—The woman had picked up the man's favorite saying.

During their travel, when the steward accidentally caught Ishino's eye, the stout fellow showed him the courtesy one pays to a king. People watching had no doubts as to Ishino's dignity.

Ishino's travels in Italy were the purest and happiest of all the accounts of travel in Italy. In a new bed the taste of kisses was new. Whatever streets they passed through in Italy he found no woman more beautiful than Florence. Not even in the pictures in any of the galleries. It seemed unfortunate that not one of the artists of old had seen such beauty as had Ishino. . . . That says it all. If we must add another episode, on the boat from Naples to Corsica a traveler who looked like an English merchant had asked Ishino about the details of the geography of Corsica. The traveler may have thought Ishino was Corsican.

At all the hotels where they stopped, everyone spoke of Ishino as "the young lord."

⋔

Reading Makio's letter, Haruè was dazed. After an hour at last she was able to cry. When Makio's brother came to console her, she showed him the letter, which she had forgotten she had folded up after reading in silence.

Brother started reading. . . .

"I've read brother's letter. As you have known ever since we were married, brother is a little unreasonable, and so I am writing this letter to you. I am now living with a woman named Florence de Tarme. She's the daughter of the owner of a château in Touraine. I trust her and I think you would trust her too. Florence. . . .''

He was reading aloud, but gradually his voice got weaker until he was mumbling.

Makio's brother read it over again one more time.

He was silent. At last he heaved a deep sigh and said: "Haruè . . . recently a reply came to my query of Inagaki, whom you have spoken of, and he wrote that Makio had recovered. Indeed, though, he is insane. . . . In fact, I didn't speak of it to you before, but Inagaki wrote in his letter that Makio was living with a woman named Florence. Though he's not in the hospital, he is crazy. . . . If he weren't, how could he ever speak of these things?"

Brother again read Makio's letter that he held in his hand.

" '. . . Mari will be Florence's child and mine. If you come here. . . . If you do want to come, I understand and you may do so . . . but . . . you could also double as servant to Florence and me.' Hm. He writes very cleverly. A superman?"

Makio's brother laughed, but at the same time tears ran from his eyes.

"If we had known it earlier, when he said he would come to get Mari, we might have let him come back."

Brother was speaking to himself. Haruè did not reply, and he continued.

"Haruè. Pay no attention to it. . . . Because they are the words of a crazy person. . . . Forgive him. It is distressing. Still, he sees Mari as lovable. . . . You must think of yourself. That's so. You have your love; you can indulge in that. He's gone crazy. . . . He's like a child making unreasonable demands on its mother. . . . If I do say so, from childhood he used to make unreasonable, selfish demands to trouble his mother. . . . Somehow since those days he has had a queer temperament. . . ."

Whether or not Haruè listened to her brother-in-law's muttering, she remained silent and nodded occasionally. She stared with tear-blurred vision at the quilt in red *yūzen*[4] pattern wrapped around the sleeping Mariko beside her.

It was cold, and brother looked through the porch glass at the snow that had just started.

"Do you think he's all right?"

Suddenly Haruè spoke.

"Huh! What did you say?"

Brother turned and asked in turn.

"It's his sickness. . . . This time I wonder if it isn't serious?"

"Well, we don't know that. I feel sorry to bother him too often, but let's make inquiries by cable to Inagaki."

Brother picked up the letter and read it again. He seems to have wondered if the severity of the illness wasn't revealed in the letter.

⚟

Return cablegram from Inagaki to Haruè

(TRAVELING IN ITALY. DEFINITELY SAFE. REST EASY.)

⚟

When Florence and Maki returned to their accustomed residence at 209 Boulevard Raspail, it was already March.

Florence had spent all the money she had received from Maki.

Maki saw that a letter had come from his brother. He slit it open immediately. He wanted to know quickly when Haruè had left with Mariko.

There was not a word about that in the letter. His blockhead of a brother said Florence was a woman of unknown lineage. (Brother seemed not to have read what he wrote about Florence in his letter to Haruè.) Rather than idling away his time in Paris, he should return home without a moment's delay, the letter said. Had he considered how anxiously Haruè was awaiting his return? Brother could not send any more money at all. He had entrusted the traveling expenses for the return to Japan to the Japanese Embassy, but this money could not be used for anything other than the cost of travel.

He found it odd that brother wrote nothing at all about Haruè's coming here but rather about her waiting anxiously. It was strange, too, that Haruè was not happily coming at once to Paris in accordance with his bidding. Haruè shouldn't be such a disobedient woman. Sitting next to Maki, whose face betrayed his bewilderment, Florence joined in by asking, "What's the news from your homeland?"

"My brother, as usual, is saying things I don't understand," Maki said, laughing. He related to her all the contents of the letter.

"You're worried about money. That will work out. We can live on the wages I bring home from my work. Don't you think so? I don't want to be separated from you on any account."

"Yes, of course. I think so too," Maki said.

As soon as he knew they were back from Italy, Inagaki came to visit at a time when Florence would not be there. Inagaki told Ishino about the cablegram from Haruè during his absence, his own reply to it, and brother's inquiry about his health. . . .

"I wrote to your brother and told him not to worry; you were not ill at all. Because that's the way it is. But," Inagaki said with a laugh, "even if it bothers you, I did reveal in my letter the facts of Mademoiselle—that is to say, Madame Florence."

"That's all right. It's the truth. I told Haruè all about it myself."

"You did? . . . I think you also got a letter from your brother. He wrote me and asked me to encourage you to return home. He added that if you didn't return, he wouldn't send any more money."

"Well, I won't return," Ishino said softly and cheerfully. "No matter what, I've got to stay here and paint pictures. After seeing the old masters in Italy I want to paint, whatever happens. Florence says she won't leave me. If I don't receive money, we'll live on our own. Our life up to now may have been too luxurious. I'm going to sell the useless stuff. Florence is paid a salary at her office. For myself, I'm thinking I can become a chauffeur. I'll profit from my spare time by painting. I'll be even happier than I was before."

He laughed cheerfully. Then he spoke enthusiastically of Italy.

Florence rejected the idea of his being a chauffeur. She rejected the idea of selling things. She agreed only that he could paint pictures.

One day he went out to buy some painting supplies that he had run out of. When he came back to his room and looked around, there were signs that someone had been there. At the foot of the terra-cotta figure of Pan was a letter. It was in Florence's scribbled handwriting. He opened it apprehensively.

My beloved Maki

That steward came to look me up. He reported that my elderly father in the Touraine Château was on the brink of death. I had to be present at his death, my poor father had said. I came to tell you of my departure for some time. You were not here. Fearing that I would be late for my train, I took off on the spot. I'm going back to the château. Probably I can greet you at my château in the near future. I will surely come to get you. Please bear with it. It's only a brief parting until then. As a sign of our short separation I enclose a thousand kisses.

Forever your
Florence

A small locket fell out of the envelope. Inside were a photograph of Florence and a curl of her golden hair.
"Forever your Florence"
"Forever your Florence"
"Forever your Florence"
Sadly, but with that rare refinement of his, he smiled.
"Forever your Florence"
"Forever your Florence"
"Yes. I think so too."

⌂

Maki Ishino turned up at the bistro Au Bon Coin where he had found his "Forever your Florence." Collaring the proprietor, Felix, he said: "Monsieur. Can you give me something to eat? Then I'd like some of the usual wine. Unfortunately I don't have a cent on me. I've sold everything that was salable. The only things left are Florence's. She's coming soon from the Château de Tarme to get me, but in the mean-time I must keep her things with care. I'm driving a taxi. But, strangely, nobody rides in my cab—maybe because the car is dirty?"

(No. Surely no one would feel easy using a king as footman—though they do say that recently in Persia a footman became king.) So Felix thought. Felix had every intention of hearing the request gladly. That was not because of their long-standing acquaintance. The words of a king, even in supplication, are heard by the subject as orders. A certain kind of people, hearing Ishino's laugh and manner of talking, think it a happy duty to comply with his wishes as they would those of a king. Why this man had such dignity they had no time to question when they were in his presence. It stemmed surely not from his per-sonal appearance alone. His dress, like a flower withering and dried but not yet dropped, grew less fresh by the day. To be receptive to a dignity like Ishino's was not for the common man. Most properly so. A trans-mitter must have a suitable receiver. Ishino continuously radiated an atmosphere like radio waves. To smell an odor, you need a healthy nose. To sense the charm and fragrance of the waves Ishino radiated the nose must be free of the stench of material things. To receive the feeling of nobility in noble works of art one must have a sense that can appreciate and submit to the art. Felix, the proprietor of Au Bon Coin, had a special ability to feel Ishino's appeal and his dignity. In a word, you should know that Felix, the proprietor of a restaurant that attracted poets and artists, and prostitutes as well, was an eccentric. Felix would always boast to his customers as follows.

"As a connoisseur of wine I am no match for an Italian. But what are Italians when it comes to judging art? I'll tell my story. I won't use the name, because it is so pitiful. The gallery is so well known that if I mention the name of the city, you will recognize it, a private gallery, of course. In its collection there was a fake red Tintoretto. I knew it was doubtful, and after some hesitation I finally said as much. To the gallery owner, yes. Apparently it was determined to be a fake after five scholars studied it over three years. Since then the Tintoretto has been removed, they say."

How true these words may be is not guaranteed. However, even within lies, random talk, or boasting one may find a personality. Felix was a man who talked like that. Felix liked Ishino. The regular customers at Au Bon Coin liked to find Ishino there too, it seems. They enjoyed hearing talk of olden times. They took pleasure in feeling that they could see in his person a noble king in exile among themselves.

"Not a cent on me."

When he said that, the impression of nobility was strengthened, oddly enough.

"It's hard to be poor."

When he said that, the romantic impression was deepened, oddly enough.

So his actual existence became symbolic and could simultaneously be seen as a figure of irony against society.

Felix had found out that Ishino painted pictures. He begged to see some of Ishino's work. Being a curious fellow, he wanted to know what kind of art this strangely noble individual had produced. He could surmise what that work might be like.

Ishino was silent in the face of this plea, but he laughed like a child who was feeling shame.

Felix grabbed Ishino by the arm. He shouted: "Come along. Let's go. I'll give you a room. I'll give you wine. I'll contribute painting supplies. . . . Come, you paint."

Felix continued talking as he led Ishino to a room four flights up.

"Who's got to be crushed to death by poverty? But what kills genius is poverty. Felix's attic is no king's court, but it does keep away hunger and cold. Felix doesn't serve it to guests, but he's got some wine saved from the year 1575. How about it? Here we are."

As Felix opened the door and entered he turned back toward Ishino, who was following, bewildered.

"Please bear with it. The light is not adequate except under the window. But you're a person who paints even with darkness as your model. Stay here; don't hesitate. Just paint. . . . I'll bring the 1575 wine at your request."

Felix was excited.

Ishino looked around the room and said carelessly:

"I'll stay—until Florence comes from the Château de Tarme to get me."

"Yes. Until then. . . . Just a little while. You look like your health is failing badly."

"Because I'm poor."

In fact, poverty, which could not wound his dignity, was spiting that dignity by wounding his health.

"At my studio at 209 Boulevard Raspail," Ishino said, sitting down in a chair, "I haven't paid the rent for four months."

"That's all right. I know about it," Felix replied. "The things you left there I'll. . . ."

"You'll take good care of them, won't you? Because they're Florence's."

"Yes. I understand."

"Until Florence comes from the Château de Tarme to get me."

Felix nodded silently in consent.

Saying he would go and get all the things necessary for painting, Felix left the room. Once out the door, he spoke from outside. "Shouldn't I leave this closed tight? So you won't be disturbed?"

"Yes. I think so too."

Felix locked the room from the outside.

Thus Maki Ishino spent two months on the third floor of Au Bon Coin. He did nothing but drink 1575 vintage wine and wield his paintbrush. He painted extemporaneously. As Felix had divined, he used space as his model.

When the regular clientele of the restaurant asked where the "penniless king" was, Felix replied: "Sad to say, he is utterly mad. I put him up on the third floor. He seems satisfied there until they come from the Château de Tarme to fetch him."

"What? The Château de Tarme?"

When the guests asked, Felix said with a disgusted look, simply: "It's a castle in a modern fairy tale. It's absurd. If he were really crazy, there'd be no problem. But he's only one-fifth crazy. I've recently come to understand the source and the depth of that man's nobility. It comes from his happiness. From happiness!"

"From happiness?"

"That's right."

That's all Felix would say about it.

One morning.

Felix opened the door of the third-floor room and looked in. Although it was the usual time, Ishino was still asleep. The second time Felix went to open the door, Ishino was still sleeping. Felix walked up and shook him. No matter what, he would not open his eyes. In plain language, the man was dead. A smile graced the lips of the dead face, like the opening blossom of a rose.

The cause of death was completely unknown. The doctor came and said it appeared that Ishino had saved up several days' dosage of the sleeping pills the doctor had given him and had taken them all at once.

"It can't be helped," Felix said. "Such nobility can't last forever on this earth. He couldn't wait for someone to come and get him from the Château de Tarme. Then, too, he despaired for his artistic talent. Alas, he had lost faith in his own talent! The more genuine the artist, the more covetous he seems to become. He cannot be satisfied."

Mumbling on, Felix stood up. Suddenly he spread out both arms like wings, and, balancing on one heel, spun around like a top.

"What are you doing that for?" the doctor asked in surprise.

Felix, his face red from the sudden spinning, spoke as in anger.

"In the old days Dr. Kresper got rid of his sorrow this way."

"Doktor Kresper, a German?"

"Yes. You don't know him."

Felix walked around the room and counted the paintings left by Ishino.

"You," the doctor said with a scowl. "It looks like you confined a mental patient when he should not yet have been confined. The deprivation may have made the condition worse. . . ."

"What are you saying?" Felix turned his glance away from the posthumous works and toward the doctor. "If he had left this room, Maki would have persisted until he found his Princess Florence of Château de Tarme, probably on some street corner. . . . A sorceress with half-magic and half-love coming back from some assembly of witches. . . . You don't understand. Because you don't know the beginning of the story. Damn. When did I ever put a hair in that woman's soup! Dear Doctor. Please go home. Many thanks for your trouble."

. . . Inagaki at the time had been staying in London for some four months.

᚛

The posthumous exhibition of Maki Ishino's works was planned by Felix. People who understand the new art all supported it. The foreword to the exhibition catalogue was written by André Salmon. Some people said this poet who doubled as critic was a man of eccentric tastes. Others said he had extraordinary fervor and foresight in discovering the new beauty. Salmon's statements were quoted in the *Journal de Paris* newspaper. The substance of his article, which caused a sensation in Paris, was as follows:

"Nowadays there is no romance, there are no miracles, popular opinion often asserts. So long as there are individuals, we do not know where and when romance and miracles will happen to occur. Anyone can say that is true, but to show an actual instance is something not every one can do. Isn't that so? You, Apollinaire, in that special heaven to which only artists go. Recently our Maki Ishino, who has moved to join you there, has shown us that example. Just as the story has it that man was made from a lump of clay, he has made a fairy from a common prostitute. He has painted thirty-one portraits of this fairy.

"She stands in front of an old castle resembling Chinon. She is riding a horse. She is feeding an owl. She's lying naked and prone under a lilac. She's embracing a child. The child is holding an oriental pinwheel. How beautifully it spins. Outside the fairy's palace is an iridescent fountain. In the windows are goldfish;—here, strangely, the fairy is not present, but clearly it is the fairy's room. The fairy cuts her golden hair with scissors—we do not know the reason why. But what beautiful hands. The fairy lifts a strand of hair out from a plate. It is some strange and fantastic food, but what beautiful hands. The fairy's most beautiful hands hold a fan on a plate. . . . Those most beautiful hands, they were the hands that El Greco once painted, but Maki's hands are not inferior. One could believe her hands would hold nothing on earth other than budding flowers and ripened fruit. There is one where the fairy sits in a boat like a gondola and holds a bunch of hyacinths. There is even one on a train. In one the fairy is surrounded by a host of pigeons. Apollinaire, they are the very pigeons you so often sang about. The fairy is naked, unabashed, in the midst of a deep-red room.

"He has thrust before our eyes all the worlds of the fairies. What we have spoken of, poor Apollinaire, you could not have seen upon the earth. Thanks to Maki, we have seen that truth for the first time here upon our earth. Thus have I come to know it. To our surprise, fairyland has within it its own fairyland reality, as there is a fairy-tale truth within the fairy tales. Maki has grasped the reality of that other world by your own inexplicable leaping technique, Apollinaire. In a completely modern way. If you were alive, I think you would surely take joy in it. This is what I say to you.

"This artist painted one theme only from the Bible. That is the 'Baby Moses Drifting on an Ark of Reeds.' Apart from whatever interest there was in painting it, how lovable is the baby floating over the waves. In every man who sees it, fatherly feelings will be aroused. In every woman who sees it, motherly feelings must be felt. Unique among his subjects, it is tremendously beautiful.

"He has the rugged honesty of Henri Rousseau. He has the fragile beauty of Marie Laurencin. Like all the school of the new art, he achieves composition without ostensible composition. Yet his art is one of the most refined of modern times. Like Modigliani but with his own unique reality he appeals to the human soul. So what is that? It is what Maki Ishino has created. In truth he has created the feminine smile after Leonardo da Vinci. It is the smile of the fairy enticing man. It is at once of the spirit and of the flesh. It is pagan. It is oriental. That is why I must call it the fairy's smile. This bewitchingly effective smile is his matchless creation. Although people may see it often on the earth, I wonder that it had not yet been made eternal. That's how real is that smile, I would say. Was the prostitute who nurtured a man into such a pure being and let him dwell in her bosom a loving woman like Manon Lescaut? Or has the artist reflected himself, using glass of no account for a good mirror, adjusting for incidental light? Either is fine—but no matter how, Maki Ishino's art is a solid reality."

And on and on.

Notes

1. Satō used the French word for "crazy" (*fou*) as his Japanese title.
2. From the Oscar Wilde novel *The Picture of Dorian Gray*.
3. The name is written in characters literally meaning "ten-thousand-league child."
4. A paste-resistant process of dyeing that produces sharp-edged lines of color separation.

The Star

Hoshi, 1920

THE 1st STANZA

The wealthy Chen family of Yingnei town near Chuanchou city had three sons.[1] For generations the Chens had been a family of wealth and honor. The oldest brother succeeded early, recently having become a circuit commissioner for the Kwangtung-Kwangsi provinces. The second and third brothers, still young, studied diligently at home. Because the youngest was the third son of the Chen family, he was named Chensan, or Chen the Third.

THE 2d STANZA

Where he got it from no one knew, but Chen the Third learned to observe and know the stars. One clear, starlit autumn night he picked out from the countless infinity of the heavens a single star. That without doubt was Chen the Third's Star of Destiny. If you wonder why, no matter how many nights he watched it, that star twinkled with every twinkle in the eyes of Chen the Third. Other than this, there was no star like it. Chen the Third knelt before his star.

THE 3d STANZA

"I beg you, My Star. Grant me as wife the most beautiful maid in the world. Grant then that the son she bears me will become the greatest man in the world."

Thus was Chen the Third's prayer to his star.

THE 4th STANZA

Tired from his reading and poetry writing for his senior licentiate examinations the next year, older brother wandered into the garden one autumn evening. There, without so intending, he overheard the words of Chen the Third. Older brother laughed at Chen the Third for his prayer.

"That's a stupid prayer. You're just asking for the happiness of the common man. If I were you, I surely would not ask for a wife and children. I'd ask for something for myself instead. Not for my child. I'd say *I* want to be the greatest man in the world."

"That's right, Brother," Chen the Third replied frankly. "I had to think that way at first. Then I changed my mind. For me to become a great man is something I think I can do through my own efforts. On the other hand, to meet the most beautiful woman in the world, to be able to win her heart, to make her my wife, and with that wife to beget a child who will become the greatest man in the world—that kind of happiness is not something I can get in my condition and through my own efforts alone. For that I must depend on the power of the stars. That's what I thought. . . ."

"Indeed yes, but," his brother interrupted. "This is what I think. Fate may be more powerful than you think. Suppose you were born under a star of evil destiny, how far could your fervent prayers turn that to the good? I don't believe in the stars at all. Yet maybe I can say I believe in them more than you do. Anyhow, there may be some use in praying to the stars. If so, what star is mine?"

The brothers talked like this, then raised their eyes again to the heavens filled with stars.

The riddlesome heavens were infinitely deep.

THE 5th STANZA

". . . Suppose you were born under a star of evil destiny, how far could your fervent prayers turn that to the good?" . . . These casual words of his brother—later one might have thought the star had granted Chen the Third his prayer through these words of his brother.

THE 6th STANZA

Some years passed. Older brother, the brother number two of the Chen the Third who had said he could become famous through his own efforts, had achieved his ambition and had been posted to the governor-general of Kwangtung-Kwangsi. That the good offices of his older brother, long a circuit commissioner for Kwangtung-Kwangsi, were influential in this we need not add.

THE 7th STANZA

Chen the Third went to Chaochou to send off his triumphant brother.[2] There brother's party gave up the horses they had ridden to avoid some frightful Japanese pirates said to be based near Amoy, and there they took ship for his post in Canton.

"Fair winds be with you!" Chen the Third called out, saying farewell to his brother.

In the June dawn brother's ship raised its sails. Rounding a cape, the little sails disappeared to the south.

THE 8th STANZA

Astride his horse Chen the Third rode through the curious city of Chaochou to see the sights. It was afternoon of the day his brother had sailed. Under a dreamy summer sky young Chen the Third on his horse

was lost in thoughts of loneliness. Brother had attained his aim. He
had been posted to the governor-general of Kwangtung-Kwangsi. He
had sought and won a beautiful wife. But as for himself. . . .

Some years had passed since he had put his heart into his prayer to
his star, but he had heard not a thing about the most beautiful maiden
in the world. Hadn't his prayer to the star been heard? Lost in these
idle thoughts, Chen the Third let his horse go its way. When suddenly
he thought he heard the sound of a lute from somewhere above, he
raised his head.

Before his eyes and beyond a splendid gate was a high Chinese balcony towering over a pomegranate tree in luxuriant full flower. It was
like a vision to his eyes. If you ask why, there leaning lightly on the balcony railing and playing the lute was one of the world's most beautiful
women. In harmony with her black gown her profiled face was as white
as a white magnolia.

Gazing in rapture, Chen the Third lifted his voice boldly in song.
His voice blended with the sound of the strings. Surprised, the maiden
at the railing turned to look. Quickly, coquettishly, she made as if to
toss something, then went abruptly indoors.

An early-ripened litchi nut dropped before Chen the Third's
horse. Fading from Chen's eyes was the slim, brightly shining figure of
an infinitely beautiful, charmingly angry maiden, her hand raised in
skillful dance.

THE 9th STANZA

Chen the Third stopped his horse. Pointing back the way he had come,
he questioned a passerby. That house was the residence of the Huang
family. The maiden was the Huang's fifth daughter. . . . Since Flower
Day last spring the people of Chaochou had spoken of her as the most
beautiful maiden in the world. . . . That's what the passerby said. Surely
Huang Wu-niang (Huang Fifth Daughter) was the most beautiful
maiden in the world! Chen the Third felt his heart pounding and his
hands sweating—the hands that held with the reins the litchi nut
thrown on the ground.

Thus Chen the Third came to see Huang Fifth Daughter, the girl said to be the most beautiful in the world.

THE 10th STANZA

Treasured for generations in the family of Huang Fifth Daughter was an old, old mirror. . . . When Chen the Third returned to his lodgings and heard again of Huang Fifth Daughter, he learned about the mirror. The casual reference to the mirror gave Chen the Third an idea. Under the pretext of the mirror he could at least see the maiden again, he said. After a night spent in thinking, Chen the Third called for the man-servant in his lodgings. Tossing off the bedding and his elegant coat, he proposed exchanging his young nobleman's clothing down to his vest for the everyday clothes of the manservant.

THE 11th STANZA

One morning a workman came walking from far away. . . . The young man claimed to be a polisher of mirrors with a secret process passed down in his family over the generations. Arriving at the Huang home, he asked to polish the treasured old mirror.

He polished the mirror assiduously all the day long in the leafy shade of a bamboo tree that let through a green light from the long day's summer sun. Finally, at evening he finished, and when he was about to replace it in its case, he dropped the mirror and its box onto the paved stone floor. The box broke into many pieces; the mirror split in two like the wings of a magpie. He dropped it by mistake, the work-man said. Actually, he told no lie. There was an inexplicable impetus, and the surely unbreakable thing had broken.[3] People scolded and blamed the workman. At last came the master and pressed him about how he ever proposed to pay the price of this precious treasure.

"It can't be helped." Chen the Third was inspired with unexpected wisdom by this unexpected event. "Of course I'm not a man of much silver. All I can pay you with is myself. I will work as a slave in this family for as many years as it takes to pay for this mirror, no matter how many years." Forthwith, the unfamiliar workman spoke thus manfully. Looking around at the crowd with a faint smile for some reason on his cheeks, he added, "With myself I think I will give this family no less and maybe more than the worth of this mirror and its case."

Fifth Daughter, hidden behind the crowd, watched the uproar. It was the first she had seen of the young workman. She blinked as if she were staring at a dazzling light. This was exactly the young nobleman who had sung with her when she played the lute as he passed her gate yesterday on his horse. Or, she wondered suspiciously, didn't the workman look like the lingering vision she held of yesterday's gentle squire?

THE 12th STANZA

The young mirror polisher thereupon became a slave in the home of Huang Fifth Daughter. From that day on, Fifth Daughter watched the slave ceaselessly and anxiously from the seclusion of her room. There were any number of opportunities to watch. If you ask why, it seems that the slave, too, ceaselessly hoped to catch the eye of Fifth Daughter. So Fifth Daughter came to believe that this was surely the young man on horseback.

"With myself I think I will give this family no less and maybe more than the worth of this mirror and its case." Wise Fifth Daughter dwelt on the words of the young man and his smile as he said them. She seemed to understand everything, or even to brood too much about it. To say that you give someone a mirror case is to offer a promise of marriage. Fifth Daughter thought he was a dubious slave. She thought, too, he was a pleasing slave.

Of course Fifth Daughter disclosed her thoughts to no one. Except one person. She felt she wanted to confide only in Yichun (Beneficial Spring), who could be called both servant and friend to Fifth Daughter.

THE 13th STANZA

Beneficial Spring came of the Hung family, but she was orphaned at an early age and was raised by the Huang family. She grew up like a sister to Fifth Daughter, only closer to her than a born sister. Fifth Daughter and Beneficial Spring were the same age. This year they were fifteen. Beneficial Spring was a beautiful girl too. As Fifth Daughter was beautiful like a ruby set in gold, Beneficial Spring was beautiful like a sapphire set in silver. If Fifth Daughter was called voluptuous, you'd have to say Beneficial Spring was enchanting. Fifth Daughter's beauty was an earthly richness; Beneficial Spring's beauty was a heavenly serenity. In Fifth Daughter's beauty there was something that excited and intoxicated. In Beneficial Spring's beauty there was that which sobered and tempted. There were some, therefore, who would say that Beneficial Spring was more beautiful than Fifth Daughter. Maybe they were right. Beneficial Spring became servant to Fifth Daughter. Thereon hangs a tale.

THE 14th STANZA

Fifth Daughter and Beneficial Spring were brought up like sisters, each adoring the other's beauty. As they reached the marrying age, each became uneasy at the excessive beauty of the other. Each began to see the other as somehow more beautiful.

"You and I, which of us is more beautiful?" Thus one day spoke the innocent Beneficial Spring.

"You are. No doubt about it. Still, that is something we do not know for ourselves, unless we get answers from another, from lots of people, to judge by." That's what Fifth Daughter said.

With this sweet exchange the two of them decided that on Flower Day each would stroll through the city to let the people on the streets decide which was the more beautiful. In jest the girls wagered their lives on the outcome. The one who lost the contest would serve the winner for life. . . . Because the two were so congenial, they never would part. The winner would choose the man she loved, or would be chosen by him, and she would make him her husband. The loser would serve the winner and her chosen man and would become the second consort of the winner's husband.

THE 15th STANZA

Soon it was Flower Day. Fifth Daughter spoke.

"Let's carry out our agreement. You go out and walk the streets first, please." . . . Wise Fifth Daughter had a scheme behind these words.

Arraying herself in her newest finery, Beneficial Spring went out to stroll the streets as Fifth Daughter suggested. The crowds, young and old, men and women, all stopped when they saw Beneficial Spring. They stared as if they were seeing a mirage. They looked back as she passed. The young ones whispered, or they yelled.

"Who's that girl?"

"She's as beautiful as any woman in the world."   "She's truly beautiful."

"Look at that blushing face."

"What a flower she is."

THE 16th STANZA

"Now it's my turn."

Fifth Daughter spoke, closing her ears to Beneficial Spring's account of what she had heard.

"Lend me the robes that you wore. . . . It's not fair if we don't both dress the same."

. . . The scheme of wise Fifth Daughter lay behind these words.

Fifth Daughter put on the rose-pink gown that Beneficial Spring had worn and went out into the streets. The crowds, young and old, men and women, all stopped again to look at the maiden in the rose-pink gown. People yelled.

"Hey! That beautiful girl is going by again." At the sound of the voice Fifth Daughter raised her smiling face and looked around at the people.

"No. You're wrong. That's not the one we saw before."

"It's not the girl we saw before. But who do you suppose that beautiful maid can be?"

"Yeah. She's no way inferior to the one we saw before."
"She's rather more beautiful."
"Yes. More beautiful."
"Definitely more beautiful."
Tottering on two of the tiniest feet in the world, Fifth Daughter walked as languidly as a spring day, slipping slowly through the swarms of eyes upon her. She smiled as she basked in the very words she had expected.

THE 17th STANZA

The people of Chaochou city spread the word that twice this day they had seen the vision of a flower walking on Flower Day morn. Some reported joyfully that the first to stroll was the spirit of the flowers of autumn, the second to stroll was the spirit of the flowers of spring. These were people of no original vision, but they liked for no reason to say outlandish things.

THE 18th STANZA

Fifth Daughter was fully aware of the peoples' feelings. Human beings can sense when they are being talked about. First of all, Fifth Daughter drew peoples' eyes by dressing in the very same clothes as Beneficial Spring—who had already been the focus of everyone's attention. She made them compare her with Beneficial Spring. The crowds who had already praised Beneficial Spring, then seeing Fifth Daughter, found it hard to say which was more beautiful. To praise Fifth Daughter as fully as Beneficial Spring they had actually to use stronger words. . . .
"This one is more beautiful."
In her wisdom, wise Fifth Daughter captured peoples' hearts. Fifth Daughter became "Beautiful as any in the world," "Truly beautiful," "More beautiful" than Beneficial Spring. So Fifth Daughter defeated Beneficial Spring. The straightforward Beneficial Spring laughed and

gave up. That's how she was brought up. Satisfied, she became Fifth Daughter's servant.

Thus did haughty Fifth Daughter augment her beauty. Thus, too, did humble Beneficial Spring augment her beauty. Each one. Day after day.

THE 19th STANZA

The beauty of Beneficial Spring had to be reflected in the eyes of the new slave. At times he felt the unadorned servant was more beautiful than Fifth Daughter. When the young man thought like this, he was startled. He was ashamed of his inconstancy in thinking about Beneficial Spring when he had come to this family with his heart set on Fifth Daughter. He was a single-minded young man. In his determination, he pinned his many dreams to the Fifth Daughter that he could barely see in the depths behind her window rather than to the servant Beneficial Spring whom he saw constantly. The feeling that he had to achieve his dream became acute. He wished to do that which was difficult. . . . The young man who aspired to the happiness of the common man seemed possessed with the character of a very uncommon man.

THE 20th STANZA

"I beg you, My Star. Grant me as wife the most beautiful maid in the world. Grant then that the son she bears me will become the greatest man in the world."

Even now Chen the Third secretly prayed the same prayer to his star. He prayed more compulsively than ever.

THE 21st STANZA

Mixed in with the rough and lowly slaves, doing the same rough and lowly work, the mirror-polishing slave surely had a concealed but unconcealable grace. Even Beneficial Spring sensed that. With a tender look Beneficial Spring watched in pity the slightly built slave among the others, turning the heavy millstone in the autumn sunset.

THE 22d STANZA

Fifth Daughter for her part was forever thinking of the dubious young slave. One winter's night she cornered Beneficial Spring to talk about the youth. What she said: "That slave is no mere low-born boor. . . . He's too refined for a mirror-polisher. . . . He has some purpose behind him for sure. . . . I saw that man myself. He was riding a big horse past my gate, dressed up in a sky-blue waistcoat worn over a pearly white, shining jacket. . . . To say it may sound fantastic, but that was neither dream nor fantasy. It was early summer." Fifth Daughter talked on with a look as if she were seeing that scene before her now.

THE 23d STANZA

These days Beneficial Spring clearly felt herself in a trying position, both happy and sad. She had thought of speaking privately to the slender slave that she secretly pitied, but he had confessed to her his love for Fifth Daughter. He never whispered, "You are dear to me."

Alone, Beneficial Spring thought of her promise of a lifetime that she had exchanged as a joke with Fifth Daughter. If that man who was too gentle to be a slave, as Fifth Daughter said, was really a highborn nobleman, that would be all right. Even if he wasn't so eminent, it would be all right to be his second consort. Yes, she could see him— riding a big horse—dressed up in a sky-blue waistcoat worn over a pearly white, shining jacket. Fifth Daughter would become the wife of the handsome gentleman. Then . . . and then at least I'll be the second consort, and that will be fine, she thought. I'd like to be his wife. But he thinks nothing of me. . . . Beneficial Spring heaved a hot sigh in her cold bed. She shivered. Was it because her skin was cold? Or because her heart was hot? She herself knew not. Beneficial Spring let out not a word to anyone. She stored her grief.

THE 24th STANZA

Each of the two became more beautiful, Fifth Daughter in charm and coyness, Beneficial Spring in purity and sadness. These two blessed with beauty from heaven became in all ways simply more beautiful.

THE 25th STANZA

At last Beneficial Spring had to report the slave's words to Fifth Daughter.

"I really did pass in front of this gate on a horse last June. . . . At the command of my star I found Fifth Daughter. . . . I am the third son of the Chen family of Yingnei town near Chuanchou city. My oldest brother is circuit commissioner for the Kwangtung-Kwangsi provinces. My next brother was posted last year to the governor-general of Kwangtung-Kwangsi. As for me, I have no post. . . . My only desire for now is to know for myself how deeply a man can love his wife, how deeply he can be loved by his wife. I don't want to be a Taoist immortal. I want human happiness. In my hometown I have a big mansion. In my heart I have only love for Fifth Daughter. I would like to tell her that directly myself."

Thus spoke the slave to Beneficial Spring.

Beneficial Spring so reported to Fifth Daughter.

Fifth Daughter hid her face and said to Beneficial Spring in a thin voice trembling with resonance, "I'll meet with him."

THE 26th STANZA

After Beneficial Spring had led the idol of her heart secretly to the door of the other maiden's room, she fell onto her bed. Fell down and wept. The next morning Chen the Third and Fifth Daughter and Beneficial Spring all kept their eyes cast down, avoiding each other's glance. Beneficial Spring, embarrassed, frightened, sad. The other two, embarrassed, frightened, happy.

THE 27th STANZA

Within a few days Beneficial Spring withered and grew gaunt like a person long in mourning. Her heart was empty; a day was as long as a month. She did her servant's work in silence, like a shadow. With a sigh she gazed from her window at the flowers blooming gloriously. Not one flower met her fancy. All were different from the flowers of spring of the year gone by. As she stared blankly, tears came to her eyes. To her surprise she felt a gentle hand on her shoulder. Fifth Daughter spoke in a low voice but with vigor.

"Though spring has come, why are you so sad? It is better not to be sad. You will become that man's second consort. I won't forget my promise of Flower Day last year."

Beneficial Spring turned warily and looked hard at Fifth Daughter. A large butterfly straggled in from the garden and flitted about the golden flowers in Fifth Daughter's hair. Vacantly watching it fly away, Beneficial Spring stared at the emptiness.

THE 28th STANZA

If she says that, how happy I shall be, thought Beneficial Spring. Now she was hearing those very words she had often whispered to herself. Now hearing the exact words that she had thought were a vain hope, she did not believe her ears. If the words were trustworthy, the heaven and earth where Beneficial Spring lived were suspect. But at last the one who said the words truly was Fifth Daughter, and Beneficial Spring could believe that Fifth Daughter spoke in earnest. As Fifth Daughter spoke in more detail, Beneficial Spring began to think the whole affair was no more than a dream. . . . Fifth Daughter had determined to go to Chuanchou with Chen the Third. Full of passion and deeply in love, she would leave her father's house with no regret. Even if Beneficial Spring hesitated to forsake the house where she had been raised. . . .

THE 29th STANZA

"Since that's agreed, let's elope as soon as possible. Afterward we will send someone from our home to yours for your hand. There's no other way. . . . It's too bad. The old people are deeply suspicious. They won't easily believe that this slave is a suitable young man for their daughter. My life was spared that day I broke the family's treasured mirror, but when they learn I have stolen the greater treasure that is you, this time I will be killed. They won't give their daughter to a slave. But when it is the Chen family of Yingnei, they will not refuse. . . . If you will be my wife at any cost, flee with me quickly. . . . The road is long but not dangerous. I know its safety well because I came that way. . . . For traveling expenses I have gold and silver buried. . . . Come with me. . . . Where there's love, there's no cause to doubt."

Chen the Third spoke thus last night to Fifth Daughter. Fifth Daughter believed the words of Chen the Third. But Fifth Daughter felt lonely at the prospect of going so far all alone, even with her beloved beside her. Fifth Daughter wanted not to part from Beneficial Spring. Her own elderly mother would be reassured if Beneficial Spring was with her. Fifth Daughter talked that way about Beneficial Spring to Chen the Third. . . .

". . . Therefore, come with us. If by chance you do not go, I will follow him alone to Chuanchou." That's what Fifth Daughter said to Beneficial Spring.

If Fifth Daughter said that, and if Chen the Third was bound to go, Beneficial Spring thought she would go to Chuanchou. She did not want to part from Fifth Daughter either. Even more, she did not want to part from Chen the Third.

"Oh, please take me along," Beneficial Spring murmured deliriously, her eyes flashing.

THE 30th STANZA

"At last, tomorrow is the day," Fifth Daughter whispered to Beneficial Spring one day. "We, that man, you and I, will leave the house in the depth of night early tomorrow morning." She spoke in a low voice, with spirit. "That man has obtained gentle but fleet-footed horses. You and I," she laughed innocently and continued quickly, "he says you and I will wear men's clothing. He says it's necessary." The mention of men's clothing brought a blush to the face of the bashful Beneficial Spring.

Jade Swallow in its cage let out a cheerful chirp. Fifth Daughter, who could not stay still, reached out her hand, and on a whim she opened the door of the cage. Surprised, Jade Swallow stopped singing. The bird sat thinking for a bit on its perch, then hopped timidly to the door. Hesitantly it flew. The little yellow bird, accustomed to the tender care of its owner, hopped onto the railing and sang briefly. The moment Fifth Daughter waved her hand, the bird flew joyfully away. . . . It disappeared into a rather far-off flowering tree.

"From tomorrow there'll be no one to feed you." Fifth Daughter gazed into the empty, slightly swaying ivory cage and spoke as if she were apologizing to the no one there. She stood and leaned on the railing. Beneficial Spring stood next to her. "This balcony is where I first saw the man," she said to herself with feeling. Bowing their heads briefly, the two of them mused on this.

THE 31st STANZA

The three arrived at the city gate. The adventurers spoke not a word. If they had not felt their hands clasped firmly and warmly, the two maidens might have doubted whether the man leading them briskly through the darkness was really their beloved. In the ominous silence no one spoke. The city gatekeeper said nothing when he saw the three. He opened the gate carefully without its creaking. Last evening he had received from an unknown young man a heavy purse of silver on the promise to open the gate secretly in the night. When they had slipped silently out through the gate, a familiar voice spoke first. "Rest easy." Slowing the pace he added, "Look." Pointing at the northern sky, he said "That is my star. Those three are now lined up. Tonight they point exactly in the direction of my home."

Then he lapsed into silence again as they walked on for a bit. "Wait here. Just a bit. The horses should be here." Hastily he rushed off somewhere.

THE 32d STANZA

Taking each in turn by hand, he helped them onto their horses. Three horses there were. "It's all right. Hold the reins tight!" Two horses followed the leader, trotting in order. The lead horse had a nimble rider, who was unflagging in his careful attention to the two who followed. The two inexperienced riders were thus able to proceed at the fastest gait. The horses ran naturally. These horses had been very well trained for use in battle. Two villainous soldiers had stolen the horses and were waiting under the largest *longan* tree outside the north gate. "These are the horses that sweat blood. They come from the Tochari Kingdom in Central Asia," the sellers insisted. Not wanting to lose a moment, the buyer of the three horses filled the outstretched hands with silver. The three horses ran. . . . Under the dawn sky of late spring. . . . Hooves beating in concert. Ridden by riders incredibly more delicate than ever the riders before. . . . Onward through the brightening night toward the three stars.

THE 33d STANZA

When Fifth Daughter's household learned from the other slaves that the reticent, reserved one had disappeared, the three were already a hundred leagues from the city. When the family learned that Fifth Daughter and Beneficial Spring had disappeared along with the slave, the three were already two hundred leagues away. After another fifty leagues within the day they slowed the pace of the horses. . . . The family was convinced that the maidens had been taken aboard a slave trader's ship, and they grieved. Fifth Daughter's mother laid the blame solely on Beneficial Spring.

THE 34th STANZA

The three horse-borne travelers tried in every way to avoid peoples' notice, but they were easily noticeable. Though they were youths in everyday clothing, one in a black coat, the other two in deep blue, they drew the attention of those they passed. People stopped. People looked back. Three such handsome riders were a rare sight around these parts. Especially the two young ones, even as they held the reins securely with a single finger, could be mistaken for women.

Indeed they were to be wondered at. Today they thought they would stay in Changchou, but a company of soldiers captured them. The world was falling into disorder. Under the pretext of protecting the virtuous, but really carrying weapons to afflict the people, the soldiers had long been oppressing the natives, obtaining meat and drink, threatening travelers and robbing them of gold and silver. They were like a gang of officially recognized local bandits. . . . The year before, the provincial government had sent a troop to meet Chen the Third. Those men were dressed in accord with proper military discipline. They showed that the peace of the area must be well preserved. Chen the Third, knowing little of the world, had believed that the route, though long, was not dangerous. This time Chen the Third was not with a government troop and he was captured.

THE 35th STANZA

The maidens in men's clothing were stripped bare in the bright daylight. The soldiers covetously compared the slender bluish-white hips of the two maidens, who were trembling prone on the ground. The soldiers took the travel money, saying they would keep it. Then they announced that these rascals must be rigorously investigated.

"You'll regret this, by God!" Chen the Third called out as he was being thrown into jail.

As he said this he knew in his heart he had no way to carry it out. All he could do was yell in mortification. But the soldiers were troubled by the authority in his words, by the presence of two beautiful maidens and three fine horses and the unexpectedly large amount of cash for traveling. It made them think these were no mere travelers. If not for that, the beastly soldiers, excited by the vision they had so covetously seen by day, would have dragged the maidens from the jail in the middle of the night.

THE 36th STANZA

"This one here is a robber who has stolen an enormous amount of gold and silver treasure, two good-looking women, and three thoroughly tamed war horses. A fellow who steals war horses must surely be a scoundrel. The offense is clear but he won't admit it. We were planning to torture him anyway, so we put him in leg irons and handcuffs. We put the young women in there too. They're only in leg irons."

The jail keeper explained this, bowing politely in greeting an official of apparent high rank, guarded by a line of soldiers. The official peered into the cell. A group of dark figures seemed to be moving in the dim interior; there appeared to be three persons. The prisoners, trembling anew at whatever it was, eyed them carefully through the cell window. The high official merely nodded and stepped out.

"Brother! Wait! Brother! It's me!"

"Don't mistreat the prisoners too much. . . . Is that one crazy?"

The high official turned to the jailer as he spoke.

"It's okay! It's me. Brother!"

The prisoner shouted again. . . . Actually like a madman. The high official stopped. His ears were struck by the familiar home dialect. The echo in his ears changed the color of his face. Paying no heed to the jailer's reply, the high official spoke calmly. . . . "Well, let me take a look at that prisoner."

THE 37th STANZA

"You'll regret this, by God!" What Chen the Third called out by chance had by chance become reality. The high official without a doubt was Chen the Third's oldest brother. He had come suddenly from his post of duty in Kwangtung on a special mission of patrol to the

Fukien coastal area, where the disorders were rumored to be at their worst. The brothers had not seen each other for a long time, but oldest brother believed it was youngest brother from the resemblance to middle brother, and youngest brother recognized oldest brother from the resemblance to middle brother. They chatted for more than an hour in Chuanchou dialect. Oldest brother, already past the prime of life, listened to the honest account by the still-young third brother. Oldest brother sympathized with his passion. He wanted to help his dear brother achieve his cherished desire. He said he would make time to visit the Huang family of Chaochou. . . . He said, too, that he would find an old mirror and case not inferior and maybe better than their old mirror and send it to the Huangs. . . . Yesterday's prisoners became today's guests of honor. Fifth Daughter and Beneficial Spring had their hair dressed without stint and ornamented fully with hairpins. The men who yesterday shamed them and punished them were today shamed and punished themselves.

THE 38th STANZA

"I beg you, My Star. Grant me as wife the most beautiful maid in the world. Grant then that the son she bears me will become the greatest man in the world. . . . It seems that you have heard and delivered half my prayer. Now please favor me by completing my prayer. Please give me human happiness."

After the lucky storybook meeting with his brother, Chen the Third gave thanks deeply to his star for its protection. He knelt more devoutly and longer than ever. Looking up at the blue sky in which his star was buried, and thinking of his love, Chen the Third felt how tiny humans were. But at the bottom of the tiny heart of a tiny human he felt there dwelt a blue sky in which was set another limitless host of stars. It made him feel that to be born human was truly fleeting and painful, but, just for that, life was worthwhile. . . . Struck with these feelings, Chen the Third's eyes sparkled like the stars.

Taught about Chen the Third's star, Fifth Daughter and Beneficial Spring believed that each had her own star ranged to the right and to the left of his. As the two women worshipped their own stars through the window, each prayed secretly.

"I beg you, My Star. Protect me and let me be loved deeply by my husband for all of my life."

The prayers of the two women were by chance the same. Identical, too, to what every bride in the world must pray.

THE 39th STANZA

In the midst of sadness the more one looks back on the happy times the less difficult it is to bear, they say. All people in the midst of sadness must look back to their happy times.

Before she knew it, Fifth Daughter was absorbed in thoughts of yesterday to relieve the agony of today. Why did the days and months run on? If new days and nights brought no new happiness, why did not the sun's charioteer *Hsi-ho* stop in his rounds at the moment of happiness? . . . "No, the sun's charioteer brings no happiness for me. He robs me of my happiness. The charioteer comes laden mountains high with happiness for Beneficial Spring. To think how much we loved, where ever did my happiness go?"

So, resentful, Fifth Daughter looked back over the year and a half that had fled. Resentful, she looked at her husband Chen the Third and second consort Beneficial Spring. Resentful, she looked at the faintest of the three stars aligned in the dusk. "That time, the happiest time in my life when I prayed to the star, was my prayer not heard?" So she brooded, fluttering her long eyelashes feverishly and blinking her heavy-lidded eyes.

THE 40th STANZA

"My husband's love—such a deep love it was—when and why did it shift to Beneficial Spring?" A thousand times over she asked herself the clear and natural question. To divert herself from sorrow, she looked at the loom. Her hands long busy with the weaving had stopped. Her thoughts instead, like a shuttle that never stops, wove a poor fabric in her heart. "The love of my husband, no doubt it was from the night Beneficial Spring conceived his child within her. How I envy her. Why have I not conceived his child? If my husband does not favor me with his love, heaven too withholds its favor. . . . I think its promise was a joke that does not encompass my protection. I rue the day that I promoted Beneficial Spring as second consort to my husband. . . . At that time I wanted to share a little of my surplus happiness with Beneficial Spring, who was in the depths of sorrow. How could it all have been taken from me? How I resent my husband's fickle feelings. No, my husband is my beloved. What I resent is Beneficial Spring. Without recalling my kindness at the time, she holds my husband's love for herself. In the end she has become proud. Sometimes she throws a furtive glance of pity, as if she should feel some compassion. I see that clearly." . . . But, sadly, Fifth Daughter had been raised since childhood in happiness as a hothouse flower. Placed in favorable circumstances, she knew not the coldness the world returns for kindness. She was born to be easily warped by adversity.

THE 41st STANZA

When Beneficial Spring thought of her beloved's child that she carried in her body, a thrill of joy engulfed her. She felt herself more than ever in love with the man who brought such unprecedented happiness. Her ever-meek heart became even gentler. While happy in feeling the depth of her husband's love, she felt that she had wronged Fifth Daughter. Often she urged Chen the Third to love Fifth Daughter. Yet Chen the Third felt that his time with Fifth Daughter was chilly and gloomy-dark. On nights when Fifth Daughter did not see Chen the Third, she thought deeply of her love for him, but when he came, she would speak first of the complaints filling and shutting her heart. Before the everlasting complaints had ended, it was already dawn. Why didn't she speak of her love? Next time indeed she would. The morning after, she regretted it all the day long. Then, next night she would speak first of her complaints. Timid-hearted Chen the Third had no dislike for Fifth Daughter, but he found it hard to listen to her barbed words. He contrasted them to the tenderness exuded by Beneficial Spring. He felt that as her heart became grim her beauty was fading. Even as he embraced and consoled Fifth Daughter, he thought only of love and desire for Beneficial Spring, with her deep black eyes beautifully gleaming. Once the foundations are shaken loose, a house will tilt. In the end a tilting house will collapse of its own weight. Thus the mutual love of Fifth Daughter and Chen the Third seemed to crumble. The harps that play the harmony of husband and wife were out of tune—the little one strung too tight, the big one too loose. Through the habitually sleepless nights of her loneliness, as she agonized at the on-and-off voice of a cricket, Fifth Daughter had to keep asking herself how much Chen the Third still cared for her. Love that must seek such proof is bitter.

THE 42d STANZA

At dawn one day Chen the Third came from Beneficial Spring's room to visit the chamber of Fifth Daughter. He must carry out his promise of the night before to Fifth Daughter. He pulled aside the curtains of Fifth Daughter's bed. Strangely, Fifth Daughter was not there. Pinned next to the pillow with a golden hairpin was a letter. In the pale white glow of the lingering candlelight he opened it with trembling hands. In dismay he pushed open the door and ran out. Noticing it was still dark, he retrieved the candle and went out again—to the well in the garden. The place she had written she would throw herself. A single small red shoe lay on the stone paving! It was Fifth Daughter's! He held the candle over his head, tipping it to one side as he peered into the well. The dark shape of one shoe floated as if dejected in the circle of water reflecting the golden light from the candle. The water was heavy in its silence. Chen the Third set the candle on the stone. He picked up the shoe from the stone. Vines with flowers were embroidered in black over the red. . . . It was the very shoe Fifth Daughter had worn that first night behind her curtains. Again he looked into the well. There on the surface of the quiet black water was reflected a single star from the heavens. Looking carefully, Chen the Third saw it was his star.

"Fifth Daughter!"

Chen the Third called out. The deep water reflecting the black shadows enticed him. Staggering, he fell—as if pushed forward. Or as if he had lost his footing in panic.

A short cry sounded sharply from the granary next to the well. It was drowned in the echoing roar from the blackness of a well swallowing a man.

In his agony Chen the Third looked up for the last time at his star directly over his head—a head shoved up above the water. . . . That star alone may have known the fervor of the feelings that pursued Chen the Third into the depths of the well. . . .

THE 43d STANZA

Next to the well the stub of the candle flickered wildly as it burned. The shadow of a figure came lurching out of the granary. Illuminated by the candlelight, it was Fifth Daughter, pale as a ghost. She ran staggering, not looking at the well. She ran staggering into her room. She grabbed a brush and wrote. The meaning:—In my shallow wisdom I thought to measure the depth of my husband's love. By feigning my own death I thought to test the extent of my husband's grief. So I killed my husband. I killed your husband. I killed the father of your child. Please forgive my distorted heart and my shallow wisdom. I go now to the land of the dead to beg that man's forgiveness. . . . This was no false letter that would surprise and kill Chen the Third. This was the truth. It was addressed to Beneficial Spring.

The posthumous note was found on the rosewood mirror stand. Wasn't it a pity that the mother-of-pearl inlay in the rosewood stand was an arabesque design of peonies and pomegranates, the symbols of happiness?

THE 44th STANZA

The silver candlestick run over with tears of wax from the burnt-out candle was placed by the well. The bodies of Chen the Third and Fifth Daughter were brought up from the bottom. With the bodies were two shoes of Fifth Daughter. Although Beneficial Spring had seen the letter, she wanted to shield Fifth Daughter and so said little to anyone. People thought it strange and they thought it sad that this young husband and wife died at the same time and at the same place. They placed the two bodies in the same outer coffin, buried them in a single grave, and erected a single tomb. Beside the tomb they planted an acacia, the tree of mutual love.

THE 45th STANZA

Beneficial Spring perceived that it would be easy to follow her husband into death but hard to live alone. She thought of the life stirring within her body and she remembered, too, the words her husband had chanced to say the night before he died. She had to live. Her husband had said, as he caressed her, "In the eyes of heaven you are the most beautiful woman in the world. You are my wife therefore. If that is so, my child is conceived in your body in accordance with my prayer. It is surely a boy. The child will become the greatest man in the world." Looking at things then, Beneficial Spring could see as her husband's last will that she protect and raise the child inside her, no matter what. Beneficial Spring grieved for the husband who died without seeing this child soon to be born. She grieved too for the child. She grieved for herself. But the resentment toward her husband was not great. To die like that for the Fifth Daughter for whom his love had waned. If he had done it for me, that would have been one thing, she thought. We had such happiness in that I could have such a truthful husband. Now he is dead. Such a tenderhearted person, thinking not to leave me lonely and alone, has left me with his child. I was from the first an orphan. Now, thanks to this man, I have this sweet child. No longer am I lonely and alone. So did Beneficial Spring strive to think in her time of sadness. Chilly tears ran in fine streaks down both her cheeks.

THE 46th STANZA

The one who grieved most after Beneficial Spring over the deplorable event of Chen the Third and Fifth Daughter was the middle brother posted to the governor-general of Kwangtung-Kwangsi. Ten years before he had overheard youngest brother's prayer to his star. When he heard the news of youngest brother's marriage, he had celebrated his happiness at thinking that brother's prayer to the star had been heard word for word. Now, with the news of these unforeseen deaths, he recalled the words he had spoken to youngest brother that night in the shadowy garden. . . . "Suppose you were born under a star of evil destiny, how far could your fervent prayers turn that to the good?" . . . These words he really had spoken casually. Now, though, as he thought about it, he grieved at the unbearable idea that his words had been a prophecy. When he heard the circumstances in more detail, the feelings were even stronger. He had long known how his brother longed for human happiness, and now he was depressed day and night to think on his brother's death. Feeling he should try to console his inconsolable heart, he naturally produced a series of elegies. One recited the following sense. . . . So long as the blue rose blooms not in color on the earth, there will be no perfect happiness in the world of man. It is no more than the belief in a dream. Unless we perceive this, all who pursue happiness will end in despair. I have no pity for the drunken butterfly pursuing a flower in the mirror, nor for the confident monkey yearning for the moon's reflection in water. My youngest brother, you who could always dream, I do not bemoan your pathetic death. You who believed there was nothing higher than the love of a long-sought woman, you were favored with that happiness. And so on.

THE 47th STANZA

Beneficial Spring's child was a boy. This child, born not knowing his father, was a sadness and a joy alike to his mother. Often a tear from Beneficial Spring would drop on the child's laughing face. After the period of mourning was over, Beneficial Spring did not again dress in finery. For all that, her beauty did not diminish. Many were the men proposed as second husband for the still young Beneficial Spring. On these occasions Beneficial Spring always pointed to the child beside her and replied, "For this child's sake." Gradually the child grew large and the grief of Beneficial Spring grew old, like the classics of music. One may know the tune but every time one plays the melody one surges with new strength. Her spirit did not break. A man with wife so chaste has happiness even after death. Thus did people praise Benefi-

cial Spring and envy Chen the Third for his love. His tomb—it was
Fifth Daughter's tomb too—was covered with moss. The acacia tree
grew to a sapling, then to a full-grown tree. Branches flourished in lux-
uriance. Pink flowers covered the tomb like an arbor. Seeds split from
the pods and fell like hail onto Beneficial Spring and her child when
they came on autumn mornings to offer flowers and incense. The red
beans were crimson as the wet shoes of the unhappy Fifth Daughter.
The days and months passed, lonely but happy for Beneficial Spring. If
you ask why, her child from an early age showed a surpassing wisdom
that happily reminded Beneficial Spring of that unhappy man's
words. . . . "The child will become the greatest man in the world."

THE 48th STANZA

Sun and moon move not for mankind. Utterly indifferent to the ups
and downs of man, the sun and the moon may move for themselves
alone. Not even they may know their way, but in habitual coming and
going they may but continue roaming that same road. We do not know
these things at all. We see the sun and moon coming from the east and
going to the west. How long will that same course repeat itself time
after expected time? Humankind, not one of us, has any way to calcu-
late. All that man can do under the endless coming and going of sun
and moon is for each and every one, thinking his own thoughts, to go
on living moment by moment, or go on dying moment by moment.
Beneficial Spring's reason for living was her beloved child—the living
reminder of her dead husband. She guarded the memory zealously. In
her mother's eyes that followed the growth of this boy child, she saw
happily, sadly, the image of his father.

THE 49th STANZA

The child of Beneficial Spring took his mother's family name of Hung.
He was called by the nickname Heng-chiu; his personal name was
Cheng-chou. He passed his doctorate in the middle of the Wanli
period.[4] Along with his joy at this success he had to grieve for the loss

of his mournful mother. Still, she died firm in the belief that her child would become "the greatest man in the world." Led to believe that himself, the child served the four emperors Shentsung, Kuangtsung, Hsitsung, and Szutsung.[5] The country was in its last period of prosperity during the reign of Shentsung. After that there were omens suggesting a gradual decline. Kuangtsung reigned for only thirty days. Hsitsung was emperor for seven years. Then it became Szutsung's time. Our man Hung Cheng-chou became governor-general of the Chi-liao district.[6]

THE 50th STANZA

The emperor Szutsung went out of his palace secretly one day, wearing commoner's clothing. He sought out a fortune-teller of good repute. As the emperor was about to open his mouth with a question, the famous fortune-teller stopped him rudely with his hand. It was his pride to tell fortunes without hearing a word from the person seeking his fortune. The fortune-teller spoke first upon variously considering his predictions.

"You came to me in distress about the nation?"

The young emperor in commoner's clothing felt the sharpness of these words from the arrogant fortune-teller. They saw into a man's inner heart, but the emperor answered lightly.

"Yes. I am a patriot. The nation is in tumult. Rebels are said to be rife in Shansi. Troops from Manchuria are advancing slowly but steadily toward the capital. People of talent love their talent more than their country. They all hide in the mountains to exercise their talent. There are few who will save the nation in its troubles. They say a star of strange new light is shining. The emperor's heart must be devastated with worry. Even people like us are concerned about the nation's future."

"All right," the fortune-teller said. "I will predict the nation's fate. Tell me a written character you are thinking of now."

"Well, then." The man who was seeking his fortune thought a bit and answered, "the written character *yu*."

"Is it the *yu* in 'patriotism'?" the fortune-teller said, picking up a writing brush with fingers that looked like a dead branch.

"No, no. It's the *yu* of 'friendship.' "

The fortune-teller wrote a large character *yu* for friendship on the paper. Then he said to himself coldly, "But that suggests the character 'opposite,' doesn't it?"

"No, no. It's not that *yu*," the emperor denied in confusion. "The *yu* I said was the *yu* in 'profitable.' "

The fortune-teller wrote again on the paper, this time the character *yu* in profitable. Then he said to himself coldly, "Hm, that's only half of the *ta-ming* cycle of favorable days. Is the great Ming empire half gone too?"

"No, no. It's not that *yu*," the Emperor denied in confusion. "The *yu* I spoke was the zodiac sign *yu* for 'bird.' That's the sign for next year."

For the third time the fortune-teller wrote a large character on the paper, this time the *yu* of the zodiac. Then he said coldly to himself, "That's 'esteem' with the top and bottom missing. What's this all about?" He threw away his brush. Looking up sharply at the man who wanted his fortune told, he said, "It's a painful thing."

The emperor tossed a piece of silver on the paper where the three big characters were written. To conceal the face that was pale and the voice that trembled, he hurried away, saying nothing. It's a bad joke, he muttered. Just trivial puns. . . . But it is a worry. . . .

THE 51st STANZA

Among the roving rebels springing up on all sides the most powerful was a man of Shensi, the son-in-law of the chieftain of a large band of mounted bandits. His name was Li Tzu-cheng. At first the government said they were like a case of scabies—annoying but not life-threatening even if they spread. Soon they became more powerful and active, and the next year, which was the zodiac year of the bird *yu*, they invaded the areas south of the capital in Hopei and Hukwang provinces. Wherever they went they burned and pillaged. They killed bridegrooms and raped brides. When they captured Feng-yang, they despoiled the imperial tombs and burned the mausoleum. All of Shensi became theirs. They were pushing toward the capital from the southwest. Becoming at last alarmed, the government mustered lots of troops and dispatched them in that direction. Hung Cheng-chou was made commanding general. . . . Meanwhile the Manchu army was advancing slowly from the north. With enough power to claim the kingdom, they began to call themselves the "Ching" empire. This new nation, with the Ching emperor at the head of his troops, conquered Korea. Just as Hung Cheng-chou was at last driving off Li Tzu-cheng, the Ching forces approached the capital. Again the Ming emperor commanded Hung Cheng-chou, this time to attack the Ching forces. The emperor relied on Hung Cheng-chou, thinking, "This is the greatest man in the world today."

THE 52d STANZA

When they met a big army, they would quickly fade away, dispersing and hiding no one knew where, then suddenly assemble again from all directions. This was the usual strategy of Li Tzu-cheng's forces. While Hung Cheng-chou was moving north to fight the Ching, Li's forces recovered their strength in Honan Province. There they killed two princes. Again they moved in strength toward the capital. When he learned the state of Li's forces, Hung was encamped in readiness for a decisive battle with the Ching. He lost heart at the news. . . . If he were able to subdue this huge Ching army here and now, and if the almost defenseless capital fell in the meantime, it would all come to naught. . . . On the other hand, if he once yielded to the Ching with its superior forces, even if he had no alternative but to give half of the great Ming empire to the Ching, that would still be better than the total destruction of the country. Yes indeed. . . . Offering to divide the great Ming empire in half, he would make peace with the Ching. He would yield in favor of the Ching. Obtaining Ching reinforcements in return, he would suppress the roving bandits. Another day would come to take up the struggle for supremacy with the Ching. These were Hung's bitter thoughts. He surrendered to the Ching. When the rumor of Hung's defeat reached the capital, the emperor believed that he had died for his country. The emperor lamented that the loss of this man was the same as the destruction of the country. He ordered an altar of sixteen stages where he mourned his great and faithful subject. But Hung, who had determined to die but had not yet been able to do so, hastened to the rescue of the capital at the head of the Ching army. He was too late. Li Tzu-cheng's forces had captured the capital in the meantime. The cowardly emperor Szutsung, losing heart, hanged himself from a willow tree near the jeweled staircase. . . . "It's a painful thing," the fortune-teller had told him twelve years before, frightening him with a cold stare.

Li Tzu-cheng named himself ruler in Anhsi. The rebel called his country Tashun.

THE 53d STANZA

Hung Cheng-chou had not yet been able to die. Knowing that the emperor who loved and trusted him so much had died for his country, Hung pretended not to know. If you ask why, Hung had to destroy Li Tzu-cheng, the enemy of his emperor. He contrived a scheme for the Ching commanding general Wu San-kuei to destroy Tashun. By this strategy Li was driven to flee, barely escaping with his life to a mountainous area called the Chiu-kung Mountains. The tyrannical rebel general was pursued by villagers. In the end the ruler of the Tashun nation died by hanging himself. Hung Cheng-chou thought now was the time to throw away his life. But he could not die—like his mother who felt it would be easy to throw her life away yet had to live for her late husband's sake. Hung had unintentionally become obligated to the Ching for benefits received when he was with the Ching army attacking Li Tzu-cheng. With the benefit of the Ching forces he had taken revenge on the emperor's enemies. Not only that. The first Ching emperor, Shun Chih, saw Hung as a rare and great man in a time of troubles. He encouraged Hung to serve the Ching, persuading him with various reasons. When Hung could not refuse such arduous favors, he finally spoke up. "If you will listen to my request, I will serve you." He asked to be allowed to determine the laws and institutions that were yet scarcely established by the new dynasty. In truth he had political talent to match his military talent. So Hung served the Ching. . . . The name of the nation was changed. The rulers were changed. The people who were ruled by the old emperor who loved and trusted me so much are the very same people now. I will suppress my shame and serve the late emperor's people. I will establish institutions to provide for the happiness of the late emperor's people. That's what Hung Cheng-chou thought.

THE 54th STANZA

Hung Cheng-chou busied himself happily night and day at his new work. He paid no heed to the criticism that happened to reach his ears. People said "Hung Cheng-chou is a disloyal subject. The emperor Szutsung, who loved and favored him, died thinking Hung had wholeheartedly given his life for his country. The emperor heard that he had surrendered to the Ching, but without asking whether Hung had survived, the emperor mourned him in grand style. That man Hung lives with no concern. Now he is serving the enemy nation. His mother was a faithful wife. He is an unfaithful high steward." . . . Hung was not angered to hear these words. He did not venture to answer the insults. What could he do to justify himself before those who distrusted him from the start? Still, Hung was lonesome. The loneliness that comes when no one understands a man's motives—that was hard to bear. He wondered if loneliness was enervating him day after day like a bitter wine that dissolves into weak poison. His loneliness drove him at his work. Laying down his brush as he worked on his drafts late into the night, he would say to himself as he guarded the loneliness that gnawed at his heart: "I don't know whether I am a great man or not. But loneliness is a tax that the greatest man pays at the highest rate. If it is paid willingly, a man becomes a hermit." As an old man he often thought quietly of the past, remembering his mother fondly. "My mother believed in me to the end. If my mother were alive today, even if she didn't understand my feelings, wouldn't she believe what I say? My mother, who often said to me, 'You are the child who will become the greatest man in the world,' why didn't she say to me, 'You are the child who will become the loneliest man in the world?' . . . Mother, the Mother who was orphaned, raised in another family, and widowed, the Mother who raised me. My lonely Mother. I am your child to the end!" He called up in his heart the image of his mother, as, like a baby, he clung to her in sorrow.

THE 55th STANZA

"I beg you, My Star. Grant me as wife the most beautiful maid in the world. Grant then that the son she bears me will become the greatest man in the world." The Chen the Third who had prayed that prayer to his star; the Fifth Daughter said by the world to be the most beautiful, who as first wife to Chen the Third joined him in his death and in his tomb; Beneficial Spring, most beautiful in the eyes of heaven, who as second consort conceived and bore the son who would be great; and Hung Cheng-chou who was that great son; and all the rest of them. Since they lived, and laughed, and grieved, and sighed, shed tears, became angry, took pride in winning, endured loneliness, and finally died, already it is more than three hundred years. In the meantime the Ching nation has been destroyed, as was the Ming. Only in Yingnei town near Chuanchou city the mansion of Chen the Third casts its shadow in the water flowing by the banks of the Pu River. The house looks as though it is about to fall, yet there it sits even now. . . . I have not seen the house. I made a trip last year to that area, but in the end I did not go to Chuanchou.

Notes

1. Chuanchou was a trading port in Fukien Province on the South China coast. For this Japanese fairy tale of old China, the translator has chosen to use a simplified old-style romanization of Chinese familiar to English readers when the story was written. The culminating events in the story are drawn from Chinese history.

2. Chaochou was near Swatow.

3. Old Chinese mirrors were made of bronze and hence were "unbreakable."

4. 1573–1620.

5. The last four emperors of the Ming dynasty, covering the period 1573 to 1644.

6. North and east of Peking.

Unbearably Forlorn

Wabishi-sugiru, 1922

I

Seikichi's younger brother's wife, Kuniko—his wife until recently, that is—had qualified as a geisha.

Yurika was her professional name.

II

This woman, earlier a geisha in the same district, had overreached herself to become Seikichi's brother's wife. True, she was hardly eighteen at the time. Now, five years later, Seikichi's brother had abandoned her —you'd have to put it that way.

Although they separated by mutual consent, the brother does not seem to have confided fully about his intentions. Immediately on leaving his wife, he left for Korea with another woman. He spoke of his notion of taking an unsuitable job, but his real reason for going to Korea may have been the woman. . . . Kuniko seems to have said as much to Sumiè. Seikichi heard it from Sumiè. The women friends exchanged letters.

Yoshizō had a woman? Now that you'd heard it, that was not so surprising. But that brother divorced his wife because he had a woman, Seikichi didn't suspect that. . . . If he had known, there was nothing he could have done. That is, when it came time for them to split, although Seikichi lived in the same house with them, he was consulted by neither. Maybe they failed to consult because Seikichi for his part avoided consultation. Kuniko's people actually said to Yoshizō, "How about consulting older brother at least once, because he's there." Yoshizō had replied, "Yes, but I know what he will say. An individual thinks for himself and does what's most reasonable for himself. There's no other way, is there? . . . That is how he talks, and I'll get the same answer. He'll just ignore it."

Yoshizō may have spoken like that because it was difficult to bring up the subject with his older brother. Still, he was not necessarily wrong in saying that about Seikichi. Although Seikichi was their brother, he never said anything to them about what was happening before his eyes. He could not. He had become that kind of person. To have an opinion that might be expressed to others, you have to cherish strong ideals of your own. Or else you have to be a person who settles for shallow views. There were only these two ways. Seikichi no longer held any ideals, and yet he wasn't so shallow as to raise opinions that were clearly of a superficial nature—especially about man–woman relationships.

Seikichi himself knew about husband-wife separation, indeed he had experienced it twice. Not only that, only a year and a half ago he had been dragged into the middle of the marital breakup of a friend closer to him than his brother. It was a terrible experience for him. Recalling the event, he thought often of the words "Made to drink boiling lead." As a result, he became the laughingstock of his colleagues; the story was exaggerated; he felt he could never meet that friend again; the wife's feelings were hard to forget. Somehow, in the two years since he was involved in the event, incredibly, when he looked at himself in the mirror, the hair on his temples was showing white, and a dozen white hairs could be counted in his moustache. . . . Not only the self that was reflected in the mirror. He looked into his heart to see if there at last he hadn't brought a little order into the confusion, and indeed he did become calm. Before he knew it, though, the feelings became negative, self-complacent, self-centered, irresolute. In his thinking at least, he was determined never, even unconsciously, to blend the lives of others with his own. When he could not fathom his own feelings, how could he understand those of another? He could not speak casually when he was not convinced it was worth the cost of his life. But if he would not give up his life for himself, why should he throw it away for another? To show sympathy for another without committing yourself from the start to life's greatest sacrifice, that is the origin of error. Sacrifice was out of the question. We can only watch intently as the someone else we are watching either dies or she lives.

Thus did Seikichi resolve his stubborn feelings. Because he was like that, he said not a word even as he felt in the air the start of his brother's marital split. But the fact that he expressed no opinion was not the same as having no opinion harbored in his heart. As he watched nonchalantly the impending break in his brother's marriage, he could think that it was even more bitter for him than for them. By nature he was a sentimental man. He was so conscious of that sentimentality that he took good care never to drop the mask that "Another man's affair is another man's affair." His own remembered feelings of separation long after the event were brought home to him anew by his brother's affair. So now his bitter thoughts on watching Yoshizō's breakup were not provoked on that couple's behalf. The feelings might be no more than his own remembrances.

Then, he did want so much for Kuniko to remain his younger brother's wife. Kuniko had known well both of Seikichi's wives from whom he had separated. She knew all the strange circumstances lately surrounding Seikichi and his friend's wife, and the compounding pains in the twists and turns of love. Since he had come to live in Yoshizō's house after his wives had left, Kuniko had come to know the quirks in Seikichi's behavior, so she could talk with him in a personal vein about any topic he became involved in. Isn't all affection a matter of relationships drawn from the sharing of long conversations? . . . By a brief reference to "that time" or "that person" the same vision flashes before both. By a simple flick of the eyelashes complex feelings can be shared. That is human intimacy. . . . Now Seikichi had almost no one left to be intimate with. Basically sentimental as he was, he put on a front, and feeling his insignificance, he found it difficult to reveal himself to others. Except with one or two people the always lonesome Seikichi would conceal himself. Through the circumstances of the past seven years, including the succession of two wives and then of his lone friend coming and going on a daily basis, and the friend's wife who had become his lover, it had now come to pass that he must lose both friend and lover at one time. There was hardly anyone left for Seikichi to talk with about old times. He had memories of everything spanning six or seven years of months and days from when he was twenty-three or twenty-four until he was thirty, especially the stormy times. The Seikichi who concealed himself was never free of misunderstanding by the people around him. For that reason, and for the sake of conversation about his life gone by, he wanted not to lose Kuniko. She understood him quite well in all his moods. She was like a kindly younger sister to him. Actually, some of the people who frequented Seikichi's house, those with less of a personal connection, did think of her as Seikichi's real sister. Wasn't that because their emotional relationship was so smooth and natural? Kuniko had said: "Now I can really understand you, Brother. Though at first I thought you were just grouchy and cold-hearted. . . . That's your unfortunate nature."

She was so comforting about it.

"You're not at all cranky these days, are you, Brother? Maybe through suffering you've managed to control your temper. . . . I have to feel all the more sorry for you."

"Don't be impertinent."

They talked that way. But when younger brother left his wife, Seikichi had to lose her into the world's vast throng. Just as Seikichi's former loved ones, dividing his earlier life with him, had gone off, taking their half somewhere unrelated to him, so Kuniko was now disappearing with a part of his life far out of his range, leaving a slight but piercing feeling that was hopeless to explain to someone who had not suffered a separation. Yoshizō and Kuniko would come to understand that too.

Whatever Seikichi thought, Kuniko was not his wife. He felt he wanted to stop offering opinions to Yoshizō even more because of his rather high regard for Kuniko. . . . That was Seikichi. On second thought, he tried to see what was going on in Yoshizō's mind. He had to understand in some degree Yoshizō's feeling of coolness toward Kuniko. It really amounted to nothing, though, if you didn't know that Yoshizō had another woman. Anyhow, there were problems with Kuniko. She was terribly inefficient at housework, not only clumsy but slovenly and neglectful. The kitchen was more devastated than one in a houseful of men. Kuniko had been born into a disadvantaged home.

When she was thirteen she was sent for her brother's sake to a geisha house. There she was raised. Surely she never knew what the life of an orderly household was like. It would be a pity to blame her too much on that score. Anyway, the tendency grew gradually worse. Although Seikichi watched in silence, he was continually chilled to recall how his first wife, though she did have an outside job, had become slovenly at the sink like that, leading in time to marital storms. He too wondered what to do about Kuniko. For Yoshizō, with his customarily tidy personality, these trivial matters may have made the house rather unpleasant. In fact, on Sundays, his day off from the company, Yoshizō would often go around clicking his tongue as he picked up and disposed of the dirty things. Unable to remain indifferent, Seikichi would say something to Kuniko about keeping a cleaner house. On one of these occasions Kuniko said: "That man" (pointing to Yoshizō). "I don't know his feelings, but even if I do keep the house tidy, he doesn't show any sign or anything. I have no incentive not to leave things scattered around."

"Yes, that may be so. But it's not good for either of you that way. Look, it's like this—whether a house is kept neat or whether it isn't is a matter of habit, not theory." He smiled meaningfully and added as a joke: "I've seen a woman like that. If you mention separation, she suddenly opens the bureau drawers and trunks and begins to undo the kimonos and underwear of the husband who may be leaving her. Then she'll say, 'If I don't keep things neat, in no time at all you'll run out of things. I don't want the person who comes after me to think that I was slovenly.' . . . As she cries she unstitches his clothes."

"I understand, Brother. That's enough talk about Ōkyo. I'm not as meek as Ōkyo. . . . It's crazy. Stop talking about your lover. . . ."

"What do you mean lover? She's not your wife."

"So! Stop talking about her. Whether she's your wife or not. . . ."

III

Ōkyo, until recently wife of Seikichi's good friend and Seikichi's lover. (Should we say "is," or do we have to say "was" his lover?) That's who.[1]

IV

Seikichi walked along looking outwardly as cheery as ever. Inwardly his head was a mixed-up flow of impressions and retrospection. Some thoughts merely flickered through his head; others annoyingly infested the surface of his meditations. Of course he had lots of topics that he had to think about, but not one was of interest to him. Those gloves he had just bought were a little too small from the start, but the clerk said they were just right and sold them to him. He hadn't liked them all along. The leaden sky of November was dreary and cold. Suspended in the early dusk was a row of streetlights, blurred and ghostly globs of yellow. Although there was nothing special about it, it was for some reason a hopeless, wretched, depressing day. The people coming and going, walking or riding, whoever they were, were hurrying homeward —at least so it seemed to Seikichi.

Seikichi had no road home to hasten, on which he ought to hasten.

Now that his brother's home was dissolved, he had moved for the time being into the second floor of the house of an acquaintance. Though it was kindly offered, Seikichi had a presentiment that he would not like it. Still, he could not easily refuse the proffered favor. That was because on three or four occasions, in response to his friend's pleas, Seikichi had loaned him fifty or a hundred in cash. There was no prospect of repayment, but his friend urged Seikichi, who had no other place to go, to move into his vacant second-floor room for a while. Seikichi did not think he would get his money back, but the fellow seemed really troubled that he couldn't pay back what he wanted to, and he had therefore offered lodging to the homeless Seikichi in order to ease his sense of burden. Seikichi thought it would be better to accept, even temporarily. Actually, the matter of a place to live was suddenly rather pressing for him. But when he moved into the house, Seikichi's earlier feelings, which for some reason he did not understand, were strengthened.

He did not like the people. Even after he came to live on the second floor, they borrowed money from time to time when they thought he had some. They said it was just for a week or a month or so, but there was little real prospect of repayment. Of course it wasn't pleasant for Seikichi. He didn't like the kindness of those who would invite another into their kind of poverty. Even when he presumed they were not asking him for a loan, they made him feel the aura of their poverty. Actually, Seikichi was impoverished by the borrowing. In less than three months it totaled something like two hundred yen. This was a severe blow to Seikichi, who lacked the means to live without working. Of course, he had intended to pay something every month for his lodging.

To have money borrowed from time to time by people with pretensions of kindness was unpleasant not only because of the money question. He could almost think that the people had wanted him to move here from the first just to borrow money from him at times. Yet surely they weren't that kind of people. It was just that day after day they had no money. They were indeed very kind. These people didn't understand Seikichi's disposition at all, it seemed. By nature he would rather be left alone than receive unwanted kindnesses from another. The unfortunate thing was that around the time he came to the house he contracted a mysterious skin ailment. He suffered for a month and a half. He kept thinking it would go away, but gradually it became worse. It spread finally to his insteps, and he could neither stand nor sit freely. Inevitably he had to receive the kindness of those who lived in the house. Of course, he was grateful for the consideration and kindness.

Still, in a word, those people and Seikichi were not at all compatible. Seikichi felt that their kindess was excessive. . . . Everything was controlled by their life-style. Even in little things, Seikichi's wishes were ignored. Here was an example. They offered to wash his hair because it was so unkempt. Seikichi couldn't use his hands because of the rash, so he was pleased. But when the husband ordered the wife to bring a basin, or a pitcher, or spread out a newspaper, or bring soap, or a towel, or another small washcloth, or a comb and hair tonic, Seikichi couldn't stand it. . . . To make such a big undertaking out of it annoyed him. Such painstaking kindness was too ostentatious, even if not intentionally so. Compared to Seikichi, who wanted nothing other than the vagabond spirit he had long possessed, this family that was so kind to him would not go for a little trip without carrying a blanket roll tied with a shoestring or a glass properly stored in a pouch. That was their way. There was just a difference in their likes. Strangely enough, while the self-indulgent, hard-to-please Seikichi was grateful for their kind-ness, he could take no joy in it. He thought it was a nuisance to have his head washed with polite but tedious and bothersome care, as if by a master of ceremonies. He felt keenly, though, that the incompatibility was mysterious. That time two years ago when he was sick he recalled in a moment of pleasure, that day when Ōkyo rubbed his back with alcohol. He was pierced by the thought that those wonderful hands had gone from him forever. He felt relieved at last to have his hair washed, when the husband who had gone downstairs returned to the second floor, his hands outstretched like a person surprised. Seikichi wondered why, until the man spoke.

"How about some oil on it?" Both his hands were covered with oil.

"Oil? No, I don't want any. . . ."

"If you don't put oil on after you wash your hair, it's not good for you, they say."

"Good or not it's all the same," Seikichi said with an unpleasant expression. He could not flatly refuse when the fellow had prepared it on purpose and was being so kindly. The man was not someone to notice another person's expression, and Seikichi's still-wet hair was doused in grease. Hardly able to wait for the fellow to go downstairs, Seikichi wiped his head with the newspaper, rumpling up his hair. He was mad at himself for being unable to refuse such an unpleasant thing. Filled with a sense of its absurdity, he smiled grimly and said to himself: "I can't stand kind people. A man's life-style should be entirely his own affair. When it's not, you get angry. That's the kindness of the man of no taste. . . ."

These words to himself mingled in his mind with the scene before him as he walked. He thought of adding: You know, a person who makes kindness into morality uses his kindness to demand kindness for himself from another. Maybe that gave them the idea it was a proper moral obligation for Seikichi in his comparatively well-to-do state to give them money in their poverty. If not for that, they wouldn't have been able to ask nonchalantly for money all those times. He under-stood their poverty. . . . As so often happens, the young husband and wife had no established plans for making a living or anything. It wasn't just them. The time when Seikichi was married to his first wife, almost ten years before, was like that. He remembered the pain of having no money. When they asked for money, there was no help for it. What can you make of their way of doing things? One heard a lot about their continuing misfortune, but despite that, husband and wife drank *sake* every evening as they chattered and joked together. Married for only six months, they were, you could say, a young married couple, the man about Seikichi's age and the woman barely twenty-two or twenty-three. Though newly married, the man had previously had money. He was said to have used it up in the pursuit of pleasure. It was one thing for the two of them to spend the evening drinking and bantering without regard to others, but from Seikichi's point of view he felt that he was providing the drink money. It made him feel mean. As they became drunk, the bantering increased. Though not to the point of being intolerable, it was certainly not to Seikichi's liking. Still, sitting at the same table he did not once show a look of disapproval. He could not. If he carelessly threw them a dirty look, and if they noticed and thought it was only because they had offended his taste, that would be all right. But if they took it that "The single guy is jealous, you know," Seikichi would feel wretched—that would be a problem for him. There was nothing he could do on those occasions but engage in the joking, while thinking, "This is my service to life." If they thought he was enjoying the merrymaking with them, the absurdity increased four- to fivefold. It would have been good to refuse right at the start. In a fit of temporary weakness he could not refuse their kindness, and heedlessly he got himself stuck with these people he didn't like. Little by little he became angrier and angrier. However, it was not as though he was the wife of that husband, or the husband to that wife. I learned to my sorrow (so Seikichi joked at his own feelings) about being intensely fond of the wife of another, but now I am disliking another wife, and that would be a source of trouble too, wouldn't it? . . .

Seikichi was learning to turn his feelings in a playful direction. Into a bitter smile to soothe himself. Into a complex joke when expressing to someone else one's sad or otherwise serious feelings. Thus did he give the impression of a rather jovial man, or even sometimes a frivolous or insincere one. Even as he realized this he made no effort to open his heart to anyone else. He concealed himself. Seikichi was a hard man to understand for someone who did not intuitively figure him out. He was especially hard for the opposite sex to understand,

Seikichi reflected in his usual joking manner. The women he had lived with for years and finally had to leave were vaguely in his memory now, not with hate but with a certain feeling of nostalgia. He recognized his solitary personality and took half the blame on himself. All these feelings were included in the short phrase "I'm a hard man for the other sex to understand. At any rate, I no longer have a home, such as it was. . . ." The sight of his former wives facing him over supper flashed before him in space, then disappeared. He said to himself, "These people observe moderation in nothing at all."

He was not speaking of his former women. He was recalling the evening dinner scene with the husband and wife he had been thinking of earlier and with whom he lived. His thoughts of them had been broken off, but now he reached this conclusion. He didn't always feel this way, especially when his mood was gayer, but for some reason, tonight he had absolutely no desire to return to the house where he lived, where his dinner was being prepared. He continued walking deliberately and briskly in the opposite direction from that house. On this evening when everyone else seemed to be hurrying home.

Dinner at Ōkyo's house—how often, how vividly that scene threatened to come back to him. Even now it went without saying. He tried as hard as he could to erase it from his mind. Over and over he let his interminable thoughts run to the Toyama couple with whom he now lived, but when thoughts of them were interrupted, he could not help but recall Ōkyo's home. This was one way to prevent that. In the end Ōkyo and her husband were linked to the Toyamas and thoughts of them popped to the surface. . . . Ōkyo and her husband knew the Toyamas well, and they must have known that he was living there now. The husband had always disliked the Toyamas, and wouldn't he be saying something to Ōkyo right now about Seikichi, like "That guy's got such a nervous, hard-to-please side to him, how can he live a single day with people like the Toyamas? I can't bear even to look at people like that." Seikichi could imagine it. He felt he could actually hear the voice saying it, and it made him angry. What could Ōkyo say in reply? . . . With slow, unsteady hands encased in his new gloves he groped for a cigarette from the morocco leather case in his overcoat pocket. He puffed on the cigarette without inhaling as he walked on, lost in thought. . . .

"How can you say such an inconsiderate thing? Seikichi doesn't have any place to go." Yes, Ōkyo, please say that.

> *I've no house,*
> *I've no love,*
> *Day after day,*
> *Ōkyo!*
> *For me. For me*
> *Like this,*
> *Only inhaling*
> *An insipid cigarette.*

These random words came to him before he knew it. . . . People passing him in the dusk that had fallen completely would turn and look back at the smell he had called so insipid, the cigarette from his new tin of Lord Byrons. He may have said that because luxury has no power to heal a man's sorrow. Seikichi repeated the random words again and again. Anything was all right. All he wanted to do was call out "Ōkyo." He repeated and repeated the words. Like an impatient mother eagerly singing any old lullaby to put her child to sleep, Seikichi was trying to put his own sorrows to sleep.

Dinner was surely finished now in all the happy households. Even those with no households would get hungry. He walked, feeling hungry, with no particular objective.

Suddenly he stopped.

V

The area where Kuniko worked as a geisha was near here. Yes, it was. Certainly she was called Yurika. Kuniko had gone back to her own place at the beginning of summer. . . . He hadn't seen her for half a year. If he met her, Kuniko too should be surprised and pleased.

Hesitating, Seikichi took out his watch and looked at it. He reviewed his thoughts. He appraised the neighborhood. Hesitating again, he turned back in the direction from which he had come. Without so intending he retraced his olden memories too. . . . Yoshizō, who was still in school in those days, used to go out in the company of school friends of bad repute. There were rumors about the places they sometimes met for amusement. He remembered hearing that the geisha house where Kuniko had worked under the name of Yaeko was called the "Plum Tree House." If you continued walking a little farther in this direction, then turned right at the corner with the large dry-goods store, and then took the next right into the first narrow street, there was a combined Western-style restaurant and billiard parlor. It was in this neighborhood. Kuniko herself had said so back when Seikichi was walking with Kuniko and Yoshizō in the area. Since Kuniko, who became Yurika, came from the house in this area, it must surely be the Plum Tree House. Generally speaking, Seikichi didn't know much about geishas, and he was totally unfamiliar with this locality. Though he thought he would like to have dinner somewhere this evening with Kuniko, whom he still looked upon as a sister-in-law, he was uneasy about going into an unfamiliar place. Before he knew it, though, he was walking in the direction he had heard about.

Seikichi wondered how Yoshizō was doing now. That time when Yoshizō at last appeared to be consulting him about leaving Kuniko (really he was reporting rather than consulting), Seikichi had said only one thing to Yoshizō, and that in a gentle, natural tone. "It's best for anyone to do what he thinks. Without consulting anyone else. In doing what you want, you don't shirk your own responsibility. That's my way. Well, aren't you doing what you want? That's how we come little by little to understand human life."

Yoshizō had listened quietly. Seikichi disliked seeing the beginnings of confusion from the packing up for the dissolution of his brother's household. As his brother's household was disappearing and there was no other place to go right away, he went on a trip. During Seikichi's absence, Yoshizō departed earlier than scheduled. After he had gone to Korea there was news from a postcard, but Seikichi was a poor correspondent and did not reply. Seikichi was famous in the family for not writing letters, so Yoshizō was probably not offended. Since then there had been no other news. Maybe he was ashamed of having taken a woman with him without saying anything about it. What kind of woman she was, what kind of life-style he had, and the like. Speaking of women, he remembered that, once when he ran into

Yoshizō late at night at some transfer station on his way home, Yoshizō did have a woman with him. Because he didn't know of it then, he didn't look to see what kind of woman she might be, but wasn't that the woman after all? Because he said nothing about taking a woman with him, he didn't want to send any details now. . . . When it came to confiding that he had a woman, Yoshizō knew that Seikichi was not one to interfere or scold him especially. Why didn't he say something about it? When it came to Kuniko, she had only an older brother who was not very friendly and who ran a little store for Western-style clothing. Kuniko said nothing in particular to Seikichi, who was naturally rather worried and asked what she might expect to do after returning to her family. And yet, seeing that she became a geisha in less than two months, she may have had that intention from the time of her divorce. She didn't say anything about it, but for his part he would have liked to hear it from either Yoshizō or Kuniko. It was as if Yoshizō and Kuniko were convinced he was coldhearted—he who kept his painful thoughts to himself. . . . He felt slightly dissatisfied with them but, coming to his senses:—Hey! I must have become a complete individualist. I won't allow people to tell me their troubles. It's my way, too, to say nothing to others, isn't it? If I ask others to confide freely in me when I don't confide in them, I'd have to say that was selfish. After all, haven't Yoshizō and Kuniko come to respect my ways? Then what's my purpose in meeting Kuniko tonight? Not really to console her. Nor to be consoled. But a pretext isn't necessary. It's enough to eat together. I'd like to go to a place where we could talk. He had no such place, though, other than wherever Kuniko was.

If Ōkyo heard that Kuniko had become a geisha again, how surprised she would be. Ōkyo, so ingenuous and completely trusting of Seikichi, may have thought of Yoshizō as "unfeeling, not like Seikichi." Or she may have wondered why when Kuniko had Seikichi nearby. . . ." Ōkyo had met Kuniko only once—"that time" (Seikichi remembered "that time" vividly). Kuniko liked Ōkyo, and Ōkyo liked Kuniko very much. Ōkyo often gossiped about Kuniko. . . . "As that's the case, Seikichi, I have to give up the idea of being with you, but I'd at least like to call you 'Elder Brother' just as cheerfully as Kuniko did."

Saying this, Ōkyo would imitate Kuniko's tone of voice in whispering "Brother, Brother." . . . Ōkyo. Why did he think of Ōkyo today?

Oh! Yes! Wasn't today the twenty-fourth of November? A day to remember! I wonder if Ōkyo isn't recalling this day two years ago. Seikichi felt strangely that he was trying to strain his ears. . . . Couldn't he hear Ōkyo's voice coming from far off somewhere? He had turned into a back street; if he strained his ears he could hear only the sound of his footsteps. . . .

> *I've no house,*
> > *I've no love,*
> *Day after day,*
> *Ōkyo!*
> *For me. For me*
> > *Like this,*
> *Only inhaling*
> *An insipid cigarette.*

VI

"Well, to start with, I'll have a hot whiskey. And some of this."

He pointed at something on the menu as he ordered, while continuing his earlier train of thought. . . . Where and how can I invite Kuniko? I don't know of a meeting place or a restaurant in which to eat quietly. I could have the waitress telephone Kuniko and ask her about it. Yes, I'm hungry, but I shouldn't eat too much before then. With that decided he looked around the restaurant again. No doubt about it. This is the place—the Western-style restaurant with its billiard parlor. . . . He could hear the clatter of billiard balls from the second floor. This must be the house Yoshizō and his friends used to visit. If so, Kuniko's —that is, Yurika's house—must surely be in the neighborhood. . . . If not near, no matter. I'll have her called on the phone.

"Miss, may I borrow the phone book?" After she brought the hot whiskey, Seikichi took the phone book, but he could not find a number for Plum Tree House.

"Miss, there should be a geisha house in this neighborhood called the Plum Tree House. No? You don't know the phone number?"

"Isn't it listed in the book?"

"I can't find it."

As they were talking, a woman's voice sounded from the kitchen out back.

"If it's the Plum Tree House, isn't that the one right nearby?" A mature woman of about thirty who appeared to be the proprietor stuck her head out of the kitchen, looked at Seikichi, and said, "Welcome." With a glance she continued: "You've got business with the Plum Tree House? You want geisha?" She laughed winsomely with an elegance that made one wonder if she used to be a geisha herself. Damn! This woman too. Though older, she resembled Ōkyo somehow, with her aquiline nose and old-fashioned hairstyle of a married woman, Seikichi thought.

"Oh, yes," Seikichi replied earnestly. "She's called Yurika. Is there one by that name?"

"Yurika? She's been gone since last year, I think."

"Really? I thought that recently, around July or August, she'd gone back there."

"She's young?"

"Yes, around twenty-three or four."

"Maybe a new Yurika has appeared. Do you want her? Then rather than look up the phone number it would be better to run over there. You, go on over. . . . To the Plum Tree House, that's easy." The latter part she said half to the waitress. She instructed the young woman, who seemed to be new and did not know the place. "Turn at that corner. . . . There's a rickshaw stand, a hairdresser, and there's the Plum Tree House." Then to Seikichi she added: "If she's there, shall I have her come over here briefly? Okay? Is it all right if we don't mention your name? . . . Yes, then" (she turned to the waitress as she spoke) "go on over to the Plum Tree House. Tell them if Yurika can come over, there's someone here who knows her. We know those people well, and if she's there, she'll come."

In her kindness the woman betrayed some misunderstanding of his purpose. Seikichi felt his cheeks burning; his face had a tendency to redden quickly. It was not particularly noticeable though, because his cheeks were already red from the half-glass of whiskey he had drunk.

The young woman put the plate of food he had ordered on the table and took off for the Plum Tree House. The answer came back that

Yurika was out. They could get her, if he really wanted, but even then it would be about an hour before she could come.

"Oh, is that so? Thank you. It's not all that urgent."

As he spoke, he gave up the idea of waiting for Kuniko before eating and ordered more substantial food.

There was no one for the melancholy Seikichi to talk to. The landlady, having done what she could for him, went upstairs to the billiard parlor. The young woman was fixing her hair in front of the large mirror. The restaurant did mostly a delivery business, and the room was shabby. That was nothing, but since the stove hadn't been tended to, the room was chilly. From overhead the footsteps of people walking around the billiard table resounded dully. There didn't seem to be many players, but the clear clicking sound of the balls mingled with unintelligible chatter and the voice of the landlady. The voices were cheerful, the footsteps those of a fat man, Seikichi thought pointlessly as he listened to the sounds. He drank another whiskey, this time a cold one to follow the hot. His face was now a deep red. His body was warm but his feelings were not at all those of a drunk. Compared to the animation from the floor above, he felt that all he had was a cricket chirping at his feet, that everyone around him was silent, that wherever he went his situation became more desolate. There is a phrase "One's shadow is thin," but Seikichi's shadow wasn't thin. It lacked the dignity of a presence. That is, his face had a kind of unease, a sense of eeriness like a portrait by El Greco. It made women and children shrink from him. He could not remember sincerely sharing joy with anyone. . . . His sentimentality was exaggerated as he became a bit more drunk. That was his way with drink.

VII

He felt he could not stand being alone. There was no one he could expect to talk with him. . . . No one other than Kuniko. He left the restaurant but walked less than a block before he turned and went back. The waitress who had seen him off was reading a fiction magazine, now at leisure with no customers. Flustered at finding he had returned to the front door, she exclaimed, "Oh, you forgot something?"

Seikichi answered, half to himself: "No, not that. Since I came this far, I thought I'd go to meet her. It's just an hour—until Yurika. I don't know anything about this neighborhood. Could I ask the landlady to show me a place to wait? It's a nuisance, but. . . ."

The landlady came down from the second floor and told him the house number. Since he wouldn't find it just from that, she and the waitress went outside and pointed it out to him. Watching him leave, the two women appeared to whisper together. Turning at the bar diagonally opposite, then turning again at the T intersection, you reached the house farthest in back. Seikichi arrived at the place instructed. He was not used to visiting places like this, and he was distinctly uncomfortable. Seikichi was tongue-tied with strangers, and he wasn't accustomed to joking with maids. When he drank he became strangely serious. He knew that Yurika would not come right away, and she did not. It appeared she did not frequent this house.

The middle-aged maid said: "It's no fun, sir. To waste time drinking alone by the clock. You've already waited a full hour. Anyway, in a place like this the time is not very dependable; shall I call someone else to wait with you?"

"Oh, that's all right. . . ." Seikichi spoke ambiguously. The place would be even more stifling with a woman he did not know. Anyway, he thought it would be better not to get too comfortable before Kuniko came. So he added: "Well, I'll just wait alone a bit longer. If someone else is here, I'll get scolded. . . ." Seikichi's joke was stiff.

"Oh my, how awful."

"Awful is awful. Because it's such a close relationship. . . . My talk tonight is confidential. I've come to consult about making money. . . . So it's better if you don't worry about it. As I'm no drinker, I'm sorry to trouble you when you're so busy. It's all right if you leave me alone. I'm a nuisance, but please just leave."

"Well, don't worry about me. Really, why is Yurika so late? When she is so lucky to have you waiting. . . . Isn't that so?"

As she spoke she seized the opportunity to leave. There was no sign that any of the rooms were busy, but the maid felt awkward and did not like this strange and gloomy guest. Seikichi was embarrassed too. He wanted to change his mood but had no way to do so. No, not only to change the mood of the moment. His whole life was at a dead end; somehow he had to find a way out. That time—from that time when he had to give up thinking he could meet Ōkyo again he had lived somehow by resigning himself to the passage of day after day, months of days. Bit by bit the feeling grew worse. Hadn't he finally given himself up to shallow idleness and sugary loneliness? There was nothing to believe in, yet without slipping into the depths of skepticism. . . . Lost in this tortured reasoning, he poured himself a cup of fittingly now cold *sake*.

The people coming and going in Seikichi's head, lots of shadows of men and women, appeared one after another. His mind was like a crossroads; the shadows there proceeded each in its own direction. All were figures from the past. Not one hinted at a direction for his future. Only one, Sumiè, loitered, blankly facing the future at the crossroads in his mind. . . . But as he stared, it wasn't Sumiè, it was Ōkyo after all —it became the figure of Ōkyo at the crossroads, walking away sobbing into the past. That was a pity for himself and for the tormented Sumiè. . . . Thus far had he come in his thinking.

"Oh! she's come." He pricked up his ears suddenly and turned his downcast eyes up toward the outdoors. The clattering-wood sound of hurrying feet reached him abruptly there in the second-floor front room. . . . Echoes resounded in the ears of his memory. They were Kuniko's footsteps! The accustomed steps of his family. The footsteps of Kuniko hurrying home from shopping in the cold. His spirits rose to his throat.

"It's Yurika. Good evening!"

"Oh, Miss Yurika, you've kept him waiting a long time."

This conversation and some ensuing chatter seeped up from below. Not only the footsteps. The voice too was Kuniko. The voice was a put-on, though. It did not echo in his heart like the footsteps. The moment he recognized the unexpected footsteps he thought them a jumble of Kuniko's walk with the illusion of a lone, hurrying geisha. That was unexpectedly sad for him. The moment he heard the footsteps his abstract distress that his brother's wife had again to become a geisha became suddenly real. With mixed feelings of sadness, regret, longing, and weariness Seikichi waited patiently for the Kuniko who was Yurika to enter the room. Absorbed in other thoughts, he sensed— suddenly, eerily, tenderly, plaintively—the sound in his ears. The quiet sound of steps on the stairs, the almost noiseless sound of the shoji opening at the touch of her hand on the far side, and there was Kuniko, striking a pose—no, it was Yurika who peeked in, her lips pursed and face stiffened.

"What a face! Wow!" Seikichi said.

The stiffened face of Kuniko who was Yurika suddenly looked dubious and then completely natural. Her mouth fell half open; her eyes opened wide. . . . It was like the serenely bright, richly innocent look of three years earlier when she first came to brother's and before she was worn down by domestic cares. Yurika's expression had changed at once. . . . It was completely Kuniko. . . .

"Goodness, Brother!" She slipped across the tatami floor and sat down at the brazier facing Seikichi.

"What's up? This is a surprise!"

Kuniko took Seikichi's big bony hands, which were spread over the heater, and pressed them lightly between her small hands. . . .

"Aren't my hands cold?"

. . . Kuniko spoke after a moment of silence. Then, as if she had just happened to notice her heartfelt action, she gently let loose his hands. She stirred the fire in the ashes and spread her own hands over the warmth.

Seikichi was silent. There was no special meaning to Kuniko's words suggesting her hands were cold.

Seikichi sensed that Kuniko sighed in relief. He wondered if she was reluctant to meet him here. He was about to ask, but just as he opened his mouth Kuniko's words collided with his.

"Oh, I'm really happy. I don't know this place, and when I heard that someone was asking for me specifically, I wondered who it would be. . . . They say you learned of it at the Shinyo Pavilion?"

"The Shinyo Pavilion? Oh, you mean that Western restaurant on the corner across the street. . . . Yoshizō used to know that place well, didn't he? I felt I was being stared at all the time. Yoshizō and I look alike, so I wonder if they didn't think I was an older Yoshizō."

Kuniko was silent as if she had remembered something. "It's all right. . . . The place has changed hands. How about some *sake*, Brother?" Changing her tack, Kuniko suddenly picked up the *sake* bottle and shook it. "Oh? It's empty," she said in a cheery voice. She clapped her hands, looked around, pushed the button on the bell cord behind her, and sat up straight again. "Brother, you're drinking all alone? You're becoming a drinker. To use a geisha expression, I'm impressed. . . . Still, you're not at all red-faced."

Had Kuniko been drinking in a previous engagement this evening, he wondered; she did seem only a bit tipsy. She saw right through the downcast Seikichi, and he wondered if she wasn't jollying him on purpose. He stroked his cheek and said: "Of course not. I've sobered up."

"How come?"

"How nothing. The first three cups of *sake* make me red. No matter how many after that, it's all the same. One after another and I sober up. My face returns to its original condition. I've only had one bottle."

"You sure can hold your liquor. How did you ever learn a crazy thing like that?"

"Is that geisha talk too? But it's not crazy. Drinking *sake* is exceptional moral training, believe me. When I was tipsy just now, I had a good chance to reflect. But *sake* doesn't taste good. To me it's bitter right away—even if I'm not drunk. It's an absurd drink."

Just then from outside the shoji door, "Goodness gracious, he's cheered up in a hurry." The maid opened the door and brought in the *sake*. Settling herself, she said: "Miss Yurika, he's a cold one, all right. Before you came, it was like being led around by a mouse."

"That's right," Seikichi said, "isn't it, Miss. I'll confess it now. I was wondering how to bring up my plan for a double suicide. I was absorbed in that scheme."

"Forced double suicide," Kuniko said.

Three together, they laughed awkwardly.

VIII

After the maid had gone, Kuniko said at last, "Any news from Korea?"

"Yeah, one postcard. I haven't sent anything from here and he didn't write again."

"They say he took someone with him too."

". . . I've heard that rumor."

"They say he's in trouble, don't they?"

Seikichi said nothing.

"It's not a matter of money. It's that woman. Didn't you know, Brother?"

"I hadn't heard."

"Well, I won't say it. It would be wrong for me to say too much. . . ."

"It's all right. Go ahead and say it."

"But it's based on hearsay. I'd be tattling."

"It's okay. You're not tattling. . . . I'm cross-examining you."

"No, do you think he really is in Korea? People say he's in Moji, in Japan. . . . It gets around. I hear all kinds of things."

"All kinds of things? Really, he does seem to be in Seoul."

Actually, it was news to him that Yoshizō was said to be in Moji. Judging from various circumstances, it seemed a fact that Yoshizō was in Korea. But, as Kuniko said, after all Yoshizō seemed to be in some trouble over the woman. That is to say, her parents were not good people. They followed their daughter, whether to Korea or to Moji. They made sure that the store and everything was under their daughter's name. They interfered in anything new he tried. Even though he left the company to become independent, he could not carry through on any special projects. The woman's parents were too severe in their way of doing things. Even good-natured Yoshizō naturally became disgusted. He wanted to drop the whole affair and return to Tokyo. Yoshizō had said as much to someone who had met him there, and someone else had heard the report. Kuniko had learned of it through the second person. With deep concern she added: "Brother. How about helping him out in some way? If that's really the case."

"Well," said Seikichi vaguely. After a bit he added: "There's no help for it. He did it on purpose. So now he should deal with it as best he can. Best thing to do is leave it to him."

"I wonder. . . . That's your nature, isn't it?"

"It's proper. If I were to interfere in things now, I should have said something when he left. There's no use saying it now. Yoshizō is a man. The kindest thing really is to leave him as he pleases. Let's just watch. It's not that he's using my money; he's wasting father's legacy. What's more, it's Yoshizō's own share. But you can't say he's about to die very soon."

"You're awfully quick to dismiss somebody else's business. . . . How about yourself?" she grumbled.

"I'm a man too. Look. Thanks to doing as I like. . . . I flounder along that way."

"Great!" The Kuniko who was born in Fukagawa was becoming drunk after five or six *sake* cup refills. She too took on a businesslike air and teased him gently. "But Brother, you've resigned yourself, haven't you? About Ōkyo."

"Lay off that tonight. . . . I remembered on my way. I was so depressed. It occurred to me that today is the second anniversary of our love, like a death anniversary. . . . Speaking of Ōkyo, I met her husband again."

"What? Mr. Soeda? When? Where?"

"Six months or so ago. I saw him on the street by chance." Recalling that occasion, Seikichi began to speak of his memories. . . ."

IX

Mr. Soeda. Since that time Seikichi had called him "Ōkyo's husband," never referring to him as Soeda.[2] At least in his heart he spoke that way. If he were to call him Soeda, he would suddenly feel fondness for him like a brother, as he used to. The loss of his best friend was fixed vividly in his memory. Indeed, that sorrowful recollection lived still in his heart. . . . Though Seikichi seldom saw Ōkyo in his dreams, his dreams of Soeda were irritatingly frequent. Nor were they dreams of bickering. He dreamt of their strolling together, joking congenially. As these dream walks became lengthy, Seikichi would suddenly recall, "But didn't I break off with Soeda!" and just then he would always wake up. . . . When inadvertently he spoke the name of Soeda, he would feel exactly like that, like he was about to awaken. That was sad, but not only sad. It made him brood over how entangled the interpretation of the event had become. When he called him "Ōkyo's husband," he felt that the same Soeda was somebody else. Yet he had lost him along with Ōkyo, and all for her sake. Whether he could say the loss was easy to resign himself to or hard, he could bear it in the name of Ōkyo. That's what Ōkyo was to him. And Soeda too.

X

You were in my dreams but twice, last night included,
Your husband I dreamed of six times over.
To you I cannot talk with ease within my dreams;
With that man in my dreams I can stroll and jest.
Even my world of dreams is mean to me,
I have doubts even for my afterlife.
From dreams of you I woke at a glance
And for long I could not sleep again.
Dreams of your husband continued at length
Until next day a headache I've got. . .
I confess. I wanted just once to dream
That I had killed your husband. To see
Whether, how much, I would regret?

This was the poem that came to Seikichi.

XI

Summer was only beginning. Yoshizō and Kuniko's home was dissolved. It was around the time Seikichi returned from his travels and settled into the Toyama home. At that time a nephew of the Toyamas, a youth of barely fifteen, was living in the house. Seikichi went out for a walk with him. Having a youthful companion was a pleasant distraction.

Seikichi was walking head down and unconcerned. The man approaching must have been looking down too. . . . As the two were about to pass, they looked up suddenly at a distance of three paces. . . .

It's Soeda!

The Toyamas' nephew, who knew Soeda, recognized him on the spot. . . . Flustered, the boy bowed and said in a low voice: "It's Mr. Soeda! Isn't that so?"

The young man tugged at Seikichi's sleeve. The latter merely glanced at Soeda. The two passed. Yes, definitely it was Soeda. . . . That man was "Soeda," not "Ōkyo's husband," Seikichi felt at the moment. He thought so as he walked, while the nephew turned and said again: "It was Mr. Soeda. . . . Why didn't you bow to greet him?"

The youth didn't know the depth of it all. He asked in wonder why such old friends would pass each other with no greeting. Seikichi did not reply. He wanted to turn and look back, but he felt too that he should suppress the idea. The friends, once wont without fail to see one another daily, had now not met for nearly a year and a half. Soeda, too, had glanced up for a second at Seikichi. Without turning to look back, Seikichi was struck again by the momentary image of Soeda. He was wearing a new white topee. Over white trousers he had a homespun jacket. He looked very emaciated.

"He's very thin, don't you think?" Seikichi said to the boy.

"Yes, he's thin. It makes him look young. But I wonder if maybe he isn't sick. I just happened to think so."

"Why?"

"Mr. Soeda grinned when I bowed to him. He's an interesting man. When I've seen him before, only when he was sick and not well, he always smiled at the children. When he felt good, he always scowled at them."

The boy was a precocious reader of novels for his own amusement. That's why he made such an observation. When Seikichi heard this explanation, he agreed that it was typical of Soeda. But then, Soeda might have become more gentle recently. Soeda! Smile at Ōkyo too. Always. . . .

But as Seikichi walked three blocks farther on, "Soeda" gave way to the more disagreeable "Ōkyo's husband" in his feelings. He went up to the second floor of the Maruzen bookstore and browsed through some books, never noticing what they were about. Or rather, he picked up books of no meaning to him as he tried to keep that precocious youth from noticing his silent brooding.

. . . Since that happened, haven't I dreamt more than ever of Soeda? He thought so. . . .

XII

As he spoke of it briefly to Kuniko, he recalled that time clearly, down to the last detail. Then he added: "It was good that we saw each other unexpectedly. Suppose we'd noticed each other a block earlier. We'd have both had to put on unnatural faces. . . . It's too painful even to think of doing that."

"Brother. Don't be like that just because you are timid. You did nothing wrong. Soeda's the one who should be ashamed, isn't he? If I had been you, I would have glared at him."

Kuniko spoke in a simple childlike tone, but to Seikichi it was strangely sweet and funny. "But Kuniko, only three days later Ōkyo went by. . . . In front of the Toyamas' house, under my second-floor window. The Toyama nephew saw her and screamed at me from the window in the next room, 'Mr. Soeda's wife is going by.' I had a guest and couldn't get up. The guest may have heard rumors about me and Ōkyo. So I couldn't take a look. The boy seems to have talked after he came home about my strange encounter with Soeda a few days earlier. He may have learned something about the state of affairs. Maybe that's why he told me about Ōkyo's passing by. . . . She went by staring at the ground, it seems, Ōkyo did. . . . Maybe she heard from Soeda about me, so she thought to come by under my window. . . ."

"Is that all? You're happy at an idea like that. You're impossible, Brother. For ever. And ever."

Seikichi fell silent, interrupted by the rather drunk and flippant Kuniko. Yes, Kuniko was right.

"All of a sudden you're quiet. Are you angry?"

"Angry? Far from it. But it's such a pity. . . ."

"For Ōkyo?"

"No! No! She should be all right, shouldn't she? The one to be pitied is me." He spoke lightheartedly, with false courage. Then he picked up the *sake* cup in front of him, drained it at a gulp, and poured himself a refill.

"Oh, I'm being rude." The moment he spoke he felt his words and his voice were so professional, so sad. He took the occasion to change his tone.

"But, Miss Yurika" (he called her that on purpose), "how's business? Prospering?"

"So-so, thanks. As you can see, I've got a good patron." She spoke momentarily in jest, then returned to her natural voice. "People like me are better known for our past experience. We are recommended for engagements. It's the new younger ones I feel sorry for. Times are bad, you know. . . . Brother, you've had a lot to drink. You'll really get drunk. . . . It's natural for me to be worried about you. As Miss Yurika too."

XIII

Indeed, Seikichi had grown very drunk without knowing it. In the toilet he recalled the phrase "The shadow is as gentle as my little sister." He murmured it over and over to himself: "The shadow is as gentle as my little sister, The shadow is as gentle as my little sister," as he staggered back to the room. In his head it was clear. "The shadow is as gentle as my little sister." It was a good line, a verse spoken by someone truly lost in loneliness. Enough to make him think so.

Sitting down again on the same cushion as before, he took out his watch, looked at it, and said: "Well, I ought to be getting along home. . . . Home to the second floor of the Toyamas is all too forlorn for me."

"Home?" Kuniko said, taking out a small watch from her sash and looking at it. "No, Brother, it's still early. Only a little after ten. Don't send me home for another hour. There's more to talk about. I'll pay the geisha fee myself."

"My, you're tough. In that case, I'll stay on for two or three days. In return for your paying, though, aren't you asking for a loan in advance if I will listen?"

"You're right. You've seen through me."

Kuniko answered flippantly, but she seemed very serious. . . . Seikichi was touched to see her like that. He said: "What do you want to talk about? Go ahead."

"I wonder if I should say it now. Brother's drunk and I'm drunk. You'll come again, won't you, Brother?"

"I won't promise, but if I feel like it. Anyway, tell me what you want. What you were about to say. I'll worry about it if you don't." Seikichi settled back into place.

He felt like hearing Kuniko out, and that feeling seemed to get through to her.

"I'll say it. . . . But it's not about me. I've decided not to worry about myself. It's about Sumiè. She called on me unexpectedly, Brother, Sumiè did. I was surprised.

"Really? It wasn't a letter? Sumiè did? By herself? That's interesting. The lady called at the geisha house. It's like an act from a melodrama. . . ."

"Brother, it's no joke." She spoke strongly, rebuking the drunken Seikichi. "Sumiè was crying as she talked, Brother. She said she can't understand your feelings at all. She had no one else to consult, so she came to me. What I told her was this. . . . I could bring it up with you. But I didn't know whether in my status as a geisha it would be proper to call on you. I had to be discreet, so unless I could do it privately, wouldn't it be better if Sumiè were to meet Brother herself? But Sumiè said she could never do that herself. Education does handicap a person, you know. . . . Sumiè hoped that Brother would tell me frankly whether he liked her or hated her. She wanted me to ask you directly. Brother, do you like her? Do you hate her? Please answer frankly, won't you."

"I like her. Speaking frankly. I've liked her for a long time. Even now I don't dislike her. I like it that she can't talk candidly with me despite her easygoing manner."

"Then what's wrong with her? Her looks?"

"Her looks aren't so bad." As he said it, he thought of the way she smiled sadly with one side of her face.

"No. I feel bad to say so, but there are more beautiful women that I find unpleasant. But then, looks don't really matter. . . . So long as they're not disagreeable. To have a good-looking wife is like living in beautiful scenery. People who come on purpose to gaze are deeply impressed. But for the one who lives there, it all becomes the same before he knows it."

"Well then, her disposition? She's got a good disposition. That's the best thing about her."

"Her disposition's not bad. . . . To live with a woman of good disposition is like living in a well-arranged home."

"That kind of nonsense is uncalled for. . . . Speak plainly. You don't care. You just shilly-shally, Brother. What's the sense to it? If you're not so inclined, isn't it better to just say no? . . . Haven't you had enough to drink? Everything's empty." (As she spoke she snatched the *sake* cup from his hand.)

"What Sumiè said was: 'If he dislikes me, then reluctantly I've got a place to go. Not someone I found, but my family did. If he clearly says no, I'll resign myself. I'll do what my family wants. But I don't know whether he likes me or dislikes me. That's what torments me. . . .' Sumiè cried as she told me this. When I listen to you, Brother, I think her feeling of being forsaken is not unreasonable. Sumiè also said: 'Since your brother's attitude appears indecisive, I suspect he can't forget someone from an earlier time. Maybe he's now in contact with that person.' So I answered that I did wonder whether, in your heart, you were haunted by someone or something. . . ."

"Haunted? Oh, that's a clever thing to say."

Stifling Seikichi's unexpected interruption, Kuniko continued: ". . . Yes, it's Ōkyo. That's why I said you may not have been able to shake off your obsession. You are not the kind of person to continue the contact with someone you have once left. I know that very well. Besides, all your former women have husbands. . . . Speaking of that, did you know that Sendagichō is going to get married?"

"Really? I didn't know that."

"She came to my house. We weren't so close in the old days, but when she heard what happened to me, she came to talk. . . . Don't be suspicious. No one speaks badly of you, Brother. . . ."

XIV

Sendagichō referred to the address of Seikichi's former wife. According to Kuniko, she was soon to be remarried. Kuniko didn't know much about it, but the husband seemed to be a photographer, or something. After the wedding they were going somewhere far away, perhaps to America. Any regrets at her decision? Kuniko asked Seikichi, half in fun. "Enough of that" (he said with a wave of the hand). "No regrets. I feel good. Relieved."

It was no lie. That woman demanded too much of him. Seikichi felt he had graduated with flying colors. . . . Seikichi had long used the phrase "School of Love." Of course, he didn't mean a school to learn about love. He meant a school where love taught about human nature. Seikichi had surely learned a lot from that woman. So far as he was concerned, it was over, and when he found she took the same position, he was greatly relieved. That's when he felt he had graduated. It was none of his business any longer, but he hoped for her sake that things would go well this time. Aside from that, though, he learned from Kuniko that the woman had occasionally seen him from behind on the Ginza. She said he was always wearing a different new suit. When did the woman see him on the Ginza? he wondered. . . . And so many times. Until just recently he had been prowling around the Ginza area every day. He was killing time because of the business over Ōkyo, but when he noticed that rumors about Ōkyo were spreading, he took to fleeing like a fool, dejected and seeking to avoid being seen by people who knew him. The woman may have seen him some of these times. He didn't notice her at all. If that's the way it was, who may have seen him, when, where, in his misery, misery all the more conspicuous because of his splendid appearance? Still, was I walking around as absentmindedly as that? . . . That thought, he felt, was a much bigger problem than the woman's remarriage. . . . There was nothing else he could have done about it at the time, but as a man he should have presented a better appearance. . . . He wondered whether Kuniko perceived any of what he was thinking. He spoke.

"How about you? Will you see her again?"

"Yes, she called recently and suggested we have a farewell dinner together now that they have decided to go abroad. We set a date."

"If the subject comes up, you can mention me. Say I'm very pleased. . . . But you don't need to make a point of it. . . . Oh, yes. There is something I would like you to say for me. When a couple breaks up, you mix up some of each other's belongings. Only trivial things. . . . I said it was okay to keep some things she wanted. But the Imari—the name of the porcelain, you know—I had a small hand-warmer of old Imari ware. I used it as an ashtray. It had a picture of a strange foreigner copied from Dutch design. . . . You probably know it. Yes, blue drawn on a white background. That one. I like that one. It's nothing, but I like it. I think she's probably got it. That's all I care about now. With the kind of life I live, I naturally get some consolation out of having something like that around. Please don't forget to mention it. I'd be very grateful if you could bring it to me."

XV

Kuniko returned to the subject of Sumiè, persisting earnestly. She was convinced that Sumiè could rescue Seikichi from his loneliness. The drunken Seikichi was struck by her solicitude, but he replied: "Of course. That's so. If I don't like her, that doesn't mean there's another woman. I've done nothing to apologize for. Then what is it I don't like about her? That's it. I don't know myself. But, as you say, the obsession won't leave me. Don't worry, though. The spirit now lives nobly in the world of my poetry. That woman taught me true love. So she lives with me in my heart forever. As for Sumiè, though, she's the daughter of a good family. . . . She doesn't yet know the misfortunes of life. It would be best if she could live her whole life without knowing. It may sound strange, but I like people who have suffered. People who haven't suffered are like big, bright-colored, southern flowers. . . . People who have suffered are little, modest-colored but fragrant northern flowers. . . . or fruit? Somebody said a screwy thing like that, but I do like people who have suffered and yet whose hearts have not been warped by what they have endured. . . .

". . . I just remembered. Long ago I knew a girl who I now think would have made a good wife. This is a digression, but listen. . . . This story must be new to you, Kuniko. Long ago. I was about twenty-two. She was a maid in a lodging house. She was a graceful girl, yes, about eighteen at the time, she said. Because she was too ladylike for a lodging house, I asked her about herself. She had no parents and no brothers or sisters, she said. She was raised in a mansion where she had worked until recently as a servant. When I asked why she had left, she said only that there was a reason, that disgusting things were said. Was she seduced by the man of the house, or was it rumored that she was a concubine, or was it something else? She was a beautiful girl of large build. She liked me a lot, for some reason. Although she was a lodging-house maid, she was concerned about her future and wanted to become a nurse. Because she had to take exams, she asked me to help her with her studies. After that she would polish my shoes three times a day when she had the time. . . . She giggled in embarrassment as she told me. Then she would come into the room so often it was a nuisance.

Oddly, on those occasions she would always have a towel on her head, maid-style, and a broom. She probably wanted to show that she had come to clean. She would always come and fidget next to my desk. At the sound of footsteps she would take the broom and leave. When I think of it now, it's quite touching. At that time, though, I was still young. I was entranced by a beautiful girl of good family. That sweet maid was silly and strange. So I forgot about her after that. I just recently remembered her. . . . I was reading a foreign novel. The man in the story says to his lady: 'Long ago I knew a young woman. She was the daughter of a washerwoman. When she delivered the laundry she would often bring along a note. When I looked at the scrawled letters, they were odd. I felt ashamed to think the girl wrote like that. I didn't dream there could be something sincere in that scrawl. . . . I was convinced that sincerity came only wrapped under ample folds of silken clothing. But then I was young,' the man in the book said. As I read it, I happened to remember. The maid in the boardinghouse. . . . Just so. 'But then I too was young.' It would be nice if that girl were here now. I wonder why. Yes, she's the same age as Ōkyo. When she said, 'I've no parents and no brothers or sisters,' I liked it strangely, as I recall. Even now. . . .

"Sumiè is a lady. She's a gentle, obedient lady. If she doesn't become Akagi Seikichi's third wife, she has lots of places to go. How about going where her family suggested? Of course when it comes down to it, Akagi Seikichi may be a bit lonesome. But. . ."

". . . Brother, does that mean you refuse? Even though at first you looked as if you would accept her. . . . Is that right? Oh, I see—it displeases you to have Sumiè say she has somewhere else to go. . . . Men are self-centered, aren't they, Brother?"

"I don't know about other men. Why do I say that? Yes, Sumiè's feelings as described are true. Truth is something another person understands directly, understands lovingly. Someone was told by a young man that he was in love. When asked, 'What do you think of her,' the youth replied, 'Oh' (and after thinking a bit), 'so-so.' It's a good answer. . . . Sumiè too. I like her because she doesn't say that if she fails to get together with that man, she'll either die or live the life of a nun. . . ."

"As everything's good about Sumiè, why do you dislike her? I don't understand. . . . Well, Brother, having a third wife wouldn't make you cranky in itself. . . . You're too hard on yourself."

". . . You shouldn't interrupt so impatiently. Just listen to what I say. . . . To be too hard on yourself is like the rotting of good northern fruit. . . . Even if I have suffered, that doesn't have to make me cranky. But I am old. Just look. I get another white hair every three days. When you get old you don't go mad over a woman. Anybody would say I'm nearly forty. . . . I'm afraid of life. I didn't intend to get so old.

> This autumn
> Why am I old
> A bird in the clouds?

Is that it?

> This autumn
> Why am I old
> A bird in the clouds?

"I am old, but I have no intention of losing my youthful spirit. . . ."

Finally, very drunk with yet another round of *sake*, Seikichi became unexpectedly eloquent. He continued speaking.

"Tell Sumiè. . . . No, I will talk it over with her when we meet next time. Until just recently I longed for happiness in life. But now I'm fed up with things like happiness. I'm sick of it before I even taste it. I think it's like sour grapes on a high branch. If happiness is good, let there be happiness. . . . But happiness is not for Akagi Seikichi. That guy" (as Seikichi referred to himself in the third person) "has a mixed-up personality. The gods didn't mete out any happiness to that fellow. Instead—yeah, what do you think they will give him? Something, I'm sure. Therefore, if you're after happiness, don't become the wife of Akagi Seikichi. Parents wouldn't want to give a daughter to a man like that. Of course not. If I had a daughter, I wouldn't send her there. To abandon parents like that and come to Seikichi, a man with no regard for a person's world of happiness, that's a dubious prospect. Be ye not afraid to mend thine error?"

Kuniko stared at his face, enveloped in smoke. She spoke softly. "Then if Sumiè is that determined, it's all right?"

"Yes. . . . Well, almost. But how can I make such a thoughtless demand of another?"

"Well then, Brother, you're saying it's better alone?"

"As to that, I just don't know at all. Because I don't have anything to believe in. So whatever trivial matter it is, I just keep on brooding and can't do a thing. I'm that way about Sumiè too. I'm rooted in irresolution. Let's leave the question of Sumiè for further study. I understand the feelings you are promoting. I'm grateful—for Sumiè's feelings, of course. . . . I'll try to get a firm grasp on my own true character. I can't stay the way I am; only that is absolutely certain. I have closed the windows and lowered the shutters, figuratively speaking. Then I grumble that the room is so gloomy and unpleasant. If I don't like it dark, I can open the windows. But if I really like the dark, I can remain quietly enjoying the darkness. Whether it's dark or whether it's light, and without looking out, I'll enjoy complaining about the darkness I created. . . . So I'm wrong; look at me. . . . Is it far from the glory of a first-class poet? Glory is a good thing. Even those I scorn are enjoying it. To find out definitely what you aim at, and to get a little closer to it day by day, that's joy, that's what I want."

Seikichi suddenly fell silent. . . . Looking down at the brazier, his eyes lit on the forest of Lord Byron cigarette tips in the ashes. He said abruptly: "Hey, Kuniko. There's a revolution! Did you know that? Probably you didn't. It's fortunate if you didn't. You'll laugh if I tell you something so out of keeping. Or you'll get angry. Anyway, Kuniko, there is a revolution. There won't be geisha any more. Debts will be overturned. You can live any time with any man you like. I don't know how it will happen, but there won't be any irresolute people like me. There won't be any lonely abandoned types like me. . . . Everyone will call each other 'Brother and Sister' and will share each other's feelings. Won't that be great! . . . Won't it be wonderful when these things are no lies. But for that time to come, they say there'll be a revolution! Until it comes, I'll—I don't know when it will be, but if it's tomorrow it may be too late. Anyway, as I think hard about it, I might be a foot soldier in the revolutionary army of that dreamed-of world. Or, putting that aside, I could perhaps observe the vanity of all things through the falling blossoms, like the monk Saigyō. Or I could just live a lonely life like the poet Bashō. At least I'd live together with my Imari hand-warmer. One way or another I'll have to break out of my present condition. . . . Well, to talk like that, am I going to live a meaningless life? That's no good. Man is a common thing. What one man of little worth can do is nothing to the gods. . . . Yet for a man there is only one life, so one cannot say one will accomplish anything at all. When you think of it, the gods are crazy. . . . At great pains they created a mecha-nism called a person, but it's a failure. . . . Especially in my case!"

Seikichi chattered on. He didn't understand very well what he was saying. He looked with strange pity at Kuniko, who had drawn back blankly in awe. Turning his attention to himself, he said, "This drunken fellow has a terribly stuck-up style." And yet his feelings turned remarkably cheerful.

XVI

By the clock it was a little after 11:30.

"Well, I should be getting along home," Seikichi said, rising.

"Wait a bit. A car is coming right away. . . . You've had so much to drink you shouldn't go home on your own."

"Yeah, am I really that drunk? Well, it can't be helped. I'll be bour-geois and go home by taxi."

As he squatted down again by the brazier, he drank up the water remaining in the glass and spoke in a more formal tone.

"Of course, since you asked, I'll think seriously about Sumiè."

XVII

When they went out, the wind had come up. The cold night breeze felt good on Seikichi's cheeks. He took off his hat and looked up at the sky.

"Oh, it's a nice moonlight night." Recalling the earlier low-hang-ing clouds, he added, "My big talk has blown all the clouds away."

Kuniko said nothing. Maybe she was on the verge of sobering up. She appeared depressed. Seikichi wanted to say to her: "You've been drinking today. But you ought to give it up. . . . " But the words died in his throat. He had bitten them off. What the words were intended to express did not fit his taste. He said instead: "But Miss Yuriko. . . . No, Miss Yurika. Your makeup's a mess. An unpainted face is much better. With the white powder and the penciled eyebrows your face is much too harsh."

"Is that so?" said Kuniko. Then, as if she'd just thought of it, she added playfully: "It's a good thing. I don't want Brother to fall for me. That's not called for."

"Well, excuse me."

The two came out of the alley into the avenue where the car was waiting. Seikichi climbed in, saying nothing. Seeing him off, Kuniko said to the driver: "Lower Atago. Go straight there. But don't go so fast you have an accident. After all, he's sort of my brother."

The car took off with Seikichi riding alone. Casually looking out the window, he felt the street lights seemed blurry, shining like spiderwebs. His eyes puckered. "Oh, dear. Am I crying? Why? What for? And for whom? I've nothing to cry about. . . . But I seem to be crying. I *am* crying. . . . It's my inner sentimentality that's crying. But I'm not crying. No, definitely not." He murmured to himself, then, suddenly in a loud voice, "Hey! Hey!" he called to the driver. But when the driver slackened his speed, Seikichi said: "No. It's all right. It's nothing."

He had thought of telling the driver to drive around anywhere at will rather than returning directly to Lower Atago. But then he thought better of it, thinking "That's crazy." He muttered drunkenly, "It's all too forlorn, that second-floor room." Watching another car approach and pass, Seikichi wondered who was riding in that car and what they were thinking about. At this irrelevant thought he turned and looked back at the car that had passed. He could see nothing well. He looked around in the car he was riding. For the first time he noticed that this was a magnificent big vehicle, enough to shame him for its contrast to the shabby cars he ordinarily rode in. . . . I don't deserve something like this. This is a car for carrying geisha and serving girls. A small oval mirror was set in the front of the splendid car. Without intending to look, Seikichi saw himself there. Once again he rubbed his puckered eyes with the back of his hand. He stared curiously at that face. . . . Reflected in the mirror, the small face with its severely emaciated cheeks was turning pale as it sobered.

Notes

1. This story, ostensibly fiction, was written at the time of Satō's bitter breakup with his close friend and mentor, the more famous writer Tanizaki Jun'ichirō. Satō had fallen in love with Tanizaki's wife, Chiyo, whom Tanizaki had sent away and was treating badly. Tanizaki was not willing to divorce her until some eight years later, however, when Satō did finally marry her. In this story it seems evident that Soeda represents Tanizaki and Ōkyo reflects Tanizaki's (and later Satō's) wife, Chiyo.

2. The Japanese text omits the common word for "Mr." (kun). Japanese men address their closest male friends by the family name only, without the Mr., and Seikichi can no longer think of his former close friend in this familiar form of address; he must think of him as "Ōkyo's husband."

A Window Opens

Mado Hiraku, 1924

On an alley some twenty-five or thirty feet back in from the streetcar line there is a block of seven or eight houses like a bunch of birdcages. My house is closest to the front of the block. A tiny rented house in the middle of town like that gives no reason to expect a garden. No more than an excuse there in the back, though, is an area about ten feet square. It adjoins the residence of a well-to-do person. There is a high brick wall and, as if that were not enough, extending above it is a galvanized iron fence, completely shutting out the sunlight from my garden. Thanks to that, there had been two withered azaleas and a dead pomegranate tree. I pulled out the azaleas and hid them in a corner, but the pomegranate tree remains a problem. It is too big a tree for me to do anything about. It could not be pulled out easily. Even if I did pull it out, there is no place to throw it. I could not take it away if I tried, because my house stands so close to the neighboring houses on both sides that there is barely enough space for a man to squeeze through. Unless you chopped the tree with its spreading branches into fifty pieces there would be no way you could carry it out. I was only living there temporarily to begin with, and there was no need to go to that much trouble. So the tree stands there, dead. It shakes furiously every time a car speeds by the front of the house. The twigs touch the galvanized iron fence on top of the brick wall, making an intense noise. The framework of the house was loosened in the recent earthquake, and the sounds of shaking make unknowing guests think it is another tremor. Besides the troublesome tree there are some worthless shrubs that the landlord must have bought at a temple festival and planted.

Strangely, they are not dead. This is my garden—without color, without fragrance. Now and then I recall our big garden back home in the country. That often causes me to curse my residence in the city. I have come to pity people who live in the city.

As of now four people live in the house. . . . Each one has better than four mats of floor space, or more than eight-by-eight feet.

Of these I am the first.

Then there is A.

Then there is R.

Then there is T.

Let me introduce the last one. She is my common-law wife. She's been here for half a year.

In general you can say I am happy. That means that things ordinarily go well.

But then there's this recent thing. . . . Hardly ten days have gone by. It was a beautiful morning after the rain. I looked out as I was brushing my teeth. R had gone out behind the toilet, carrying a garden broom and dustpan to sweep the small open area. . . .

"Hey! Excuse me. I'll sweep it later."

The voice came suddenly from the old man in the tofu bean-curd store that backed up to us. His head stuck out from an unexpected place. My goodness! What a strange place to poke a hole. That was the first I had noticed it. Directly facing the window of my toilet a new window had been cut into the tofu store. No, it wasn't finished yet. It was just being installed. There was no carpenter or anything. Two men had simply sawed a hole in the back wall of the house. It was about two feet square. We were late sleepers in my house, and most of the work was done before we noticed. Now they were just finishing up the details.

I went back to my room without saying anything in reply to the man in the tofu store. The rather taciturn R didn't appear to say anything either.

"Was that fellow talking to us?" T asked.

"Seems so."

"Why didn't you answer?"

I didn't like that window. I couldn't complain about the man's opening his own window in the back wall of his own house, but it was too close to my toilet. There wasn't even a bare two feet between his house and mine. If I stuck my hand out of my toilet room window, it wasn't just that I could reach his window; I could put my hand through the window and grab a fistful of the air in his house. . . . What's more, I had always hated that tofu-store guy. Whether because someone had spit from my house onto his roof or had thrown something, or we were having trash burned behind his house and it would make the good quilts he had stored there sooty, he had gone with protests like these to my landlord to get me evicted. It was true that his roof had become dirty. It was a fact, too, that in burning trash we had by mistake slightly scorched the siding on his house. We were, after all, just a houseful of men at the time and so were rather messy. But nobody in my house would do anything like that on purpose. Anything dropped by accident from a second-floor window would fall on the roof of his house. The problem was that the houses were too close together. True, you can say it is bad to burn things in the city, and even at best the cigarette butts did pile up into a big, dirty mess in the trash. Wasn't that something he could have warned us about directly rather than going deliberately to the landlord? But since the matter was raised and we were in the wrong, we were left to apologize. If we had wanted to quarrel, we had the same kind of complaints against him. When it rained, a cascade of water from the roof of his storage shed poured violently into our hallway, so you couldn't leave it open. That was because his roof stuck out our way. Then, his house was a business that used a cooking fire, and the chimney was very low. When there was a wind, the smoke blew into our second floor. Also, he burned wood shavings and scraps of paper and they could be seen spewing from the low chimney. Sparks fell in profusion. Our white clothes hanging out to dry in the summer would become dirty. With a chimney as low as that, one should certainly be permitted to burn nothing but coal. It is useless to argue about these things in a neighborhood with common walls. It made us smile grimly at the selfishness of one who knew only the offenses he receives while failing totally to notice the offense he does to others.

If that had been all, it would have been nothing, but then there is the matter of this spring. I received a puppy to care for from another family—they were moving to a newly built house that didn't have a fence yet to separate it from the neighbors. As a fence would be built right away, I would only have to keep the pup for a little while, they said. (I'm famous for my love of dogs.) It was less than two months old and the puppy soon became used to my house. Then one morning it disappeared. When someone went to look for it, we learned from the neighborhood children that the puppy had been killed and taken away somewhere by the old man in the tofu shop. It seems the reason was that the puppy had been frisking about with the tofu man's only child, and the child had cried out in a loud voice. According to a somewhat older child, the old man had come out suddenly and said the dog could be killed because it had no license tag or anything. It might be a mad dog, he said, and he beat it on the head with a thick iron bar. The puppy ran around once in a circle and fell over. The old man picked it up and tossed it into the muddy ditch alongside the main road. An errand boy from a neighborhood noodle shop came to tell us that he had seen the dog writhing in the ditch, not yet dead. He had picked it up and poured water over it to wash off all the mud. An old lady who cooked the rice for us came to report all this to me while I was still in bed. She asked what should be done about the puppy, which was on the brink of death. It couldn't be helped. Leave it alone. It would be bad to move it when it was about to die. I didn't want to see it suffering like that. Instead, if it died, I myself would see it thrown into the front entrance of the tofu shop. I said this as I was getting up. The old lady apologized as if it were her fault. Although she had been warned not to let the dog out of the garden, it had gotten out by itself, she said. Of course the tofu man may have been vexed for two or three days. The dog, finding its bed cold, had crawled under the floor of the tofu shop to sleep there. The dog whimpered sometimes and this may have annoyed the tofu man, she said. The old lady intimated that she found it annoying too, and that made me more cross. The spring rains outside the window made everything clammy. I spit out onto the tin roof of the tofu shop. I even got angry at the people who had left the dog with me in such a cramped space.

A crowd gathered to look at the dying dog by the roadside. A visitor told us this. "That's our dog. Isn't it dead yet?" we asked. Four-fifths dead was the answer. Meanwhile a noisy crowd had gathered in front of

my house. The neighborhood children were calling all together for the
old lady. . . . "Hey, lady, the dog's here. Lady, the dog's here."

Staggering, barely walking, it came. Sniffing the ground intently, it
looked up and howled but seemed unable to focus its eyes. More gruesome than pitiful. Its head was swollen, its body soaked in mud and
smashed flat like a board. It had not yet eaten this morning. We gave it
food, but it took no notice. For two days it would not even drink water.
But it recovered. I was happy, and I imitated the dog who had come
reeling and sprawling home; that made everyone laugh. I did a monologue in fun, trying to portray the dog's state of mind. . . . I may die. . . .
This crowd of people around me have come to see the sight of me. . . .
Where am I? Yes. Isn't this a roadside somewhere? . . . I'm going to die
by the side of the road. Everybody surely thinks I'm a stray dog without
a home, but I'm not that. I have a proper home. My people at home are
worried about me, you know. Yes indeed. To die here like this would be
shameful. Somehow I've got to get back to my home. That's my urgent
business. . . . At that point I would fall over, imitating the dog, then
stagger and stand up. . . . But in what direction is my home? . . . Dog
that I am, I squint my eyes, sniff along the tatami floor, and totter as I
walk.

All this was before T came to the house. That's why she didn't know
why I didn't like the tofu man and would not speak to him. You would
never have guessed how much I hated that man. At first I just thought
he was selfish. Then according to my maxim that "The man who loves
flowers is a poet; the man who loves animals is a virtuous man," I put
the tofu man in the company of the evil men. I didn't like his odd sense
of justice that it was all right to kill a dog that had no dog tag. We
decided that our household would not buy tofu from him. Of course, I
don't like tofu all that much. This man, without consulting us, had
opened a window that had as its only view my toilet and my garden (a
joke of a garden, as I said just now). Then he would say, in a common,
half-genial voice at some inconvenient time, "Oh, excuse me!" I could
not answer the man. I don't remember ever insulting anyone on

account of his social class. I thought of him not as a tofu shop owner; I hated his impudence. And yet I can hardly recall the old man's face. This bigotry of mine was queer and childish, I thought. It may be odd, but I can't help it.

Anyhow, I did not answer him. It was my intention not to recognize that the tofu man had opened that window.

With window facing window like this I had an unobstructed view of the room next door from the toilet of my house. Because they had put a window arbitrarily in such a strange place, I had no reason to worry about leaving my toilet window open. They put a papered panel over the glass window, but for some reason they always left it open. My toilet window came to command a new scenic view.

That room, a detached room but hardly a parlor, but anyway it was a room under its own independent roof. That was the tin roof that he had complained we were making dirty, and it was under the floor of that room that the puppy had crawled. From the size of the roof you could judge the room to be about six mats big, but from what you could see from the toilet there appeared to be a closet, so the room was really about four-and-a-half mats. A single man lived there. He seemed to have moved in recently. Maybe the tofu man had rented out the room. He may have put in the window because the room was so dark. The lodger, my new neighbor, was a man over thirty. I had no interest in anything else, what he looked like or what he did. However, it did somewhat cool my hostility toward the new window. My feeling that if it were the old tofu man he would scream at us if even a scrap of paper was tossed out by mistake—that feeling no longer applied to this window. . . .

"You might say it's a widower. I wonder how he gets along." T said this with an appearance of some interest as a woman. When she saw that did not become a topic of conversation, though, it ceased to be a particularly interesting discovery. Then, night before last. . . .

There was a guest and everyone was on the second floor. Suddenly T called from downstairs.

"Mr. A. Mr. R. Come down and take a look. Here's something new."

It sounded like a joke, but her voice was for real. A and R both went down. They said something together at the bottom of the stairs.

Because my guest was a close friend and I was wondering what was happening, I left him to go downstairs too. T was halfway up the stairs, pointing out the window and whispering urgently. . . .

"Now, there's a bride in there. . . . Yes, it's a wedding. The marriage broker is there. The broker is collecting fifteen yen from each of them. He's got the money. I can hear him saying something about visits to the bride's family. . . ." T was as happy and curious as a child at discovering this trivial affair. "How quick. They've done up her hair already. Take a peek."

I was a bit interested too, and I took a look. Yes, I could see in front of the window a woman of twenty-five or twenty-six in a married woman's coiffure. But that was the extent of my curiosity. I did think it was kind of strange to watch a wedding ceremony from a place like this. I thought maybe this was the real meaning of humor. I was told that my neighbor was wearing a formal serge hakama skirt and haori jacket. It was a proper, propitious wedding for sure. The marriage broker said to the bridegroom something like "Some time soon, after a week or even half a year when you can afford it, the both of you should go back to the bride's family home for your own peace of mind and to set them at rest." He did collect fifteen yen. It appeared there were three or four other people there. Voices in happy chatter induced by *sake* could be heard close at hand.

"Yes, yes," T said, as if she had just remembered. "That is, yesterday somebody like a friend came and talked. It was about the bride. One was eighteen or nineteen. There was another a little older. She was twenty-six or twenty-seven, so the younger one was probably better. That's what he said. I guess he liked the older one, though. As he was about to leave, the friend said, opening his wallet, 'What a bore. I don't have a flat copper cent.' So the neighbor said, 'Have a bite to eat here.' I wonder if he isn't from Niigata. That way of speaking."

Then the taciturn R spoke up. "Now as I think of it. Something interesting happened the day before yesterday. . . . Maybe it was yesterday's friend. The two of them talked of 'free marriage.' "

"What do you mean by 'free marriage talk?' "

"Oh, nothing. But if the man is over thirty and the woman is over twenty-five they can legally marry on their own authority. That's all."

"What kind of man is he? I didn't get a good look."

"Well, I don't know. His hair was parted. He wore glasses. He had a summer kimono in a soft *kasuri* pattern.[1] I don't know what his business is, but he has a sideline of night work making envelopes. He must be working hard because he's getting a bride. He's got a kind of dresser, and he bought a rat-proof cupboard for food."

The happy chatter next door went on until about 11:30. We talked that long about them. Then, as we said we were going to bed and went in turn to the toilet, T made a new discovery. We were mistaken in thinking that the bride was the one with the well-prepared, married-woman's coiffure. That one seems to have been the wife of some frien who was helping out. She left. Instead, the one who stayed behind w: the seventeen- or eighteen-year-old with her hair in the unmarri woman's Shimada style, like the one they talked about yesterday. This was T's discovery. . . . "With a muslin sash on a lustered kimo and the Shimada coiffure done up ornately." I didn't see anyth myself, but I heard a man's voice. Then I heard the words "so lor you do it right," but I didn't know what it was all about.

Before going to bed I stuck my head out of the second window. The moonlit night was supremely peaceful on this the teenth night of the moon's cycle. Perhaps because I was affected moonlight, I had a feeling of good neighborly blessing for the married couple where the man had said "so long as you do it rig'

The next morning—that was yesterday morning—I peek neighbors with some curiosity. The man had his back to the and faced a desk in the brighter area. I was a little surprised had a desk there. He seemed to be writing a letter. Five or s written letters were stacked in the back. The woman? Leanir tiously, I saw her sitting bent over on the tatami with her h man. It suggested a simple shyness in the natural state of a woman placed on a new frontier. Strangely, there was a kin peace about it. Wasn't there something displeasing about it bit concerned, although it was none of my business. Af breakfast and reading all through the newspaper, I stuck over the garden to spit. When I casually looked that wa the little window from here, and there was the woman l elbows, staring down at the ground in my awful garder

pectedly rainy this morning in contrast to last night's clear moonlight, and the woman's appearance, sad to say, was rather gloomy.

Still, I did hear a quiet laugh escaping from next door.

Wasn't there more chattering talk today than yesterday?

Even now I can hear laughter. There is something like the sound of a saw again, but they are probably not opening another window. More likely they're closing it up. . . . They'll be remaking the defective shoji paper screen. That's to the good. We don't intend to watch any more, but anyway, don't we feel the autumn chill already?

> *Aki fukaki*   *Deep in autumn*
> *Tonari wa nani wo*   *The man next door*
> *Suru hito zo*   *What does he do?*[2]

Notes

   1. A blurred design created by the ikat technique of dyeing the threads before weaving.

   2. Written by the haiku poet Bashō on his deathbed in 1694, the autumn of his life, when he could no longer go out to see what his neighbors were doing.

Essays

A Discourse on "Elegance"[1]

"Fūryū" Ron, 1924

I offer this little discussion of principles to
all those people ancient and modern whose names
have come up in this text, perhaps at some
annoyance to them.

I. INTRODUCTION

It is a difficult subject. Undeniably I am no scholar. To open my mouth
rashly like a scholar is most unnatural for me. Well, how should I
speak? As who or as what kind of person? I don't know. But as I was
born into this life a talkative thinker, I am most comfortable when I am
expressing my thoughts in talk. I love to be comfortable, come what
may, even in my writing style.

Be that as it may, elegance is definitely not something talkative.
It's like the opposite. For the man of elegant taste, it's a thing that must
be felt, not a thing to be thought. If one tries to grab for it, it's like the
smoke from an incense burner that vanishes without trace. From
ancient times, therefore, the man of elegance, if he did say a word or
two about elegance, would not pompously explain its essence. As for
me, however, I don't just think about elegance. I plan to clear up just
what it is by talking about it. The man of elegant taste will surely find
fault or laugh at my own lack of elegance. They'll call me a man of no
elegance. Therefore if I were a man of elegance, there would be no little discourse. That's how passive a thing I think is elegance.

If I assume that I have been able to penetrate to the true meaning of elegance in this discourse, the very fact that I publish a talkative discourse on elegance may be eloquent proof that I am not a self-appointed follower of elegance nor am I trying to expound elegance.

Well, it's all right with me if they say I'm no follower of elegance.

I am of course a modern man. . . . I know the words "materialistic interpretation of history." I know the words "realistic idealism." I know a little even about the imported words "pragmatism" and "élan vital." Not only the words. I can get the sense of the meaning, maybe dimly. As a modern man I even have a feeling of scorn for anything like elegance. As a modern man, a cosmopolitan man. As that kind of man I believe I have surely found elegance to be absurd.

Still, I often see myself in fact as a Japanese, as a man of tradition who cannot ignore that thing that is elegance. Sometimes, indeed, I'm far from ignoring elegance. Moonlight in the evening, flowers in the morning, I feel these things enchant me. I have felt the enchantment so intensely that I never even thought about it.

In the past when I was still on friendly terms with Tanizaki Jun'-ichirō,[2] who was popularly called a diabolist or a hedonist, and we lived close together and came and went day and night, I often talked with him about elegance. We both felt that the other understood, and we had no particular arguments about how to judge its true quality. The so-called elegant taste of the ancients persists within us and cannot be perceived from the standpoint of the Western arts. Its reality wields a power over our persons and our hearts that Tanizaki called a delicious vegetarian diet. I remember that he seemed to be terribly frightened at the fascination exerted by the vegetarian arts, which he said robbed people of their youth and made them lethargic. Unlike him, I was not particularly frightened of this. In contrast to his delicious diet of vegetarian arts I remember speaking tentatively of the ecstasy of moonlight. Indeed, around that time Akutagawa Ryūnosuke knew of Tanizaki's fear of the vegetarian arts; he had probably heard the discussion from Tanizaki. "We need not be afraid of Tanizaki's fear and trembling," he told me. Presumably he was speaking about what in a word should be called elegance. Why did I bring up these names so suddenly? I wanted to say that among modern men there are others beside me who feel the enchantment in something that without much mistake can be called elegance. Even if you say these are rather few examples, I know any number. Nagai Kafū, author of "Quiet Rain," comes to mind. It is probably no great error, is it, to say that his present-day sphere is elegance? Fifteen years ago people called him a hedonist. At the beginning of his artistic life, his art, at least in its outward form, was, as we all know, not a bit Eastern. I also remember some members of a group of artists that met ten years ago under the name of the Fusain[3] Society. In the beginning their style accorded with a new movement that was the most vehement and eccentric in the Western arts. Today, on the other hand, doesn't it seem they have come to love the world of Nanga[4] art, a product of our tradition of elegance? A man like Kishida Ryūsei is the principal example.

I have counted up a lot of names. I have noted the fact that I am certainly not alone among present-day artists in feeling a certain fascination that comes from the absorption with elegance, even if for the moment we don't consider the reasons. Rather than looking around the outer world for more examples, I ask my readers to turn their eyes inward and examine first whether there isn't something of that fascination within themselves.

I'd like to ask my readers, sometimes when the world has become fleeting and the mind floats free, haven't you ever experienced an inexpressible feeling—at least it seems that way to me—a feeling that you perceived something, even from the inanimate things of the world, a feeling of emotion, sometimes quiet, or rapture and intoxication that made you think vaguely, "That's what the ancients called the feeling of a lonely moment, the pathos of things?"[5] It is a kind of dim, unceasing oddness that briefly purifies body and soul, a feeling that when we call it sad it is joyful, and when we call it joyful it is sad.

You probably know that I am irritated. My way of speaking is really impatient. Even if my way of speaking is bad, please don't make an issue of it, and if you understand please tell me, "Oh! I've had that feeling." If you don't, there is no reason for me to keep on writing. . . . It can't be helped. I would ask anyone who does not know this feeling at all to stop here and read no further. Actually, I'd be a little offended by anyone who said that. I don't believe there really is anyone among mankind who hasn't experienced the feelings I am talking about, even if infrequently, even though there are differences in degree. I would like to say that frogs must experience it, birds must experience it, dogs must experience it, but that would be a fairy tale. It is no fairy tale, though, to say that any and every human being may enjoy this experience. I think these feelings are that universal. It may be that these feelings will emerge more or less differently according to the customs and climate of the country where people are born. The same kind of flowering plants, for example, may vary some or even greatly in color and fragrance according to where they are grown. I believe there is a similarity of feeling in what we Japanese experience. This conviction leads me to conclude that these feelings I have tried to describe are shared by all Japanese and are common and easily understood despite my exasperating, roundabout manner of speaking. So I suppose that if there is someone who says, "I don't know about that," I'll just have to think he is perversely and deliberately refusing to excuse my poor way of expressing it. . . . That's how much I believe that it is universal among humans and that a people share these feelings in common.

Well, my friends who forgive the powerlessness of my pen sympathize with what I am trying to express, and are willing to read on: In explaining what kind of thing "elegance" is I want first to speak of the matter of "that."[6] Sometimes within us, not within our mind or within our body, but simply in the "within of us," as I think it more appropriate to call it, there is a "that" that passes subtly through the within of us. Subtly, like the beautiful shadow of someone who has left us. Exquisite but fleeting, a truly strange shadow that resembles joy. . . . Tentatively let's call it a shadow. We must have received that shadow from our ancestors. Our ancestors must have received it from their ancestors. Their ancestors in turn from their own ancestors. . . . Then who first transmitted it? And why did he transmit only those feelings? . . . Who would know these things? If there is someone who knows these things, why do the insects cry of an autumn night? Among insects why and when did the cricket choose his chirping voice? That's what I'd like to have the first person teach me!

As we look out across the flatness of today there appears a point so obscure we would never have noticed it without mention, and whose very existence we want to doubt. If we look closely, we see the cross-section of the cut-off end of a piece of thread. Actually, it is a long thread running through a three-dimensional link between past and present. It is a simple thing that needs no further explanation. I will repeat it, though. Can't we identify a "that" revealed elusively and dimly as a dot in the plane of our daily life and representing a long thread running through the three dimensions of human existence? I want to add something more metaphorical. Just as a single thread may look like a single point, may not a sheet of paper look like a single line if it is covered by something? Just as a single point may be one manifestation of a single line, so a single line may be a manifestation of a plane surface. What can be seen only as a dot when its view is obstructed may turn out to have length. Something that is revealed only in length, if you take away whatever is covering it, may then have width. Our actual lives, appearing as specks on a simple cross-section through the third dimemsion, may yet have more to them than these contrasts will allow us to see. If we take a slice of that space called the "cosmos," cutting at that part designated as human life, or if we take a slice through the space called human life, cutting at that part designated today, we may imagine human life today as the infinite cosmos. If we do, though, we may have only a pitiful fragment. Unfortunately, what we have been given is no more than that fragment! With the little fragment we have been given we try to unravel some big things. Each person will grasp the speck that most forcefully controls his life and will develop from that nucleus, either unconsciously or with a strong consciousness. From there, various thoughts, philosophies, and religions—that is, various and sundry ways of life sometimes completely incompatible—may thrive, even simultaneously and within like-minded persons. In this sense, countless worlds blend and overlap in the single world of today. . . . We need not go deeply into that now, though. All that I hope, dear readers, is that you know the "that" that runs through the within of us at times, and that you recognize that the ancients also must have experienced "that."

"That!" Don't laugh at me, readers, for talking like a child. Even someone who calls himself the king of words, so long as he is truly wise, will probably keep his mouth shut when he seeks to depict the kind of feelings that touch the poetic spirit of our people. Many geniuses among our ancestors devoted their whole lives in their zeal somehow to grasp precisely and express directly the "that" that I am so hardpressed to describe in words. In seeking the true expression of "that" our ancestors happened to discover a kind of literature closer to silence than that of other peoples. This our ancestors embodied in the 31-syllable and 17-syllable poems. They discovered, too, a technique of art closer to nothingness, which transforms substance into a shadow world by ignoring shadows in favor of a precise existence of real substance. That is because the poetic sentiment demands this kind of expression. *The nearness to silence and nothingness.* That was the elegant art of our ancestors. Our ancestors interpreted "that" to be close to silence and nothingness. As they took joy in their elegant arts, the followers of the elegance to which they devoted their lives really felt the "that" and perceived the truth that lies in that joy. In discovering therein an agreeable life for themselves, they were moved, too, by that momentary flash of profound joy that unites with sorrow in a deeply touching experience of the two polar extremes at one stroke. They wanted to perpetuate that flash of truth that they felt tied the momentary emotion to eternity and the universe. They brought the "that" which lies forgotten in a hidden corner of mundane life into the center of man's life, or rather they shifted the center of man's daily life to where the "that" lies. They tried to make into daily life exactly those things that could never be part of everyday life. . . . A preposterous reversal of values! They stared at that speck that could perhaps not be counted among the things of the everyday world. In that speck they found length. They endowed it with width, and on that surface they tried to build a country, a world. In that strange carefree land, however, they were not satisfied merely to let their spirits play like butterflies; they planned to have their bodies live there too. . . . The great poet from Florence who wandered around heaven in the flesh guided by a pure maiden was nothing in comparison. One might call it the creation of a daily life of the most extreme poetic aesthetics. They elevated all life and made of it a flower bed for the arts. They doubted not the unity of life and the arts. Considering how they looked on the extreme creativity of life, I must admire their radical leap. In the fullness of my affection for this group of strange romantics, and without regard to whether I rank among them, I commend the arrogance with which they regarded the mass of people living in a world they found vulgar and quite different from their own. You can say that they who created this absurdly poetic and aesthetic life undertook silently by that act to challenge the everyday world.

Nonetheless, their daily life of poetic aesthetics is the next thing to that of a beggar! Their art is next to ugliness! Their literature is next to a riddle without an answer!

But yet! For another surprising thing, aren't people with a basic appreciation of this kind sometimes charged with an unshakable power of enchantment? . . . Speaking for myself, even when I think I must deny it with my reason and my will, don't my feelings make me long for the world of that strange and silent rapture?

Well, what complicated stuff is elegance! That's why I am so eager to see the true nature of this thing called elegance.

You my readers are already aware that I have determined on the "that" of baby talk for the principle of elegance or elegant art, that most paradoxical ecstasy. Scholars call the same thing the "sense of impermanence" rather than "that"ness. If I had to use those words to describe it, I wouldn't just say impermanence but would ask that you let me make up the words for the "feeling for the evanescence of beauty." But that isn't so different from just saying "that." In coming this far I can't settle the matter simply by choosing the words "that" or the "feeling for the evanescence of beauty." We must try again to ascertain clearly the "that" which was the driving force for the remarkable unfolding of the lives they staked as adherents of elegance. Surely the secret of that incomparable and anomalous beauty must have germinated in the driving force of "that." They must have fully encouraged its abnormal growth. The exceptional that seemed not anomalous when it germinated became naturally and noticeably more anomalous as it grew.

I'd like to consider in detail the essence of the "that." Then various interpretations the followers of elegance drew therefrom, the various styles that came from the interpretation—that is, I'd like to consider the essence of elegance and the elegant arts. Then we should of course consider whether we—or I should say I—should plunge into that enchantment.

II. AN EPISODE

Recently I participated in a surprising discussion sponsored by the magazine *Shinchō*. Perhaps my readers who are not members of the literary establishment are not familiar with it, so I will explain. It's a monthly evening meeting for the idle discussion of the literary output of contemporary novelists published in the previous month—that is, a chance for novelists to talk about their art. It may sound rather elegant, but if you think so, you are quite wrong. Actually it is not a very elegant meeting. To begin with, the modern age is not at all elegant and the people who write novels are not elegant either. Moreover, meetings in themselves do not turn out to be elegant. When you consider that these three things, "modern times," "the writers of novels," and "a meeting," are none of them elegant, and you put them all together, won't the results be especially lacking in elegance? Please don't misunderstand me. I am definitely not saying that a discussion between any particular contemporary novelists is lacking in elegance. I just insist that these things, "modern times," "novel writers," and "meetings," are not elegant. Later I will take the opportunity to discuss all these things in themselves, so I won't speak in detail now. Tentatively, though, don't you have a feeling simply for the word pairs modern times/old times, novelist/poet, and meeting/solitude? I say this to test how much of a common feeling you my readers and I can share about the word "elegance." It strikes me that there is sometimes quite a difference in the way we use these words that we think we use entirely or nearly in common.

Well, it all started when the topic in that discussion sponsored by the magazine *Shinchō* shifted to a critique of the work and style of Murō Saisei. At one point somebody casually mentioned the word "elegance," and when Kubota Mantarō said that what Murō Saisei was aiming at was the "loneliness" of the ancients, Kume Masao expressed his opinion that this work differed from the "elegance" of the ancients, adding that it had more sensibility to it. I was not a little surprised that Kume seemed to think that the elegance of the ancients was lacking in sensibility. I had always thought that the thing called elegance was indeed the sensibility of olden times. When I let out without thinking that I was surprised at the difference in our viewpoints, Kume explained his opinion again, concluding that "the true elegance of the ancients was a matter of will." I was greatly astonished. In this way some thirty minutes of this not particularly elegant occasion were devoted to the discussion of elegance. Lacking in elegance from the start, the occasion became even more "nonelegant"—in other words, each of us was busy expressing his own opinion. I'd like to test my readers' feeling for words again. To sit nodding in agreement without speaking, or to express one's own opinions in a swamp of words—which after all is "elegance?" which is "inelegance?"

In saying this it is not my intention to fault the participants for being inelegant. On the contrary, of those present I was by far the most "nonelegant." Actually, I talked the most. That was because the opinions unexpectedly gleaned at this meeting, as expressed on this topic by all present, were strangely very uniform in differing so much from my ideas. They may have felt that my personal views, although I expressed them only fragmentarily, were shallow and eccentric. . . . In fact I think they did feel that way. The grand old man Tokuda Shūsei, for example, went so far as to reprove me, saying I did not perceive things "with wisdom." Yet, subjective as I am, I have a strange feeling even now as I write that their views were quite extraordinary in seeing as so divergent what I am convinced is normal. Their views were in general agreement among themselves; only mine were different. I was the exception. They may have thought I made bold to dissent only to shock people. How should I know? All I did was to say what I had always thought. Therefore, I could not help but feel a certain sense of unhappiness at how their feelings differed from mine. As what I said was no more than my usual feelings and was not a theory reached after due consideration, I felt I could not let it go at that by just saying, "The conventional view is what the greatest number of people will agree to. . . . " As the discussion progressed I was fired to reexamine in detail my views and feelings which so many thought to be so strange. However, it was not the purpose of the meeting to pursue that same topic forever. I realized too that, just as it was difficult for me to perceive fully the opinions they held so unexpectedly, I could not easily get my views through to them either. So though I greatly regretted that I could not get them to understand my feelings even superficially, I refrained from expressing my views about "elegance" any further.

My companions in that meeting and I lived in totally different worlds when it came to our views on "elegance." So what were their ideas? (See the article "Shinchō Joint Review Session No. 10" in *Shinchō* magazine for March 1924.)

Kume Masao said: "The mental state of elegance is if anything a matter of will. If elegance were a matter of sensibility, it would end up in the modern 'decadents.' Before you can arrive at those sensations, a discipline of will is necessary. Then you attain the true elegance of the ancients." After thus explaining the "true elegance of the ancients," he gave the name of "elegance of the new times" to a "narcissism of sensibility which lacks a stable view of life." That may be why it corresponds to the the modern decadents. If Kume and I could share a common view for the term "modern decadents," I think there must be one aspect in which there is a very subtle resemblance between the followers of elegance and the modern decadents. . . . I'll speak more of that later. Concerning elegance, Kume also made a distinction between "genius-style elegance" and "elegance interpreted by an expert," saying this was the source of our difference. Kume tentatively used the phrase "genius-style elegance" for my way of thinking, which he said was no more than a plea for my own kind of sensibility—a complete indulgence in just what I like. He characterized my way of speaking as "describing the ultimate elegance after the form has achieved its height." By this phrase he seems to have made a distinction between the process and the culmination, and he appeared to believe there was a difference between them, at least in regard to elegance. I found it very hard to agree with Kume's views. If the culmination could not be contained within the process, how and when could you reach the culmination by going through the process? There was no such thing as culmination. That's because it is only an ideal. . . . But because wherever we may be in the process, we can feel the prospect of reaching the culmination, however feeble that may be, can't we see the ideal for what it is? Therefore, if elegance was a matter of will in the process, wasn't it correct to say that the ultimate stage, the culmination, would also be a matter of will? To make a precise distinction between process and ultimate, between body and soul, between life and art, between expression and content, or between normal conversation and edited writing would surely be a delusion, I thought. Yet it seemed that Kume did make that distinction in his view between process and ultimate. If so, that was all right. Then he added, with his characteristic gentle smile, "If it's Satō, rest assured it will be elegance. But that's not true of everyone." As I think about it, is elegance really something so splendid that a person who doesn't like it should work so willfully for it? The ancients said, "Freeing oneself from the world, one enjoys elegance." Kume with all his rich charm had spoken my name at this time, but I could not take it seriously. Here I am reminded of Tanizaki Jun'ichirō, who feared the enchantments of elegance so much that he willfully rejected them. (To prevent any misunderstanding, I should say that although I respect him highly I have never thought of Tanizaki as a genius. I think of him as a poet, as a romantic, a man of sensibility and a person of great will in a worldly way. Therefore I do not think of him in terms of Kume's "genius-style elegance.") In this respect Kume may be flexible enough to admit an elegance in some people that is not based on will. Still, he concluded by saying, "I feel there is surely a power of will in the mental state of elegance." I would like to hear his explanation for the basis of these views, but he ended by asserting, "I think the literature of Bashō is a literature of will."

Tokuda Shūsei said: "I think the elegant taste of the ancients was more a psychological thing than a matter of sensibility. It was a rigorous course of study, like the cultivation of Zen. A little different from the tea ceremony as practiced by rich people today, I think." And: "The elegance of the ancient elite was not an art of amusement. It was rather a kind of Eastern religious thing." Shūsei construed my use of the word "sensibility" to conclude that I had confused elegance with the pleasures of the wealthy. Although it would be rude, I wanted to say I was a bit mortified at being instructed in the theory of enlightenment. Though I was a complete novice, I had no intention of talking about elegance without some understanding of it. To reinforce my point I would like to put it this way: the life of a follower of elegance was exactly like a rich man's tea ceremony. The only point of difference is that the follower of elegance stakes his body and soul on feelings that the common man takes as pleasure and that in the original intrinsic meaning are in fact pleasure. The common man enjoys pleasure as a sideline. The follower of elegance, however, makes that feeling the only thing in life. This one point is the greatest difference! In Part 1 of this essay I have already spoken in praise of that complete reversal of values which occurs for the follower of elegance, so I won't discuss it further. This may clear me of the stupid allegation that I think the rich man's tea ceremony and true elegance are one and the same thing.

Shūsei, however, called my way of talking about sensibility superficial, and he said elegance was "more psychological." On this point I could agree, of course, that it was psychological, but I wanted to ask whether the "psychological" was closer to "mind" or to "heart." I thought it was closer to heart. I thought, too, that the follower of elegance attained that feeling through what could be seen by the eye, heard by the ear, touched by the hand in daily life. Hence I had used the word "sensibility." Even if the word "sensibility" was contrary to the idea of will, I did not feel that it was in conflict in any way with the broader meaning of "psychological." If sensibility (it would be all right to use the word "sensual" to associate it more with the body) could be said never to be psychological, then all art, especially the creation of music and art that can exist only through direct sensibility, the masterpieces that appeal to a person's heart, would be impossible! Generally speaking, sensibility to the arts is a psychological thing. It is built on the mystery that spiritual feelings can simultaneously be physical, or that physical feelings can simultaneously be spiritual. In the mingling of the feeling of bodily ecstasy with the feeling of spiritual ecstasy, the modern decadents found their artistic meaning too.

I'd like now to respond to Kume's statement, which I earlier passed over, that, "If elegance were a matter of sensibility, it would end up in the modern decadents." As I just said, the art of the modern decadents can be understood as art where the feeling of bodily ecstasy can exist simultaneously with the feeling of spiritual ecstasy. I'm not alone in this interpretation. Where I look on elegance as sensibility, I feel that the so-called followers of the decadents, those with the pale passion of the Baudelaire spirit, have a touch of something very much in common with the followers of elegance. If I speak of them as having a pale passion, let's tentatively call ours a pure white passion. The point where the two differ lies entirely in what may be called the product of Eastern culture and the product of Western culture—the dim scent of man and the strong scent of man. (What do I speak of as Eastern culture? I'll try to explain.) Just as the followers of the decadents are thoroughly artistic despite their hint of religion, I recognize that the followers of elegance, as Shūsei says, have an "Eastern religious" component. I do not feel it is a "rigorous course of study like the cultivation of Zen," but I do see them as devotees of art. Followers of art for art's sake, I'd like to say.

These devotees of art have combined the intoxication of sensibility simultaneously with the "psychological" intoxication spoken of by Shūsei. The pursuit of art made their lives unite with art. Or made them try to unite. That is not a matter of will, however. It is the pursuit of intoxication. I see them as hedonists of high degree.

Let us consider the elegant writer Nagai Kafū, whom I have mentioned, or Tanizaki Jun'ichirō, who shuddered so in fascination at elegance, or Murō Saisei, who was the starting point for the question, or someone like Kitahara Hakushū, the leisured poet of Odawara. If we lay aside for a bit the question of whether they penetrated to the essence of elegance, anyone will recognize that their hearts seem to be drawn to elegance. No one will doubt that they are artists of pleasure and sensibility for our times. I think we can understand that pleasure and sensibility have an important relationship to elegance. Natsume Sōseki, the author of "Recollections," must be called the literary man of the age. I don't know whether he was the novelist of the age, but I don't doubt that he surely was the literary man of the age. If we consider his early works, like Pillow of Grass and The Poppy, we find even in Sōseki a strong aspect of sensibility. When Sōseki pointed to Izumi Kyōka, a writer of rare sensibility, as the greatest writer of the Meiji period, I think that fully proved the level of Sōseki's sensibility. I wonder about Kōda Rohan, along with Sōseki the other literary master of our time. I find an element of will rather than of sensibility in his elegance. He is the only exception I can mention. Is that why I think of him as a philosopher and not just a devotee of elegance? We can see in this an example of the delicate closeness of the follower of elegance to the Eastern philosopher.

I don't know many facts about the ancient Bashō. Not much is known generally. I plan to write more about him another time so I won't go into detail now. But, so far as I know, he was seen and understood by the people of his day and by those of later periods to have the characteristics of a man of pleasure. I think it is interesting to note that Bashō lived in that pleasure-loving period of Genroku (1688–1704) and that the source of his proper style has been found in the serene and deep, indeed very deep, earlier reaches of the popular, artificial, pleasure-loving danrin school of haiku. Bashō fully savored the popular atmosphere of the time. I fancy him accomplishing in ten years what it took popular attitudes a century to do. In a word, his genius was with the people. He could appreciate at a glance and with unfailing taste what it was the people craved. He did not oppose the popular taste. He was led by his sensitivity, not his will. I don't think his nature was rigorously stern. I see him as warm and genial. Let us take a look at his literary creations. Kume said, "I think Bashō's was a literature of will." This baffles me completely without some explanation. Indeed, a world of grayness characteristic of the elegant arts is inherent in his work. But in that gray world, how sensitive he was! "From which tree's bloom it comes, I do not know: This fragrance." "Oh, awesome! The young leaves, the green leaves, sparkling in the sun." "Along the mountain road somehow it tugs at my heart: A wild violet." "Left over in the rains of May, the Golden Hall of Chūsonji." "Quietness—Sinking into the rocks, a cicada's cry." "Against the wintry gust how sharp are the rocks, Amid the cedars!"[7] As I quote a few of his memorable poems, I feel they are all extremely sensitive. I see his writing as enduring for all time. But that sensitivity is not something modern; it is downright elegant. There can be no argument about that. Only one among Bashō's writings, "Rules for a Pilgrimage," can arguably be called a matter of will, as its title demands, but actually it reveals his cultivated taste for "discretion." Beyond that there is nothing in it to trouble about. It can be left out of his collection of artistic writings. Speaking not only of Bashō but of the art of elegance generally, when literature fails to reveal an elegant sensibility but shows simply an intent for elegance, a will for a "stable view of life," that elegance is no more than a vulgar, commonplace thing! I would affirm that to look on elegance as a matter of will is to destroy elegance! Just think. That refinement whose pulse the followers of elegance demand as the highest form of their art they call a "scent" in their kind of technical terminology.

Shūsei said that "Bashō works hard." Obviously. Everyone must work hard. Isn't life itself a kind of hard work? But don't all people who excel find enjoyment in all hard work? People who find their pleasure in no hard work are no more than libertines! People who work hard with no pleasure are no more than slaves! Bashō was no libertine and he was no slave. He was a great poet. A poet works hard for poetry. A human being works hard for life. The greater they are the more their work becomes pleasure.

Other than Kume and Tokuda, Kubota Mantarō explained elegance as "the effort to awaken to the primitive spirit." Kanō Sakujirō said only, "It is the effort to find peace through some sense of reliance." The two were very sparing in their words. It may be explanation enough for them, but for me as someone else, it is vague and hard to grasp, just like Buddhist intuition. I feel somehow that the two of them look on elegance as a product of a religious will.

I hope these writers will forgive me for wasting a lot of words in abrupt rebuttal to the fragments I have quoted. If I have not been able to interpret their opinions correctly, I hope they will be willing to take the time to enlighten me, as I have gone into such detail just because of our unfortunate differences. Actually, to understand "elegance" clearly and correctly is to explain the greater part of the arts of our people, and noting how very important "elegance" is to the clarification of our national character, I believe it is no idle pursuit to consider the question in general and not only for the benefit of these writers. Criticism is surely not just a matter of discussing new works each month, nor is it limited to choosing the same themes we use for imported Western books. . . . It seems that the four people gathered there looked on elegance as something very difficult. If I dare to criticize freely, it appears that these writers have great reverence for something the essence of which they know nothing at all about. For me, elegance is not a popular illusion of men of taste who blindly respect the "elegance" of tradition. . . . Shūsei, for example, went so far as to say it was not the same as a rich man's tea ceremony. Perhaps they were attracted by these sentiments so strongly that they made an impetuous mistake in their determined efforts to find reasons for placing a high value on them. For that or some other reason, they ended up by brazenly ridiculing the very "elegance" that they seem to love so much. This they did unintentionally through the absurd irony of "The theory that elegance is a matter of will." Really, for me, "The theory that elegance is a matter of will" was an amusing and unexpected paradox! Many thanks, friends. You've given me a very appropriate topic for an essay.

Well, let's go along with them and look on the followers of elegance as religious people. Why didn't they make it religion itself, not merely something with religious aspects? Let's look at it as a matter of will. Why didn't they become Stoic philosophers of self-denial? Why didn't they exhibit that much will? If they really took it as a matter of will and religion, there are several other reliable positions they could have resorted to. Why didn't they take their place among the ascetics sitting erect on a rock under a tree with their fingernails piercing the palms of their clasped hands? Why didn't they join with the followers of Saint Francis, who chose "noble poverty" as his bride and coiled a belt of rope around his hips? Or why not appeal to the teachings of the Cynic Diogenes, who lay in a tub asking only for sunlight? We must say that unfortunately they lack the originality for that. Then why didn't they become Buddhist disciples like those around them they resemble? Why did they make a pretext of strong feeling for the arts in a vain pursuit of pleasure? If they are creatures of will, how deficient is their will. How shallow are their efforts. If you say this is what is expected of will, I find no fascination there. From the first I could not resist a feeling of scorn for them as mean-spirited, inconsistent, shallow thinkers. I may despise their artistic achievement as if it were a frivolous, ugly, half-deformed child. . . . I'll despise it without giving it another moment of consideration.

I must think it over again, though. It was not I who saw them as committed to will. I saw them only as out-and-out hedonists committed to the enjoyment of the arts. That's what I said. . . . But they relied on something else. With their sense of a single truth they produced a grandiose new world of artistic intoxication quite apart from that of ascetics, hermits, and monks. This they did with their conspicuous all-or-nothing attitude.

This led them to a strange poetic and aesthetic life, so strange they could reasonably mistake it for religious asceticism or jump to a hasty conclusion that all was a matter of training the will.

All these mysteries are to be found in only one thing: the "that"! And this thing called "that" is mysteriously a "certain something" in which human will cannot exist even in the minutest particle. . . . I do not relish sophistry. I do not play with irony. I am speaking as frankly as I can the truth that I feel. As I recall it now, it was not unreasonable of me to be astonished the moment I heard the phrase "Elegance is a matter of will," because just then "these ideas" were lying in idle confusion in my innermost heart.

Now I must turn to the explanation of what I call "these ideas."

III. THE MAIN THEME

I said earlier that elegance was "the pathos of things," or "the lonely moment," or rather it was the assimilation of those feelings into everyday life. I conclude that the essence is what scholars call "the sense of impermanence." You can't say in a word that "the pathos of things" and "the lonely moment" are the same thing. As the words differ, there is no question that there is some difference in their spirit and their content. I intend to explain later just how they differ. Even as they differ, they are like a couple of twists and turns in the same stream as the water flows back and forth from one bank to the other. That's my conclusion. In stating my conclusion so clearly I may be making an arbitrary decision. . . . It is not that I haven't thought about this at great length. Even if I can't get beyond this point however much I think about it, I have no doubt about my decision. I intend, therefore, to base my theory on this judgment.

After all, isn't any theory based on the judgment of its advocate? When people agree with that judgment, they call it original. I think it rather doubtful that people will call my conclusion an original one. But for me I have nothing else on which to base my inescapable conclusion. For people who agree with me, or at least for people who find no contradiction in my proposition, I will speak a bit about my theory. From those who at the start do not accept the basis of my theory I would be happy to learn what is unreasonable about my conclusion after I have heard their explanation of the theory of elegance that they would substitute for mine, and the basis for that theory. . . . First let me say this in extenuation. . . . Then add another thing. I don't myself know whether my interpretation of elegance is the same as that conceived by the ancients. How can anyone know the "authentic mental state of elegance among the ancients" when we cannot call them from their graves and hear it from their own lips? What we can do, though, is to look into those impressions of elegance living in our own hearts. We can delve to see where we can agree, what we can explain for ourselves, what satisfies us. Therefore, if I find no impressions of elegance within me, my view of elegance will be total nonsense. I have no intention of ever explaining anything to those who are prepared from the start not to understand me. But I do not demand that everyone agree with my ideas. I would just like to have you, my readers, see that it is natural for me to hold my ideas. I should like to have it under-stood, too, that if your ideas differ from mine, it is most natural for me (though not of course for you!) to oppose them. No matter how discor-dant your ideas may be with mine, so long as they are consistent I will have no thought of criticizing even though I may disagree. Everyone should look on things from his own viewpoint; that's all we need. . . . I'm an individualist, don't you see?

I just make the length of my sleeve fit my stature.

I have said that one kind of sensibility, the "sense of imperma-nence," was the basis of elegance. What is this thing called "the sense of impermanence?"

"The sense of impermanence" came in with the introduction of Buddhism. As evidence, literary historians have generally said there was no "sense of impermanence" in the Manyōshū.[8] I don't disagree with this established view. As Buddhism, that religion with the most philosophical background, was being propagated among our people, but before it was adopted as a philosophy, the sensibility to or the senti-ment for "impermanence" took root first. This is an interesting point in considering the ethos of our people. The bent or the ability for specula-tive thinking is actually very weak in our people. It is our national character to look down on those with a propensity for speculation. We call them disputatious. It seems that from olden times we have been a people without thought and without philosophy. That being so, where and from what class of people did the "sense of impermanence" first spring? "With a cherry blossom in our hair, let us enjoy today as well." Living thus, didn't the court nobles, tiring of their play, express their sadness on the edge of joy? It was the court nobles of the Kokinshū[9] who discovered the poetic world of the "pathos of things."

As the "pathos of things" is the sentiment or the sensibility drawn from Buddhism as a pessimistic religion, it is quite natural that ele-gance built on that world has a religious aroma to it. This is not what interests me. It is like people who say there is no problem in knowing that tofu is made from soya beans because tofu has a bean flavor to it. What interests me is that what was simultaneously a religion and a phi-losophy was perceived only as sentiment and sensibility and was later transformed into the artistic sphere of "the pathos of things."

Then what is the true nature of "the sense of impermanence?"

In thinking about humanity, whether as a people or as an individual, humans become aware of the existence of self at an age when one can think about such things, perhaps in one's youth. It doesn't take too many years to reach the age of discretion. A person must notice the existence of "nature," of things quite different from the other human beings who are like oneself. A person will stare in wonder at the contrast between nature and mankind. That very wonderment will change into a feeling for the total contrast between the eternity and infinity of nature and the momentary and minuscule status of man. After sensing the infinitely vast, a person will see the thing nearby as infinitely small in contrast. The self that they had felt was rather large they now see to be infinitesimally small. . . . You may say this is the beginning of wisdom. You may say it is the awakening of the soul. . . .

Friends, don't you remember ever being struck, at some moment when you were low in body and spirit, by a weird feeling? You thought a part of you like a hand or a head had suddenly grown infinitely large and then in a twinkling had shrunk to become small as a pinhead. I've had this feeling again and again. I've interpreted it to myself as follows. . . . There came a moment of wonderment for our ancestors or for ourselves when we were too young to know on our own and we perceived in a flash the grandeur of nature and the smallness of ourselves. Don't we now unconsciously recall when that vague moment was first etched deeply into the bottom of our hearts? Our hand, uncannily so big, that hand uncannily shrinking as if to disappear, wasn't that a symbol of the universe and of man? . . .

This is only a digression. I have no doubt, though, about the depth of our human wonder at discovering the contrast between nature and mankind. It may seem too fanciful, but to say that all human civilization stems from that fact is no mistake. All man's religion, his philosophy, his art derive more directly from wonder at the contrast between man and nature. The grievous reality of the contrast between the infinity of nature and the minuteness of man is the stimulus for mankind. In that flash of self-realization some people have boldly tried to establish something immortal in human striving—a separate human kind of permanence in contrast to the permanence of nature. Some people believed that by devising certain rules mankind could be made as eternal as nature, and they searched for those rules. Other people have felt

that, considering the minute and momentary nature of man's existence, the price is too high for the pain that must be expended for us
humans to get through our fleeting lives. Those people saw nature as
deceiving man in giving us an instinctive tenacity for life. The effort to
prolong our lives they saw as a form of kneeling in reverence to nature,
and instead they were determined to repudiate this life. All the history
of philosophy, the history of religion, is nothing but a catalogue of
these facts. Art had a different means. It undertook to construct an
especially agreeable and beautiful world to enable one to confront eternity within the moment, even if momentarily. Whatever the method,
whatever the direction, these people devoted all their energies to it.
All those who strove with hope for human life, and even those who
were skeptical or negative, have displayed a human will. Rather than
praise human will, some religions and philosophies have denied such
praise. Those who positively repudiated will in their religion or philosophy were as willful as those who praised it. If we call the will of those
who praised will a plus power, we can say that the others worked with a
minus power. As soon as human beings have noticed the minuteness of
man in relation to nature, each person has demonstrated will in trying
to escape his grievous condition. Like a wild animal trapped in a cage
that it cannot break out of. If you call it shameful, it is shameful. But if
you call it heroic, it is heroic in the way that man has fought. . . . I
don't know why we do it. We do it because we have the same desire to
live as does the wild animal. You can even say the will that works with
a minus power is after all a means to savor our feeling for life. It is quite
reasonable that this power should so suddenly be displayed at that
moment when we fully realize how limited is the power of our lives,
just like the wild animal in the cage.

When this spiritual awakening to the contrast between man and
nature occurred among our people, nothing less than the "sense of impermanence" was born. That "sense of impermanence" is no more than
the sensibility, the sentiment arising from recognition of the momentary, minute nature of man and the eternity and infinity of nature. It is
definitely not a philosophic view achieved through hard work. It is the
source from which all mankind has fought the willful, heroic, bitter
struggle. It is the kind of sensibility or sentiment that a people must
acquire without effort while they are still youthful. Among other

peoples, too, a prototype of this sensibility or something much akin to it has induced the anguish of their religions, philosophies, and ways of life. Those same feelings that called forth such anguished screams and actions among other peoples were born among our people but grew, not into religion or philosophy, but immediately became aesthetic and then grew easily into the artistic state of the "pathos of things"—the sphere of that single subtle principle where the instant and the eternal become identical.

I say "easily." Yes, before it became art didn't the reality of anguish linger in the cultural history of our people, whether the anguish came by will or by reason, in the plus direction or the minus direction, in life itself through its grounding in art, through philosophy or through religion? What era shall we see as the spiritual awakening of our people, before the development of the artistic state of the "pathos of things" or after? The culture of the Nara period[10] along with the art of the Manyōshū was a lively, innocent culture of human superiority, unaware in its youthfulness of the awakening of spirit. It did have premonitions of spiritual awakening. That was all. Because that was all, it was all the more precious.

I believe it was the poets who felt the "pathos of things" and caused the true awakening of our spirit. They pioneered the artistic sphere with no feeling for pain. You can call it too easy a miracle. It may have been the influence of Buddhism, but I would like to call it rather more accidental. From my point of view, the poets of the Kokinshū were all in a certain sense decadent. They were exhausted at the limits of their pleasures. They were just plain sentimentalists. But they really harbored a rich talent.

In truth, the strenuous activity of life, even when not a life of misery, often makes us think of death. In that moment when we are so tired that the thought of death is pleasing, however, we cling to the instinct for life so long as we live. We can conceive how, by thinking of death, we can enjoy life. The attachment to life, the joy of life in these circumstances constitute life at its irreducible minimum. "The pathos of things" and "the sense of impermanence" are no more than the joy of life, the attachment to life at its irreducible minimum. At that moment when a person who is exhausted by his activities thinks unconsciously of repose, his will becomes faint like a shadow. The feeling for nature's eternity that comes to such people is expressed in a sad affection, like nostalgia, for the final home that will in time envelop us. But as long as one is alive, one does not wish for death. . . . The instinct to long for death was given never nor in the least to mankind. What was given was the instinct for life. When a feeling like the desire for death occurs, the instinct for life is tired, pained, or crazed. Those who commit suicide have displayed only insanity in respect to the instinct for life, goaded by their dissatisfaction with that life.

The court nobles of the *Kokinshū* did not wish for death out of dissatisfaction with life. Considering their excessive exhaustion from the pleasures of life, their desire for quiet must have been a search to renew the pleasures of life. Once they noticed the eternity of nature and the momentary nature of themselves, they must have looked at themselves with undreamed of terror. Those people, tired in their contentment, their life's power faded like a shadow, could display no vigor in their terror. Nor did they. As soon as they thought of eternity and infinity, they felt a kind of grief at the total impossibility of their happiness continuing forever. In their faded vitality their grief was fleeting. The grief never deepened. The Buddhist conclusion, and nothing more than the conclusion, may have helped them then. But I wonder if what saved them was not their very rich poetic talent rather than their religion. In their fleeting but deeply rooted grief, they first discovered a new world of poetry. In their joy at discovering this new poetic world, and enraptured by their art, these poets easily resolved the sad wonder they had discovered in the contrast between man and nature. That is why I want to use the words "the feeling for the evanescence of beauty" for "the sense of impermanence." The joy of sadness. The joy of weariness with life. The poetic sentiment of "the pathos of things" is with no further explanation a kind of decadence.

Yet why does this poetic feeling for decadence forever touch our hearts? No doubt we have long been brought up with that sentiment. Why did it become the poetic interest of our people and not lose its fascination over so long a time? . . . Don't we sometimes sense it vibrantly alive in our hearts even now? This is worth considering. I find rather good reasons for it. First of all, the poetic sentiment of "the pathos of things" is rooted in an important and long-lasting new human condition that we can call the awakening of man's soul. We can say it grows almost directly out of that condition. Second, in discovering this universal and perpetual human problem it offered at the same time a solution to that condition. It is no exaggeration to say that the solution was reached simultaneously with the discovery of the problem. . . . At times we find ourselves fully satisfied with this solution. What kind of solution does "the pathos of things" offer, after all?

We know how different peoples in their confrontation with nature, sometimes even wishing to conquer nature, have boldly and decisively devised diverse ways, only to find in the end that their anguish was heightened. The novel solution our ancestors chanced on as they faced the problem was, I think, undreamed of by other peoples, especially the Europeans. . . . Nothing less than that. Our ancestors happened (really by chance!) to feel themselves a part of nature. They did not feel themselves to be humans confronting nature. They felt themselves humans embraced by nature. They recognized man straight out as the child of nature. That's all there was to it. "What a big deal!" You mustn't laugh. When we think about it in comparison to the way in which other peoples have struggled like the wild animal caught in a cage, of course it makes us laugh. As innocent as child's play, like Columbus' egg,[11] it was a solution improvised, intuitive, and yet undeniably appropriate.

But. (This "but" is so important it should be printed in red ink.) What we must not forget in feeling ourselves to be part of nature is that, as we have greatly relieved the anguish in the confrontation between man and nature, we have in so doing depreciated our human will to its irreducible minimum!

Some kind of internal discord is surely needed to limit a burning will to its lowest level. One must display a will that works in the minus direction. Buddhism needed a comprehensive philosophy in order to limit the self to its minimum. To give up will is an act of the human will. If human will were not fired up from the start and were already at the minimum level, there should be no need to exert additional will. Our ancestors—at least the poets of "the pathos of things"—did not resolve the problem through exerting a minus will, a will to abandon will. It seems to me, instead, that they accidentally achieved a solution at the moment when the power of life faded on its own—we might better call it the moment when will dropped away, not when will was abandoned. I can see no sign of any effort to achieve that solution. Rather, I see proof to the contrary. As their poetic feeling was acquired in this way, their poetry was realized only in the briefest poetic form, like no other on earth. Dr. von Koeber[12] was very perceptive when he expressed the opinion that the poetry of our people was nothing more than theme or title for what is contained in Western poetry. Actually, our people never left the starting point from which other peoples went on to construct a philosophy, or religion, or art. They made a world with no room to develop anything beyond theme and title itself.

The dropping away of human will—that is, the dimming of our life-force of itself to its irreducible minimum—is not a condition that a living person can keep going for very long. This alone is why the poetry of our people is sufficient in its shortness. It is why, in the long form of poetry that existed from the Manyōshū era, shadows disappeared completely as soon as "the pathos of things" had become the poetic feeling of our people. Because the moment of exclamation in wonder followed immediately after the momentary sensation, it was impossible for the poetic feeling of "the pathos of things" to flourish in long poetic forms. (Try comparing this with the long novels of the West!) As a sign of further development of the poetic feeling for "the pathos of things," even half the poetic length was enough by the time of Bashō's poetry. . . . The more our people's artistic style progressed, the simpler it became—isn't that strange? When we think about it fully, however, that strange phenomenon strikes us as entirely appropriate. The stark secret of literature close to silence, art close to nothingness, is not at all mysterious if we understand that the "sense of impermanence" which forms its base lies in human activity at its irreducible minimum, in the sensibility of an instant existing on the border between being and nonbeing.

The poetic feeling of "the pathos of things" needed 31 syllables. That was to make room not only for the momentary sensation but also for the emotion or even the sentimentality that followed from the momentary sensation. In the art of Bashō, however, the sentimental exclamation of wonder at the "sense of impermanence" has gone. The only thing flung out point-blank is the sensation of the moment when the self has shrunk to its irreducible minimum. All there is is nature, the sound of the wind, the murmur of the water, the crying of birds, or the blooming of flowers. As the wind made the branches sound, nature itself made man shout. It was so direct that it was symbolic. It was a great leap forward in the literature of elegance. Because "the pathos of things" was an exclamation of wonder, it was subjective. Because it was subjective, its poetic world spoke more of man than of nature. When the poetic world abandoned the exclamation of wonder—no, when it became so instantaneous that it failed to make time for the exclamation, it took the next step. It captured the moment when the subjective world and the objective world—that is, man himself and nature— were exquisitely united, thus depicting precisely one aspect of man at a time when he is embraced within nature. Revealed there is not man living as man, but man existing at one with the universe.

Human will at its irreducible minimum was concealed deeply in "the pathos of things." That is because the exclamation of wonder could neither synchronize nor coincide with nature. In other words, it was a manifestation of an attachment to life at its irreducible minimum. Because it was the lowest level, it created no contradiction in the mother-and-child relationship of nature and man that they had sensed. It was, however, one step removed from the aspect of man wholly embraced by nature. Not the relationship of a baby at its mother's breast, it is like that of a fussy child with its mother. The solution was shallow because of their subjectivity—a solution reached expressly by intuition (not by demonstration), by sensibility (not by will), by improvisation (not by asceticism), by sensing (not by spiritual enlightenment).

One more step, just one. With this subjectivity in the exclamation of wonder, with this elimination of will, will itself in its true sense had dropped away. The man who achieved this was Matsuo Bashō. Actually, in Bashō's poetic world, nature and man have readily melted into each other. That is because human will—or rather human existence itself—was expressed at its irreducible minimum. In this world of elegance, leaving aside the fine arts for the moment, there was no one who could approach Bashō in the literature of elegance, that is, in the poetry of utter impromptu sensibility. Consider Yosa Buson, for example.[13]

Buson was to the end a man of elegance. But, regrettably, compared to Bashō his elegance had something about it of "elegance for the sake of elegance." Too much so. What do I mean by "elegance for the sake of elegance?" Elegance in Buson was no longer the direct child of nature. Buson built a separate world of elegance. The art of Buson lay in that separate world of elegance he built. I see that art not as the child but as the grandchild of nature. His poetry has an excess of elegant retrospection, of elegant fancy, of elegant exclamation, of elegant emphasis.

> *Seventh day of flowers*
> *Even eating nothing*
> *The painters meet.*

Reciting that, one feels too much elegant will in Buson, beyond the instant sensibility. Buson was a master. So we can say his views on elegance were not mistaken, but even with his correct understanding we feel he presents the thing that is elegant as counter to nature. That may be an exaggeration, but at least one does feel he is posing a world of elegance quite outside the world of nature. Risky, isn't it? If Buson had missed by a step, he would have degenerated finally into the elegance of a vulgar man's elegant wild fox,[14] the tea ceremony of a rich man! The only thing that saved Buson was that he pursued a life of elegance with sensibility just elegant enough to match his elegant intentions. But for those who have elegant intentions without elegant sensibility! Frightful even to think about in the cause of elegance. Actually, so-called commonplace elegance is a doctrine of intentionally created elegance. Such elegance is destroyed by its triteness. . . . The opinion of the *Shinchō* writers that elegance is a matter of will is, I hope, not the same as that kind of vulgar elegance. True elegance, what I consider elegance, has an aversion to human will, to intentional elegance.

What do I consider true elegance? I can assert it now without the least hesitation. For the spirit of elegance the less human will there is, the better. Will should be at its lowest level possible, its irreducible minimum. In the language sense, it is the ancient rather than the present, the poet or poetry rather than the novelist or the novel, solitude rather than company, telepathic understanding rather than eloquent discussion. All the former make us think of elegance more than do the latter. That is precisely because less human will is required by the former than by the latter. If you were to show to some artists of elegance a modern novel with all its meaning constructed from the complications in the entanglement of human wills, and you explained that this was a great work of art, they might fall over in an instant swoon. Balzac and Bashō are at the two poles of literature.

For its main form in literature the art of elegance chooses impromptu poetry, closest to silence. For its main technique in art it chooses monochrome painting, closest to emptiness. That is surely no accident. It is not total silence, not total emptiness. In the end something must be expressed. . . . Why does it remain art? While very closely resembling some pessimistic religions and some negativistic philosophies, why is elegance essentially an art and not something else? This fact demands fullest consideration but is easily explained. Although elegance resembles those pessimistic religions and negativistic philosophies, there is a very great difference in the most important point. Elegance has not basically denied or rejected our existence. It feels for life at its irreducible minimum. But in no way have the followers of elegance denied life. Rather they enjoyed life, though at its irreducible minimum. To put it another way, as people who were embraced within nature, they felt acutely that life was worth living. . . . That's why I call it the pure white passion. They may have had a special distaste for human society that was built on human will, but they had no dislike for man himself. In the minimum world of human beings perceived as something minimum, they took pleasure in the presence of man. So long as it was a matter of human beings stimulated by nature—by a world that was not empty, that was close to silence but not silence itself—they spoke out happily, whether it had meaning or no meaning for the common man, whether the voice came in joy or anger, smiles or wails. So long as it was a matter of human beings stimulated by nature, they gazed happily, whether at the beauty or the ugliness of the commonplace, at whatever shapes of trees and grasses, fish and insects, clouds and smoke, streams and mountains. They communicated with joy the voices they uttered, the things they watched. The works they left behind were their objects of proof. . . . Who would have done as much without the joy of life?

Their joy was lit not by man's will. Joy's radiance originated in the reflection of nature. That's why I call it the rapture of moonlight.

They valued their feelings for beauty, truth, and goodness when those feelings were free from the rules made by human will. They enjoyed themselves for their freedom from the rules of human will and their liberation through the absorption into nature. As they loved nature, so they loved those works written with a sense of pleasure by others of like persuasion. They hailed a refinement free of overbearing will. To perceive it, a nose was seen to be needed, so they called that refinement a "scent." There is a phrase "the mind's eye." I think it would be good to coin the phrase "the mind's nose." Both the people who coined the phrase "the mind's eye" and those who used the word "scent" must, I believe, have been aware that the soul can achieve sensibility and sensibility can reach the soul. Those were the ancients.

The serenity the followers of elegance ceaselessly pursued also denoted the time when they were liberated from the various commitments of human will that they saw as trivial, the time when man and nature were thus merged. How they disliked the overbearing quality of will! They did not necessarily dislike rich brocades. Nor did they necessarily hate magnificent buildings. They must have thought of these more as tedious. Not pleasure but grief is what they must have felt at the anguish that naturally accompanies the pleasure in these things. They lived with ease under low ceilings. Will was at its irreducible minimum in every way. Basically pleasure-lovers, they disliked a total absence of people. They needed the arts, even in their plainest form. To drink other than springwater they had man's bitter tea. For talk beyond the beauties of nature they might seek friends of like form and like heart to themselves. Besides "a cup of wine, two or three good books, and a congenial friend" didn't they hold in their eyes and in their hearts "nature in its infinity?" What fruitful richness! But my colleagues who want to indulge in many worldly luxuries, are they satisfied to cut back and make do with what they have? Do they call that an act of will? Let me open the window for people who say so to show them the brightly shining winter moon, and they will shiver and say: "Master, isn't elegance a trick contrived by a doctor or a priest to make a person catch a cold? . . . They'll get the patent rights for that"—(a joke).

The followers of elegance—the followers of true elegance—did they think of their lives as something extraordinary? If so, they would by virtue of their human will have had to fall into the worldliness they hated. I believe they remained firm in their inclinations. Just as at times the life-forces dim and we think of elegance as a good thing, so indeed can man have an inborn disposition for elegance through the highest enjoyment of the minimum level of pleasure for the self at its own irreducible minimum. Elegance exists only for people like that. For example, if someone uses logic to construct the philosophy for a faith, he will not attain that faith if he lacks an active spirit in his beliefs. Likewise, if someone wills the minimum self, that person cannot know elegance unless he has the poetic sensibility of a man of elegance.

This is what I say. Elegance—at least the elegance perfected by Bashō and others—in essence is the extreme intensification of sensibility. No matter how religious or philosophical it may be, it is thoroughly artistic. It is not achieved through religious will, nor through philosophical intellect. It comes from the same original womb that could conceive religion or philosophy. Thus, when our people chanced to develop this grand, new, limitless concept, it turned out naturally to be very religious and philosophical. That is obvious. When a man subjects himself entirely to nature and exerts no human will, plus or minus, he naturally dons a pantheistic philosophy and becomes a brother to all the other beauties of nature. However, those followers of elegance who were not in the least philosophical could not find themselves in the principles of pantheistic philosophy. They could merely express their feelings as a "companion of the beauties of nature"—an expression that surprised that most elegant Western literary man, Lafcadio Hearn. Because they were not clearly aware that they had achieved brotherhood—at least in the poetic realm—with all the things of nature, they could never have asserted emphatically their delight in the romantic mystery of "Here I have arrived so soon at enlightenment," a realization that would have come easily if they had been aware of their brotherhood in nature. Likewise, they could not have asserted the immortal religious pleasure of achieving eternity through merging the smallest shrunken extremity into the greatest infinity of nature, which they could otherwise have enjoyed. If they spoke in religious terms, it came out Buddhist. If they spoke by chance in philosophical terms, it came out Taoist. They did not seem to perceive any divergence from their own thinking. . . . As I said before, they did not at all deny life. They were not believers that "To do great things is to do nothing." They just enjoyed life at the irreducible minimum. What tantalizes is that they always lived life at its minimum level. After all, we are the beloved children of nature. However self-indulgently they might have exerted their will, they would have remained the beloved children of nature. . . . If they had made that leap, there would have been no elegance now. . . .

What did the followers of elegance do to achieve their ends? We can't ask the ancients. The reasons that followers of elegance have gained eternal life—eternal insofar as man has moments when he is tired of life and has a disposition for grief in human society—lie in that profound sensibility uniting mind and body. They spent a lifetime to achieve so much. It was surely a faith they clung to without regret. But it was also willful. It took effort. If you say they were therefore people of will, that is no sound argument, just as it is not correct to say that if a famous painting is purchased with money, the painting's true essence is money.

Still, what did Bashō, the most important person to achieve this rare art, have to say about his own lot in life? As an experiment, let me quote the following and trust my readers to savor it.

> All this, however, does not mean that I am an avid lover of solitude who wishes to hide in the mountains once and for all. I am more like a sickly person who has retired from society after becoming a little weary of mixing with people. As I look back over the many years of my frivolous life, I remember at one time I coveted an official post with a tenure of land and at another time I was anxious to confine myself within the walls of a monastery. Yet I kept aimlessly wandering on. . . . with no other talent or ability to resort to, I merely clung to that thin line. . . . (From the prose poem *An Essay on the Unreal Dwelling*.)[15]

Author's postscript: For this uncompleted manuscript I think it would be good to add some remarks on things like "Elegance and National Character," "Elegance and the Decadent Arts," "On the Civilizations of East and West," "The Elegance of China, the Elegance of the West," "Why from My View of Life Is Elegance of No Value?" I have not had the time, however, and I have expressed my feelings on the general topic from time to time already. Because I have written hastily on this topic, I may have been too verbose and repetitive while lacking in emphasis. I have explained as much as I could about the things that interested me, and I have condensed the four additional topics for now. When I have a chance, I may say more later.

Notes

1. *Fūryū* may be translated as "elegance," "refinement," or "taste," including the aesthetic appreciation for fine ornamentation and for classical style. I use "elegance" and "taste of elegance" interchangeably for *Fūryū*.
2. Tanizaki Jun'ichirō (1886–1965) was a more famous and successful writer who encouraged Satō at first. They were very close friends until Satō fell in love with and later married Tanizaki's wife.
3. *Fusain:* the French word for charcoal pencil.
4. Nanga was the "literati" school of Japanese ink-brush painting, developed especially in the eighteenth century.
5. *Mono no aware:* a key Japanese aesthetic term for sensitivity to the pathos of life, the sad beauty of impermanence.
6. *"Aré,"* the pronoun meaning "that," is also used as an expression of surprise—"Hey!"
7. These translations of haiku of Bashō are by Makoto Ueda except for the second and fourth, which are my translations.
8. *Manyōshū* is the oldest collection of Japanese poetry, compiled in the mid-eighth century but including earlier poems.
9. *Kokinshū* is a collection of court poetry compiled around A.D. 905.
10. The Nara period: A.D. 646–794.
11. A figure of speech meaning "The difficulty is in the daring." According to legend, when Columbus was told "Anyone can discover a continent," he replied, "Try standing an egg on its end." The questioner tried and could not. Columbus then stood his egg on end by cracking its base, and said, "Anyone can do it but the difficulty is in the daring."
12. Raphael von Koeber, 1846–1923, was a German philosopher who taught at Tokyo University and called himself a transcendental pantheist.
13. Yosa Buson, a leading haiku poet, 1716–1783.
14. The "elegant wild fox," as portrayed in the theater of *kyōgen* and *kabuki.*
15. Translation by Makoto Ueda, in his book "Matsuo Bashō" (Tokyo: Kodansha International, 1982), p. 120.

The Joy of the Artist and Other Critical Selections[1]

The Joy of the Artist

Geijutusuka No Yorokobi, 1920

What is the joy of the artist?

To begin with, the joy of the artist is not the making of good art. Nor the glorification of the art he creates. It lies not in being understood by the critic or in being read with pleasure by the reader. All these are less than secondary for the true artist. What, then, is the joy of the true artist?

It lies just in the true satisfaction of the artist himself. No, it is rather in the joy of creation. In the moment of creation the artist can enjoy the joy of the gods. He sees a sudden birth rising out of chaos. The deeper the chaos, the greater the birth he sees. Art is no more or less than the pursuit of that condition. The joy of the artist is no more than that. As art is its own objective, the joy of creation is simply to create. In all the highest of human activities, there is no other aim but that. To think there is a further aim for the highest of human activities would be like thinking there is another divinity above divinity. Everything with any aim but this itself is but secondary in significance.

That is what I believe.

So I pray only that I may taste deeply of those moments of creation.

Artists with other thoughts than these (and to my shame I some-times find myself with such ideas) I would consider to be inferior artists. Not artists at all, I think. When I work thinking of the critic, when I work thinking of my craftsmanship, when I work with thoughts of my readers, when I work thinking of my editor and his deadline, when I work thinking of fame, when I work to establish some princi-ples, when I work thinking of my own skill, when I work thinking of any other aim or result, I feel I have lost the joy of creation. I feel I have lost that highest joy that I myself am with the gods. When the artist works under any restraints whatsoever, he is no longer a creative person. If you ask why, there is something over him, something placing restraints on him. The restraining person above is the creative one. The artist must feel he is working under that restrainer, who is the creative one. The artist, then, is not the creative one; he is like the artisan working on commission with no choice of his own.

Whatever aims and restraints he may have started from, the great artist is, I think, liberated from all those aims and restraints through his work. In his unrestricted and utmost efforts he is sure to become absorbed solely in the joy of creation. When he has tasted that joy of creation to the fullest, his good work of art remains to commemorate that joy.

What about you?

For me, as of now, that has too often failed to be the case.

Don't be ashamed for nothing. Just hope.

Creativity

Creativity is a divinity revealed in humans. It is the first child of the highest ability and the highest will. There anguish is joy, toil is play. There are days of internal struggle and days of festivity. . . . How sad it is. I have only the haziest dreams of that state. I can speak of it only in the haziest way. I am shamed that I can speak only as it were a whit-ened graveyard.

Play and Hard Work

Does the word "play" mean joyful play? Do the words "hard work" mean agonizing work? Then who said play is ignoble and hard work noble? The slave dreams that when he plays, the master will whip him; when he suffers, the master will praise him. If the master doesn't, then it's a paradox the master has taught the slave he oppresses. The person who is free to love his independence will choose what pleases him for his lifework. . . . Haven't all artists chosen the arts because they despise the conventional occupations?

Let's make hard work as enjoyable as play.

Let's make hardship into the greatest pleasure. Let hard work be the highest joy. Only the true artist knows that state, knows the alchemy of life.

Through play find the greatest rigor.

Through hard work find the greatest joy.

Even thus is life worth living.

The Social Significance of the Artist

As conventional people shouldn't we realize that there is another value to life beyond the conventional values? That can be achieved if the artist will persevere to the utmost in his stand as an artist. Can't we stop completely from doing those things we do not wish to do? Can't we as artists make our currency something other than wealth and fame? Can't we therefore endure poverty bravely at times? Can't we build that kind of society upon our existing society? Can't we drive out, so far as possible, all conventional values from the world of our art? Can't we thus defy conventionality? Only in this way can we create a social significance for the artist. If the artist participates directly in social movements or takes social problems for his topics, yet lacks this attitude and spirit, his work will be naught but a trifle.

Art as a Vocation

I curse the making of art into a vocation. . . . Now, in these times when *the spirit of the true artist* is most needed, how can we afford to let it vanish?

I'd like to see all of man's occupations converted into the arts. All those occupations without meaning derived from the self I'd like to see abandoned by humans. In this sense, I'd like to see all mankind made into *true artists*. I'd like to see all human life made into art. Then would man be close to the gods.

There will be no utopia until every occupation has become an art.

Solitude

The gods gave man solitude. Yet at the same time they gave man a disposition that cannot exist in solitude. . . . What a thing for the human race. Maybe therein lies the origin of the arts, of religion, of philosophy. . . . At least I feel that way.

Crowds are hell. . . . They knock the breath out of people of stature. A person cannot be independent in a crowd. A person not stifled in a crowd must be a slave. A person stifled in a crowd must head for solitude. Solitude is nothing less than purgatory.

In solitude, let us look deeply at the self. The only way to cure solitude is to submerge the self in solitude. When we pierce the depths of solitude, *something* is surely there. To my distress I do not yet see what that *something* is. But the fact that I feel it dimly, that there is a something there in the solitude, lends a faint glory to that solitude. Glow—let that glory shine out. Then that shining solitude is no longer solitude.

In solitude may we expand our self to its greatest. Let us comprehend at the same time that the greatest self is something very small. Then we may know the self that is a tiny phenomenon in limitless space. With this as our scope we may then reflect that the minuteness is itself limitless. Let my solitude be deeper. Let me thus understand these things more clearly.

The Zen Sect of the Arts

"Where there is content, the manner of expression matters not."

This is surely true. As for all truths, the truth depends on who is speaking. But if we stop halfway, these are dangerous words. Or maybe meaningless words. Rather we should say it this way:

"Where there is content, it matters not even when not expressed."

When I say that, I know I am a long way from those so-called arts that place infinite faith in the power of expression. I know, though, that there is another sphere for art. That sphere is comprehended in the spirit of the Eastern arts. Its scope for the arts is scope too for religion.

We might call that spirit of the arts a Zen Sect of the Arts. Thus anyone who says, without this implication in the background, "Where there is content, the manner of expression matters not"—that person may be talking catechisms made of jelly with neither expression nor content, a kind of laughable Wild Fox Zen.

An Admonition to Myself about Expression

When you think that expression is the only thing that counts, you artists, just because you do think that way, you not only must have a love for expression, but you must fear it like the gods. Because expression is everything, everything can be seen through expression. In truth, if you are to speak *words of kindness*, they must come from the heart with kindness, at least while you speak them. . . . If they do not, then *words of kindness* that would deceive a stupid person will sound like doubtful *words of kindness* in the ears of those who hear with intelligence. Even if the words can deceive the sharp of hearing, they will likely sound doubtful in your own ears. The words will be an expression that is not really *kind*. Try not to deceive others through your expression. Take your joy in not misrepresenting yourself in your expression. Love your expression. Love it to the fullest. To love your expression without fear is the love of the playboy for the prostitute. The artist's love for the expression that must be his god must be his deepest love, a love that makes him fall prostrate in awe. The artist who flaunts his expression is of the gang of Pharisees and Sadducees of the arts who flaunt their god.

. . . You artists. Love your expression in this manner. Then the question of expression and content will disappear of itself.

The Critic within Me

That which should be respected in the arts is true feeling. Reality, that is. Lacking that, the arts cannot be a living thing, cannot be compelling to man.

When there is true feeling and reality, there is still doubt whether it must necessarily touch all people.

If you show a barbarian a sculpture in marble, and even if it is a masterpiece, I am told that, far from knowing whether it is good or bad, the barbarian will not be able to distinguish whether it is a human face or something else. Not only that—the barbarian will not even recognize that an image is carved there. The whole sculpture will appear to him as no more than a flat white lump. This is no fable. It is fact. Yet this fact may be an allegory for the many critics we have around us these days.

Rather than stand on my own little dignity, I have more regard for my strong desire for growth. I take pleasure therefore in listening to the critics, but I do not want a barbarian for my critic. The critics of a published work, whether or not they understand or speak in good faith, are free to speak out whatever they wish to say. If they have not fully staked their conscience and wisdom on their judgment, the only way to prevent their speaking is through their own reconsideration. There is no other way. Nor is there need for one. Indeed, it is not impossible sometimes to get an accidental hint from a critic who is totally without understanding or good faith. In that case, rather than rushing to combat the critic who was the source of the words, the artist who is confident and seeks to strengthen himself will be grateful for the hint he has been given, the hint that adds interpretation to his highest meaning. That is surely a valuable way to cultivate one's art. The value of a work may be decided only by criticism based on understanding and good faith, but the value of a work is never harmed by criticism that lacks understanding and good faith. How can that destroy the joy of its creation? The only thing lost or damaged is the work's commercial value. Its empty popularity. It is better if the work lacks just that. For the true artist that is relief; it is freedom from care, freedom itself.

At the same time, just once (!) and soon (!) I would like to have a work that the artist in me can assert to the critic within me, no matter what anyone else may say: "I carved that from my own blood and flesh and bone and spirit. It is full of my true feelings." When the critic within me will allow, I shall be able to believe in myself and in the future of the work. What is to be feared and to be grateful for at the same time is the critic within me: my artistic conscience. He understands and sympathizes to the full, but does not let me off so easily.

The Art, That Is the Person

Geijutsu Sunawachi Ningen, 1919

It is often said "The person, that is the art." That's common sense. "The person is necessary; the poet is not." I wrote that seven or eight years ago. As I think it over, that was a curious thing I said so blithely. In those words I may have had some vague intention of saying, "The poet works with no true effort," but there was no meaning at all to the words themselves. Even if true, the words overstate the meaning. I think part of my reason for thinking and saying as much was the result of swallowing whole the words "The person, that is the art," and understanding them superficially in the popular sense.

The thought "The person, that is the art" is of course true. "Where there is no good person, there is no good art." "Where there is no person of depth, there is no art of depth." (I could substitute any other adjectives for "good" and "deep.") There is clearly no doubt about that. My conclusion—however I work it over, in the end comes out there. My present thinking, though, takes a wandering course, a little different from the ordinary (as seen by others), before it comes out there.

Now as I consider further the relation between the person and the art—the artist and his work—I have to conclude that "The art, that is the person" is truer for the artist than the words "The person, that is the art" that I had too quickly accepted. I am deliberately substituting B = A for A = B. Just as the expression is completely reversed, so the resulting thought is reversed.

Why am I deliberately doing such a troublesome thing?

Tentatively, let's see first if we can elucidate candidly and literally the words "Where there is no good character, there is no good art." Has there never been a case where a person who fails to evidence virtuous conduct (in its broadest meaning) in his real life, or a person rather who exhibits somewhat contrary behavior, has shown us something appealing, something moral (in its broadest meaning) in the artwork he has created? If there have been such cases, were they always transparent deception?

Tao Yuan-ming,[2] who wrote "Returning Home," was not really a very upright character. In his conduct he was a mean-spirited petty official. Some people say so. If so, haven't we for a long time been completely deceived by his apparently lofty writing?

Brandes[3] argued like this in the second volume of his "Main Currents of Nineteenth Century Literature."

> In his youth Clemens Brentano was a mischievous romantic. This inconstant rascal would through his own faults lose the friends he had made. He could not control the actions that would destroy the moods he could so skillfully evoke. We find in him an ability rarely seen in other romantics, a refinement linked to his fervor. *As with many writers, he was as a writer rather more serious and sincere than he was in his life. Though he was thus flawed as a person, as an artist he often gave an impression of purity.*

The italicization in the text is my addition—to draw peoples' attention to it.

In the case of Tao Yuan-ming, in the case of Clemens Brentano, was the impression they gave through their conduct the true one? Was the impression given by their art the true one?

I for one think that both are probably true. Especially the impression given by their art is the more true, I believe. Why is that?

Between people, can one person receive without prejudice what another is expressing? That is doubtful. Can a person reveal his true self before another?

Here is a man cheerful in the presence of another. How melancholy he may be when he is alone is unknown to the person who comes into his presence. . . . His nature is to stop being melancholy when he sees another face. Here is a man. He's very weak. Meeting another person, he is swept into that person's atmosphere before he knows it, quite losing his own peculiar humor. Others cannot discern his true and natural form. . . . (It would take a novel to portray his likeness.) These and other similar characteristics are often found in people. Artists have complex personalities that may differ in type and degree from these human characteristics, but they do share peculiarities in common. Complex enough for the artist alone, the combination of peculiarities becomes more complex when the artist meets people in the outside world. Sometimes he cannot control himself.

When the artist is engrossed in himself, it is normal for him to encounter obstacles that make it impossible for him to work to the full. At this point his true self emerges, and drawing on everything within him, he begins a complex and miraculous activity. In the case of poets and writers, who are artists of words, the workings of the mind flash into the head in the form of words. From these the artist adopts the *letters and words* that he thinks most suitable and best for him, that are in effect *his own spirit*. He creates a self for himself, the self he believes is the best self. He provokes a revolutionary upheaval within himself and rules over it by his highest self. He throws all of himself into a crucible. From what of the self is burned and melted in that crucible he picks out only the precious metal part of the self. This operation of the spirit is called the artistic drive. The person who can thus reveal the highest self is called the artist. He is said to have artistic genius.

A person's spirit has no form. It is not a fixed thing that people may grasp in their thoughts. It keeps on flowing. In moments it may go through innumerable changes. At times it may be the residence of the gods, at times the residence of devils, at times the residence of beasts, at times the residence of angels, at times the residence of humans— that is, gods without divinity, devils without magical powers, beasts without bestiality, angels who do not proclaim the gospel—at times the residence of all jumbled disorder. Often it is gold; again it is lead. Often it is silver; again it is clay. There are some strange minerals that we cannot guess what they might be.

The good artist sees his own spirit in the jumbled disorder of flood tide. Absorbed therein, he grasps what he intuits, recognizes, and believes to be his true self. In seizing it tightly he attains his true being.

As he acknowledges those various selves, he shows to the world his highest self. What he shows through his art is his ultimate self. . . . That is how the man of character reveals himself to the world as a self of coherent character.

Thus it is possible for the artist, who may normally seem a worthless person, to integrate his joys, his sorrows, his anger, his love, all his thoughts and feelings into his highest sentiments and exhibit them in his art. He becomes a polished mirror. He does not portray himself falsely by displaying lead as gold plate. He has merely picked out those mysterious minerals that are beyond comprehension, that are the very self made from the precious metal of the moment.

When the artist has found himself amid the highest activity of all his faculties in full integration, he calls that "the eternal, immortal me." He calls it the "absolute me." The words "eternal," "immortal," "absolute" are a kind of allegory. They are symbols. They are verses that sing of his supreme joy in the moment. He is drunk with his self-awareness. He is not in a stupor like the drunkenness of wine and opium. He is intoxicated by his complete awakening. Precisely here is the world of artistic absorption, of ecstasy.

The artist can reveal his true self fully only in the arts—only through the technique of searching for the self in his own deepest recesses. That may be the easiest and the perfect way. In the true artist, therefore, the arts are supreme beyond question. Feeling that keenly, he consecrates himself to the arts. If you cannot understand these words, quit being an artist! Find another way to reveal your highest self. Because you are not an artist. Because it is immoral to put your confidence in, to be faithful to something that you do not believe is supreme.

Where there is no good person, there is no good art.

Where there is good art, there is a good person.

Even where there is a good person, if he is not a good artist there is no good art. In that case, maybe there is no need for good art. (?)

Anyhow, where there is good art, there must always be a good person.

To be a person is necessary. To be a poet may not be necessary. (?) But the poet can become a good person only through his efforts to be a true poet, a better poet.

For the artist the act of production does not lie in making a record of his life. In fact it lies in that life itself. A good work of art of itself directly reflects the good artist's life.

The Ascetic and the Frog

Kugyōsha to Kawazu, 1919

Once upon a time there was a man. He sat on a rock in the mouth of a cave. How long he had been there, how long he sat so fixedly, I do not know. . . . There he was, anyhow.

One day a frog appeared before him. The frog did not at first notice the man sitting in front of him. The man was sitting so quietly. When the frog learned that a man was sitting before him, the frog was surprised.

"Who's that sitting there like a rock?" the frog asked, looking up at the man.

"Me? I'm an ascetic."

Thus answered the man. The frog did not fully understand the word "ascetic." The frog asked again.

"An ascetic? You're sitting there fixed like that; what on earth are you doing?"

The ascetic replied again.

"I sit here motionless. I fix mine eyes on the star that makes my world happy. I set my heart on the core of my very own earth. With undivided attention I thus control the movements of the earth and of the heavenly bodies of my universe. . . ."

"Don't speak in riddles." The frog interrupted the ascetic's words. "Please speak in a way that an ignorant frog can understand. In short, why are you doing that?"

"To put it in one word," the ascetic answered, "I seek immortality. I wish to make eternity coincide with the moment."

Hearing that, the frog leapt for joy.

"Oh! This man is the teacher I have been seeking. The gentleman I have heard spoken of. Teacher, please take me as your disciple."

Then, in his peculiar eloquence, the frog explained his circumstances and his reasons for wanting to become the ascetic's disciple. This frog, it seems, had been a frog in an old swamp in Aesop's Fables. In the old swamp that was his home there had been a terrible upheaval. The frogs in that old swamp had asked the gods for a splendid, strong king, not one of themselves, to rule over all the frogs. The gods first gave them a log to be their king, but when the frogs again asked for a stronger, more splendid, more able ruler, the gods then granted them a frightful crocodile as king of the old swamp. As soon as the crocodile was invested with this authority, he began to eat up all the frogs he could reach. So then some of the frogs cursed the gods, and some others planned a revolt against the new king. Many of the frogs' fathers and mothers and wives and children were eaten by the crocodile.

"Thus," said the frog to the ascetic, "I witnessed many deaths. I saw the wretched struggle of many of my kind scrambling to escape from the crocodile's mouth. So I came to understand that the world is a sad place. One night I escaped from that swamp. Turning upstream, I traveled far and long. Along the way I heard news of Teacher, and I decided somehow to become Teacher's disciple. Teacher, please take me as your disciple."

"Anyhow, stay here with me."

Thus replied the ascetic to the frog. Thus did the frog become disciple to the ascetic. The frog squatted down and placed both hands flat on the ground before the teacher. They squatted facing each other. They were silent. The light of the sun and the light of the moon shone down upon them in succession. At times they were completely enveloped in darkness. Owls came then and hooted at them from the tops of nearby trees. The frog trembled in fear. The frog endured and kept his silence. Around and about the frog bloomed beautiful mossy flowers. The flowers scattered, bloomed again, and again they scattered. The green moss spread around the frog's body. It crept up from the feet he sat upon. At length moss grew over the frog's body. The frog became green from the moss, like a tree frog. But he held his patience and sat unmoving. Then one morning it happened.

"Teacher!" the frog called out. "Teacher, I'm fed up with being Teacher's disciple."

Then spoke the ascetic.

"And why is that?"

The frog replied.

"I want to return to my homeland. I'm homesick for the old swamp. I would like to know how my fellow frogs are doing. I miss my dear friends; I'm anxious about them. I'm ashamed that I deserted my fellows in that awful turmoil and escaped here by myself, I have come to realize that here I am doing nothing to help my fellows."

The ascetic spoke.

"You are not your friends. You are yourself."

"If so, Teacher," the frog asked again, "what am I doing for myself, then?"

The ascetic spoke again.

"It appears we are doing nothing. But we are doing invisible work. Our happiness and our compensation are equally invisible, just like that of others. You should look at your friends within yourself. For now, don't look at yourself within your friends. Gaze instead at the world within yourself. Forget for now the you that is in the world. Don't be afraid. Just for a while. In the end they are the same."

"Teacher's words are noble, if I can understand them. It's like going in search of something that's not there."

The moment after he spoke the frog was gone from before the ascetic. The reason was the frog leapt up triumphant on his hind legs.

The frog jumped down from his rock and followed the route back down the stream he had earlier ascended. After a long trip he was again home at the old swamp. By the time he neared the old swamp, however, his thinking had changed. He thought he would like to go back to his teacher, to the ascetic. When he took one look around the old swamp that he had reached by going downstream, he could not but feel, without regard to whether it was good or bad, that it did not suit his essential disposition. The way the ascetic had taught him to think may then have become easy for him to understand. . . . Was there a clearer reason? I do not know. For a fact, though, the frog who had with much trouble made the long trip home to the old swamp now took the long road back and once again appeared on the ascetic's rock.

The ascetic was still alive. Living and sitting as before on the rock. The frog, who had returned to sit again below the ascetic, then spoke. "Teacher, please take me again as your disciple."

But the ascetic said nothing. He merely nodded with an expressionless face. Thus again the frog sat and placed both hands on the ground before the ascetic. They sat facing each other. They sat silently. The frog stared intently into the teacher's eyes—he believed they were the stars that would make his world happy. The light of the sun and the light of the moon shone down upon them in succession. At times they were completely enveloped in darkness. Owls came and hooted at them from the lower branches of nearby trees. But the frog no longer trembled. Around and about the frog beautiful mossy flowers bloomed. The flowers scattered, bloomed again, and again they scattered. The moss stopped blooming flowers. The old moss withered. New moss grew in its place. The new moss grew over the frog's body and blossomed into flowers. That's how long the frog sat there unmoving. The frog forgot things like the flowering of the moss. That is because the frog stared only at the teacher's eyes. There the two of them remained, as always, silent. Then, one evening:

"Teacher!" the frog called out. "Teacher, where are you going? I can no longer see Teacher's eyes that I have stared at till now as my stars. Teacher's figure is disappearing."

The ascetic remained silent.

"Teacher, say something please. Put my heart at ease."

Then came a voice speaking. The voice came like a breath out of the air, fainter than the wind. It came intermittently to the ears only of the frog, who for long had heard no voice, neither his own nor that of another. But he could hear it clearly. The voice spoke:

"Frog. My disciple. Be at ease. Now you have enlightenment. Now that I am disappearing from your eyes. You have long since disappeared from mine. Therefore, do not fear that I am disappearing from your sight. Those of us who began as shadows disappear when we enter the world of shadows. There we exist everywhere and for always. Just as the light that shines from the moon shines everywhere and for always. You can see it with your eyes but you cannot scoop it up with your hands. It is surely there even though you cannot scoop it with your hands."

As the echoless voice spoke thus, the moonlight, its brightness enhanced by the deepening evening darkness, shone through the dense leaves of the trees. The light struck upon the rock. The moon saw there was nothing on the rock but the moss. The sound of the murmuring stream told of silence.

The Genesis of the Prose Spirit

Sanbun Seishin no Hassei, 1924

The article "The Place of the Art of Prose," written by Hirotsu Kazuo and published in the September issue of *Shinchō* magazine, is somewhat lacking, diffuse, and incomplete, I think, but: "Among the many kinds of art the art of prose is very close to man's life. Various arts are lined up close on the right, like poetry, the visual fine arts, and music. Immediately to the left of prose is life itself."

His conclusion is certainly true.

"Ignorant scholars of aesthetics consider prose to be the most impure of the arts. In its closeness to human life, however, the art of prose has a special character of utmost purity. There is no impurity in that. It has a purity unlike any of the other arts."

That's a penetrating, clear-sighted observation. He has incisively pointed out the fallacy of applying the aesthetics developed for poetry to the judgment of the art of prose, a habit we have unwittingly lapsed into.

The argument I am proposing here owes much to Hirotsu's article. I am only trying to say the same thing in my own style. I am trying to write in my own way how I concur in the truth of Hirotsu's stated conclusion. It will be good if you read it according to your style.

Properly speaking, the art of prose in its form can undoubtedly be called as old as words. Isn't the spirit of prose art relatively new in its origin, though?

Of course, I can't deny the clear historical fact that the form of prose as written in letters derives from ancient times. What I am saying, though, is that ancient prose was a kind of prose poetry—an un-rhymed epic poetry. It was a more complex form of the epic. Because of the complexity it seems to have been treated as prose. In short, prose in ancient times was no more than a deformed child of poetry.

The real art of prose came much later in its spirit than in its form. It was born in modern times, when a new spirit was instilled into the old form that was really one with poetry in ancient times. Thus I think was born the art of prose to stand equal with poetry. We might say the origin of prose came with the origin of naturalism along with the likes of Honoré de Balzac. Rather than say such a difficult scholarly thing it might be better to say it came from having to tell how the hero in a story ate his meals or made the money to enable happy assignations with his lover. No, it might be correct to say that prose is even newer, that it is still developing today. I believe the spirit of prose as an art has taken root and produced a view of mankind quite independent of the spirit of poetry.

Aristotle wrote the "Poetics." But nobody has written a "Prosaics." Clearly the "Poetics" was a discussion of all literature in ancient times. If we consider the fact that the word "prosaic" has a kind of shameful meaning to it, we should note how unconsciously poetry has been respected in ancient times, and even now.

The word "prosaic," used to describe any reality, is today a word without meaning. "Prosaic" is not a word of contrast subordinate to the word "poetic." I believe indeed that "prosaic" should stand in open confrontation to "poetic." In the same way that the words "classical" and "romantic" are used to define two major trends—no, in even bigger confrontation—I think "poetic" and "prosaic" should be used as respectable opposites in spirit. Depending on how you look at it, the modern romantic movement may have been an unconscious fore-runner of the prose spirit I plan to discuss here. . . . Of course, some explanation is necessary about calling romanticism "prosaic" when it glorifies poetry.

First it is necessary to know what the "poetic" spirit is.

The fundamental beauty of poetry, as its form would suggest, and its spirit too, lay in a disciplined balance, harmony, and unity. Even if someone deviated from these, he kept in mind the balance, harmony, and unity, and used them to strengthen the effect. Irregular harmony produced a beauty of contrast. In the poetic life, beauty was created by control of the chaotic world through the heart of the poet, that is, through the purification of the world into coherent harmony as the world passed through the poet's heart. This thing called "poetic" in its broadest meaning, however we interpret it, was nothing more than joy in the beauty of coherent harmony. In this sense, poetry resembles religious faith. The poetic spirit was the one and only artistic spirit. All the literary arts, no matter what their individual character and without regard to exceptions, have always been in essence classical.

Romanticism resisted classicism. It rebelled against the fixed harmonic unity. The romantics, armed with real-life activities and enlivened by their curiosity, tried to create something different and original in contrast to classical unity and harmony. They found beauty in the exaggeration and contrast in whatever irregular beauty there was in classicism. At times they dared to tear down the harmonic creation they themselves had built. We can see a good example in the children's plays of Ludwig Tieck.[4]

The poetic impulse of the romantic movement breathed a new vitality into the poetic spirit and sought to change the way of looking at man's nature. At the same time, the romantics inadvertently came near to discovering beauty even in chaos. . . . That's why I say that an unconscious forerunner of the spirit of prose was in the modern romantic movement.

I have already said that the tradition of the poetic spirit was in its orderly balance, unity, and harmony. The prose spirit opposes these ideals. It is the exact opposite of the poetic spirit. Disorder, disunity, disharmony—that is, chaos. In contrast to the religious nature of poetry, prose may be more scientific, skeptical, and rather closer to the satanic. In that chaos we find beauty.

Prose in its opposition to poetry, that is, modern-day prose, is an art where we do not find the unity and harmony that come from poetic values. Yet we often experience something there that appeals to us beyond the poetic. When we look at it minutely, we know that prose comes from its grasp, in a chaotic way, on chaos itself, the reality of chaos, and a sustaining power that keeps things from flying apart. Of course, this is something that moves us primarily as truth beyond beauty. Yet we can also feel the ample presence of beauty. It is very far from the poetic beauty I have described. This unfamiliar kind of beauty I would call the spirit of prose. I see no reason not to assert that it is the beauty of chaos.

The beauty of chaos is in one aspect a beauty of deep skepticism. We can see that it derives from a view of life that recognizes the very lack of unity and harmony as a mere fragment of a larger harmony.

In any case, when the beauty of chaos was discovered, prose found a very suitable spirit for its form. The prose spirit, in other words, can be called the spirit of all modernism. The spirit was liberated from the harmony and unity based on the subjective, and rather than letting the subjective control the literary universe, prose allowed for the observation of the chaos of real life in its chaotic condition. That was naturalism. The rise of naturalism made for the flowering of prose. The prose spirit that was already gestating within romanticism was brought to full birth with the baptism of naturalism. Poetry, which controlled the literary world for a time, had its ancient crown plucked off by the sudden rise of this new spirit. Hasn't the development of modern prose in fact driven poetry into a literary corner? The poetry of today, especially modernistic poetry, is no more than a "prosaic" poetry, in its best meaning and in its worst. . . . Just as the prose of ancient times was no more than poetic prose.

Following long-established conventions, don't we often judge our diametrically opposite art world of today according to the aesthetics formulated by the scholars of former times that made poetry the ruler over literature, indeed over all the arts? Don't we hesitate sometimes to accept all the beauty that strikes us simply because there are no appropriate grounds for us to judge and to endorse that beauty that lives and echoes in our hearts? I wonder if someone like Arishima Takeo, mentioned in Hirotsu's article, isn't an example of this. Because we set our values on convention and not on our actual feelings, we know we should respect the poetic writers who see the world in a state of harmony perfectly achieved, but we may not have been able to accept in full the modernist, the artist whose prose spirit is unperturbed at flinging out chaos as chaos, skepticism as skepticism.

Or maybe Arishima's nature was incompatible with the prose spirit. He might have had a kind of classical poetic nature.

Those surging tides of the poetic spirit and the prose spirit may after all be one the product of idealism and one the product of realism.

So long as no one develops a valid aesthetics of the art of the prose spirit we shall encounter apparently very inconsistent people who are in a hurry to make poetry out of chaos. They are dadaists, who have discovered the word "simultaneity." They are the artists who contrived an effect called cubism. They are the futurists who advocate an activism that supports chaos. They oppose the artistic world of poetic tyranny that has made unity and harmony its life and soul. They brought into the art world the beauty of chaos similar to or even greater than the cosmos, a beauty that reached its climax in an insistent prose spirit but with a poetic subjectivity. The enigma of these artists, who are specific to the age, is that they have casually lumped together the prose spirit and its opposite pole, the poetic spirit.

We must wonder at the fact that a new aesthetics centered on the prose spirit has not developed in this age, even without necessarily replacing the old aesthetics.

If the spirit of poetry is a product of those times when mankind was yet young and drunken with a kind of subjectivity, shouldn't we say that the prose spirit finally appeared after mankind had reached the prime of life, come to know the self, perceived a deeper world, and undergone a baptism in reality? Or is it just that I, shedding my adolescence, came to cherish in my innermost heart these ideas of the world of prose?

The Basis for the Beauty of the Japanese Language

Nihongo no Utsukushisa no Kontei, 1941

I may not be the right person to explain the beauty of the Japanese language. One reason is that I am not well versed in the languages of other countries. Another is that as a person who has penetrated even rather superficially into the literary groves of my fatherland and has become enraptured by the beauty, it may be supposed that there is nothing there for me but the beauty. Even in many aspects of the Japanese language for daily speech and modern writing that lots of people enumerate as weaknesses I find much beauty. Then don't I love my mother tongue so much that *pockmarks* look like *dimples?* I fear, if so, that the beauty I describe in my mother tongue might not be accepted by people who don't love the language as I do.

Japanese is probably not without defects. But these are not failings in beauty. On the contrary, in a beautiful language like Japanese the defects that appear to have developed with beauty as the sole aim may be rather fragile and unserviceable for practical language. The weaknesses that many modern-day Japanese and people who have learned European languages may find in our language seem to me to be nothing other than the beauty of Japanese.

The Japanese language uses a very self-indulgent and unrestrained phraseology. For reading or writing or learning it is inconvenient. Once we are familiar with it, though, there is nothing more beautiful. It is the self-indulgence of a little bird flying at will from one flower to another. It is definitely not the way an insect crawls. The strong point of beauty for the Japanese language is in the frequent leaps, the habitually prescribed omissions. The reader and the listener must always make up for these omissions. Japanese does not consist only of the speaker saying something by himself. Confident of the listener's understanding, the speaker entrusts an extraordinary amount to the listener's freedom of interpretation. The speech is formed in concert between the speaker and the listener. There is a oneness of speaker and listener. Of course, this may be the rule in the formation of all languages, but it is extreme in the case of Japanese. Herein lies one of the beautiful qualities of our language. It is manifest in the hearts of the Japanese people who developed the language. Speech is formed in the belief in, the anticipation of, concord with the other party among people who are greatly reassured in sharing a common spirit and life. We can't expect it to be suitable for disputation or the negotiation of interests. It was developed instead with the aim of establishing friendly relations. The inadequacy of Japanese for practical use originates in the depth of affection and sympathy for the other fellow. It might be called a *soft-hearted* language that jumps to conclusions. Shouldn't we see a strong point of beauty in this inadequacy?

In Japanese it is hard to know where to find the subject of the sentence. It is extraordinary how the language conforms to life. Japanese is hard to understand from the words alone, but help can easily be found in the thick of life. In the case of writing, the strict attention of the reader is demanded. The style is naturally derived from the essence of a language rich in omissions and leaps. The grammar resists being read through with ease; the extravagant style demands reading between the lines. It is not a clever, crabby extravagance, but in exchange for excluding readers who lack devotion and qualifications, Japanese progresses in a cooperative manner, sharing part of the author's responsibility with the devoted and well-qualified reader, just as speech does. It's a very aristocratic style.

The Japanese language has a life of lyrical beauty and tenderness. That's quite natural when you see it as a language based on a spirit of concord. Gently enveloped in its haze of lyricism, it expects always to act in concert with the other. How can you expect cooperation when you start out with a combative, argumentative manner of expression? So in Japanese one's assertion is always reserved. A hint, so to speak. Here a beauty of graceful refinement is spontaneously created. Can't we say that Japanese has a kind of protective coloring over its fragile makeup? The ideal in the art of Japanese speech is to incorporate the masculine mind gracefully into an outwardly feminine appearance.

The Japanese language that presupposes friendly relations has always valued generosity above all. It is a matter of enjoying great similarities and overlooking small differences. As cramping words are not pleasant, the language has not developed very much in the direction of detailed delineation and the pursuit of theory. It is therefore weak in vocabulary. Because of a sensitive spirit that respects small differences among great similarities, there is no lack of provision in the language for the compensatory use of adjectives and adverbs and for the use of postpositions. Japanese is naturally different from monotonous languages that are clear and simple and lack tone color. In the richness of tone color, even in its simplicity, there is great beauty in Japanese. The richness is in the extent of the dim shadows, which do not produce any sharp distinctions to hinder the broad spirit of concord. I think there is a strong possibility that the Japanese language will develop further in this direction of beauty. Be that as it may, we should never forget that the beauty of generous language is the essence of Japanese. That is why I fear our fragile Japanese language may degenerate if we overindulge in the subtlety of its tone colors.

Making a virtue of the beauty of its gentle curves, Japanese as a language of concord has a power of easy graceful invitation for the other fellow to enter our own world, but it lacks the quality to persuade forcefully. In that respect it is not without its stupidities. In our awkward Japanese I often feel I will end up repeating the same old tedious, trifling, inarticulate story. The fact that the Japanese language prizes simple, naive words and sets store by a sparsity of vocabulary may be taken as a warning.

In becoming an art, the Japanese language of concord gave birth in Japanese literature to a poetry of joint composition of linked verses and to a manner of telling stories that anticipated and respected the listener. That may be an incomparable achievement in the world.

The International Quality of Japanese Literature

Nihon Bungaku no Kokusaisei, 1938

Original Title: He Who Understands Will Get It

The international quality of Japanese literature? Not a bad title. But it is too difficult. The content is not difficult. It just sounds like empty bluster. If foreigners read Japanese literature, do they understand it? Do they find it interesting? That's what it's about. I'll write about it with that intention.

"The Tale of Genji," which is respected in Japan as a representative work of ancient Japanese literature, has been translated into English and praised abroad, I hear. It appears that the international quality of Japanese literature has been tested and proved. Of course, there may be a question whether foreigners have read and understood "the pathos of things"[5] in "Genji." Still, there is another problem.

The first difficulty for the foreigner in understanding Japanese literature is the problem of the Japanese language. There is special expression and relish in the distinctive wording that makes up the Japanese language. That is not only difficult for the individual foreigner to understand; it is probably quite difficult for the modern Japanese who has become more than half a foreigner. In this sense, it is interesting that Hakucho[6] confessed to an interest in "The Tale of Genji" only after reading it in English translation.

One of the outward characteristics of Japanese literature is that it takes the form of prose poetry, not of pure prose, and therefore begins and ends in expression and not in description. It may be correct to say of Japanese literature that many things which are not written are depicted in a mysterious way that may somehow make the reader feel them. Dr. Koeber[7] made the interesting observation that Japanese *waka*[8] poems are "no longer than the title of a European poem." Actually, Japanese poems do give a title to the reader and allow him to make the content for himself. Japanese prose is thought to have developed from the forewords written to the *waka* poems, and it has almost the same purport. The *renku* linked verse developed as a unique form of Japanese poetry where there is a wonderful interaction between the roles of reader and author. When it is hard to know who is the subject, we shall be able to judge correctly if we read very carefully and become accustomed to such reading. But it may be rather difficult to read between the lines along with the author. The difficulty applies without distinction to foreigners and to Japanese. Japanese may understand better, though.

Leaving aside the style of expression, which may be considered symbolic, we should not hastily conclude that Japanese literature cannot get through in foreign countries.

Japanese literature, like all others, is based on the vindication and development of human nature. Japanese literature does reflect the fact that there is a uniqueness to Japanese civilization. Hence it treats human nature in a unique manner. Japanese literature is very hard to comprehend without an understanding and love for Japanese civilization. The difficulty applies both to foreigners and to Japanese. I do think Japanese should be able to understand better because of my preconception that Japanese understand Japanese civilization more quickly and have a greater love for it. The example of Lafcadio Hearn shows that understanding and love for Japanese civilization is not necessarily impossible for foreigners. Literature teaches the national character of a people. The understanding of that national character adds a deep flavor to a country's arts. That may be called an axiom not just for Japanese literature. The reverse is true too.

The form and style of Japanese literature derive from the national character and national ideals. The Japanese people live in constant grief over the discord between their instincts and the ideals that are inherent in the family, the nation, and the loyalty and filial piety demanded in daily life. Japanese find humanity in their awareness of the sorrows of life. This is the special characteristic of Japanese literature. The distress between the ideal and the real is not peculiar to Japan. The beauty of Japanese civilization lies in the life of the man and woman in the street, the duty and humanity of the common people, not just in the torment of the lone philosopher. The life we must live is not all happiness. There is tragedy in it. The Japanese people have known for themselves a philosophy like Nietzsche's. They have lived in the midst of tragedy and died in it. Japanese civilization idealizes a humanity that, in shame for indulging in pleasure and the love of life, has the spiritual awareness to accept death boldly in order to take joy in meeting the ideal. That is the angle from which Japanese literature treats humanity. So long as one fails to understand this, it will be difficult to understand Japanese literature. When one knows and feels this spirit, Japanese literature will be understood equally by foreigners and Japanese.

There are no gods except in living with ideals and dying with ideals. To throw off the instinctive life is to be a Buddha. The understanding of these national beliefs becomes the footnote to understanding Japanese civilization and Japanese literature.

In sum, although Japanese literature may be somewhat difficult for foreigners to understand, it is by no means incomprehensible. The truth in this statement may be illustrated by the fact that Hearn's "A Woman's Diary" first inspired him and then came to be admired by many foreigners, and that at the same time this "Diary" was taken as a work of literature by a woman of special talent rather than the actual diary of an anonymous townswoman. Much of Japanese literature, or actually all ancient literature, is as simple and beautiful as "A Woman's Diary." To know that was the source of Hearn's genius.

Hearn and Dr. Koeber had a good understanding of both the poetry and the prose of Japanese literature. As for other foreigners, there are those who understand and those who do not. That's not just foreigners either. Can't the same be said for Japanese?

I think foreigners can understand Japanese literature just as people can understand the literature of ancient Greece. Those who do not understand the humanity of Japanese literature may belong to that crowd that knows no more than the exoticism of "Fuji-yama" and "geisha girl."[9] It can't be helped.

If modern Japanese literature is translated, maybe it will be understood too well. I'm afraid it may give the impression of something made in the country, though.

In modern literature and the classics alike, the works that we want to see translated may in fact be only those which are most difficult to translate. That is, not for the content but for the especially beautiful concepts and expression. Modern Japanese literature that can be easily translated may strike them as no more than a reverse import of a displaced Western literature. Typically Japanese elements that are drifting, however indistinctly, in these works may simply be extinguished in the translation. Yes, the spirit of Japanese literature through all ages may be expressed only by nuance. Regardless of whether or not Japanese literature circulates abroad, it is surely not well suited for translation.

Let's think, then, about what Japanese writer and work from old times could be most effectively translated. How about Saikaku? Rather than his salacious stories, wouldn't samurai stories be appropriate even though they have been considered inferior? Among the moderns how about, for now, some of the works of Shiga Naoya? Then maybe we should add Mori Ōgai's "The Abe Clan" and "The Takase Boat."

Notes

1. The translator has arbitrarily selected these few unconnected selections of Satō's critical writing as samples of his thinking and style. The greater part of Satō's nonfiction prose writing covers detailed criticism of other Japanese writers and recollections of his own life. These are not represented in this selection.

2. Tao Yuan-ming, A.D. 365–427, Chinese hermit poet.

3. George Morris Cohen Brandes, 1842–1927, Danish art historian translated into Japanese by Suida Junsuke.

4. Ludwig Tieck, 1773–1853, German romantic writer.

5. *Mono no aware*. See note 5 to "A Discourse on Elegance."

6. Masamune Hakuchō, 1879–1962, Japanese novelist and critic.

7. See note 12 to "A Discourse on Elegance."

8. Traditional poems of 31 syllables.

9. An aspersion cast on those who do not know much about Japan, as, for example, the facts that Japanese call Mount Fuji "Fuji-san" not "Fuji-yama," and that geisha professional entertainers are not "girls" in the derogatory sense.